IFIP Advances in Information and Communication Technology 335

IFIP – The International Federation for Information Processing

IFIP was founded in 1960 under the auspices of UNESCO, following the First World Computer Congress held in Paris the previous year. An umbrella organization for societies working in information processing, IFIP's aim is two-fold: to support information processing within its member countries and to encourage technology transfer to developing nations. As its mission statement clearly states,

> IFIP's mission is to be the leading, truly international, apolitical organization which encourages and assists in the development, exploitation and application of information technology for the bene t of all people.

IFIP is a non-profitmaking organization, run almost solely by 2500 volunteers. It operates through a number of technical committees, which organize events and publications. IFIP's events range from an international congress to local seminars, but the most important are:

- The IFIP World Computer Congress, held every second year;
- Open conferences;
- Working conferences.

The flagship event is the IFIP World Computer Congress, at which both invited and contributed papers are presented. Contributed papers are rigorously refereed and the rejection rate is high.

As with the Congress, participation in the open conferences is open to all and papers may be invited or submitted. Again, submitted papers are stringently refereed.

The working conferences are structured differently. They are usually run by a working group and attendance is small and by invitation only. Their purpose is to create an atmosphere conducive to innovation and development. Refereeing is less rigorous and papers are subjected to extensive group discussion.

Publications arising from IFIP events vary. The papers presented at the IFIP World Computer Congress and at open conferences are published as conference proceedings, while the results of the working conferences are often published as collections of selected and edited papers.

Any national society whose primary activity is in information may apply to become a full member of IFIP, although full membership is restricted to one society per country. Full members are entitled to vote at the annual General Assembly, National societies preferring a less committed involvement may apply for associate or corresponding membership. Associate members enjoy the same benefits as full members, but without voting rights. Corresponding members are not represented in IFIP bodies. Affiliated membership is open to non-national societies, and individual and honorary membership schemes are also offered.

Hiroshi Takeda (Ed.)

E-Health

First IMIA/IFIP Joint Symposium, E-Health 2010
Held as Part of WCC 2010
Brisbane, Australia, September 20-23, 2010
Proceedings

 Springer

Volume Editor

Hiroshi Takeda
Osaka University
2-15 Yamada-Oka, Suita City, Osaka 565-0871, Japan
E-mail: takeda@hp-info.med.osaka-u.ac.jp

CR Subject Classification (1998): H.4, J.3, H.5.2, H.3, H.2.8, H.5

ISSN   1868-4238
ISBN-10   3-642-42337-X Springer Berlin Heidelberg New York
ISBN-13   978-3-642-42337-6 Springer Berlin Heidelberg New York

springer.com

© IFIP International Federation for Information Processing 2010
Softcover re-print of the Hardcover 1st edition 2010

Typesetting: Camera-ready by author, data conversion by Scientific Publishing Services, Chennai, India
Printed on acid-free paper   06/3180

IFIP World Computer Congress 2010 (WCC 2010)

Message from the Chairs

Every two years, the International Federation for Information Processing (IFIP) hosts a major event which showcases the scientific endeavors of its over one hundred technical committees and working groups. On the occasion of IFIP's 50th anniversary, 2010 saw the 21st IFIP World Computer Congress (WCC 2010) take place in Australia for the third time, at the Brisbane Convention and Exhibition Centre, Brisbane, Queensland, September 20–23, 2010.

The congress was hosted by the Australian Computer Society, ACS. It was run as a federation of co-located conferences offered by the different IFIP technical committees, working groups and special interest groups, under the coordination of the International Program Committee.

The event was larger than ever before, consisting of 17 parallel conferences, focusing on topics ranging from artificial intelligence to entertainment computing, human choice and computers, security, networks of the future and theoretical computer science. The conference History of Computing was a valuable contribution to IFIPs 50th anniversary, as it specifically addressed IT developments during those years. The conference e-Health was organized jointly with the International Medical Informatics Association (IMIA), which evolved from IFIP Technical Committee TC-4 "Medical Informatics".

Some of these were established conferences that run at regular intervals, e.g., annually, and some represented new, groundbreaking areas of computing. Each conference had a call for papers, an International Program Committee of experts and a thorough peer reviewing process of full papers. The congress received 642 papers for the 17 conferences, and selected 319 from those, representing an acceptance rate of 49.69% (averaged over all conferences). To support interoperation between events, conferences were grouped into 8 areas: Deliver IT, Govern IT, Learn IT, Play IT, Sustain IT, Treat IT, Trust IT, and Value IT.

This volume is one of 13 volumes associated with the 17 scientific conferences. Each volume covers a specific topic and separately or together they form a valuable record of the state of computing research in the world in 2010. Each volume was prepared for publication in the Springer IFIP Advances in Information and Communication Technology series by the conference's volume editors. The overall Publications Chair for all volumes published for this congress is Mike Hinchey.

For full details of the World Computer Congress, please refer to the webpage at http://www.ifip.org.

June 2010
Augusto Casaca, Portugal, Chair, International Program Committee
Phillip Nyssen, Australia, Co-chair, International Program Committee
Nick Tate, Australia, Chair, Organizing Committee
Mike Hinchey, Ireland, Publications Chair
Klaus Brunnstein, Germany, General Congress Chair

Preface

For the first time in history, the International Federation for Information Processing (IFIP) and the International Medical Informatics Association (IMIA) held the joint "E-Health" Symposium as part of "Treat IT" stream of the IFIP World Congress 2010 at Brisbane, Australia during September 22–23, 2010.

IMIA is an independent organization established under Swiss law in 1989. The organization originated in 1967 from Technical Committee 4 of IFIP that is a non-governmental, non-profit umbrella organization for national societies working in the field of information processing. It was established in 1960 under the auspices of UNESCO following the First World Computer Congress held in Paris in 1959. Today, IFIP has several types of members and maintains friendly connections to specialized agencies of the UN system and non-governmental organizations. Technical work, which is the heart of IFIP's activity, is managed by a series of Technical Committees.

Due to strong needs for promoting informatics in healthcare and the rapid progress of information and communication technology, IMIA President Reinhold Haux proposed to strengthen the collaboration with IFIP. The IMIA General Assembly (GA) approved the move and an IMIA Vice President (VP) for special services (Hiroshi Takeda) was assigned as a liaison to IFIP at Brisbane during MEDINFO2007 where the 40th birthday of IMIA was celebrated.

For the first liaison action, the IMIA VP attended the IFIP GA at Addis Ababa in 2007 and discussed future collaborations. In the 2008 IFIP GA in Milan, the IFIP-IMIA joint symposium as a part of WCC2010 was approved and I was nominated as an organizer of the symposium.

The call for paper of the symposium was announced in the beginning of 2009 and the conference topics were described as follows:

Healthcare Computing and Communications (e-Health), as a new interdisciplinary field, address how to enable ICT to help people perform and receive more efficient, effective and safe healthcare services. To foster scientific discussion and disseminate new knowledge on e-Health, we invite you to submit papers and posters describing original research, applications, or practical use cases in any of the areas listed below.

Access control, bioinformatics, biosignal applications, clinical decision support, clinical informatics, consumer health informatics, data and systems integrity, database management, data protection, data mining, data warehouse, e-Health grids, e-Learning, electronic health records (EHR), electronic patient records (EPR), healthcare information models, hospital information systems, human computer interfaces, the Internet and Web, knowledge representation, medical imaging, mobile computing, mobile networks, multimedia databases, nursing informatics, privacy-enhancing technology, patient safety management, security in healthcare, smart cards, healthcare standards, telecommunication, ubiquitous networks.

Peter Croll, Southern Cross University, Australia (HISA), and Hiroshi Takeda, Osaka University, Japan (IMIA), served as Co-chairs of the Scientific Program Committee (SPC) of this symposium. In total, 44 papers were submitted by February 15, 2010 and the Co-chairs of the SPC made their selection with an average of 2.3 reviews per paper. As a result, 22 papers for oral presentation (one paper withdrawn) and 10 papers as posters (two papers withdrawn) were accepted. The remaining 12 papers were rejected.

I hope this symposium will continue to be held at every WCC conference of the IFIP and will form a bridge between basic and applied science of information processing in healthcare.

Finally, I express sincere thanks to Reinhold Haux, Augusto Casaca and Klaus Brunnstein for their overall guidance and encouragement, to Peter Croll and reviewers for deciding the program, to Arie Hasman for the attending IPC meeting, to Jan Shaw, Jon Mason, Michelle Hills and Nick Tate for the administrative assistance, to Mike Hinchey for publication matters, to Qiyan Zhang of Osaka University Hospital for the continuous assistance from the beginning, and to all those who were involved with the program, publication and operations.

July 2010   Hiroshi Takeda

Organization

Program Committee Chairs

Hiroshi Takeda — Osaka University, Japan (IMIA)
Chris Avram — Monash University, Australia (IFIP)

Program Committee Members

M.M. Altuwaijri, Saudi Arabia
D.W. Bates, USA
A. Geissbuhler, Switzerland
R. Haux, Germany
C. Kulikowski, USA
J. Li, China
N. Lorenzi, USA
A. Margolis, Uruguay
G. Mihalas, Romania
K. Minato, Japan
R. Moghaddam, Iran
L.A. Moura, Brazil
P. Murray, UK
H.A. Park, South Korea
G. Wright, UK
T. Yamazaki, Japan

Reviewers

Hiroshi Takeda — Osaka University, Japan
Peter R. Croll — Southern Cross University, Australia
Enrico Coiera — University of New South Wales, Australia
Micheal Legg — Health Informatics Society of Australia (HISA), Australia
Lakshmi Narasimhan — East Carolina University, USA
Vitali Sintchenko — University of New South Wales, Australia
A.R. Bakker — The Netherlands
David Hansen — The Australian e-Health Research Centre, Australia
Anthony Meader — University of Western Sydney, Australia
Neil Burdett — CSIRO ICT Centre, Australia
Penny Sanderson — The University of Queensland, Australia

Joan Edgecumbe   Health Informatics Society of Australia (HISA)
Andrew Georgiou   The University of Sydney, Australia
Susan Smith   Queensland, Australia
Fuminobu Ishikura   Osaka University, Japan
Ondrej Krejcar   Technical University of Ostrava,
                             Czech Republic

Table of Contents

Poster Presentations

Updated Topics in Healthcare Informatics

Hiroshi Takeda[1,2,3]

[1] Professsor Emeritus, Osaka Univeristy
2-15 Yamada-Oka, Suita city, Osaka, 565-0871 Japan
[2] Chief Research Fellow, Osaka Jikei Research Center of Healthcare Management,
1-2-8 Miyahara, Yodogawa-ku, Osaka, 532-0003, Japan
[3] Vice President, International Medical Informatics Association
h-takeda@jrhm.jikei.com

Abstract. This key note lecture introduces the role of IMIA, scope of healthcare informatics and some topics in healthcare informatics. Among updated topics, electronic patient record (EPR) and electronic health record (EHR) are featured. A new paradigm of clinical information systems, a document archiving and communication system (DACS) is also described and discussed.

Keywords: IMIA, Electronic Patient Record (EPR), electronic health record (EHR), document archiving and communication system (DACS).

1 Overview of Healthcare Informatics

To overview the scope of Healthcare Informatics, the Scientific Content Map (Table 1) that was developed in 2002 by IMIA's (then) Vice President for Working and Special Interest Groups, Dr. Nancy Lorenzi, is one of good references [1]. Current IMIA President Rheinhold Haux described ten major long-term aims and tasks for research in the field of medical informatics, including health informatics. These were the further development of methods and tools of information processing for: (1) diagnostics ('the visible body'); (2) therapy ('medical intervention with as little strain on the patient as possible'); (3) therapy simulation; (4) early-recognition and prevention; (5) compensating physical handicaps; (6) health consulting ('the informed patient'); (7) health reporting; (8) health care information systems; (9) medical documentation and (10) comprehensive documentation of medical knowledge and knowledge-based decision support [2]. In recent years, healthcare informatics would be gear up in accordance with advancement of internet and Web technology.

2 The International Medical Informatics Association (IMIA)

IMIA is an independent organization established under Swiss law in 1989. The organization was established in 1967 as Technical Committee 4 of the International Federation for Information Processing (IFIP). IMIA plays a major global role in the application of information science and technology in the fields of healthcare and research in medical, health and bio-informatics. In its function as a bridge

H. Takeda (Ed.): E-Health 2010, IFIP AICT 335, pp. 1–4, 2010.
© IFIP International Federation for Information Processing 2010

Table 1. Scientific Content Map of the Healthcare Informatics (N. Lorennzi and IMIA, 2002)

Applied Technology	Information Technology Infrastructure	Data-Infrastructure Related	Applications and Products	Human - Organizational	Education and Knowledge
Algorithms	Archival-repository systems for medical records- EPR-CPR-EMR	Classification	Biostatistics	Assessment	Bibliographic
Bioinformatics	Authentication	Coding systems	Clinical trials	Compliance	Cognitive learning
Biosignal processing	Chip cards in health care		Computer-supported surgery	Cognitive tasks	Computer aided instruction
Boolean logic	Distributed systems	Concept representation-preservation	Decision support	Collaboration	Computer-supported training
Cryptology	Health professional workstation	Data acquisition- data capture	Diagnosis related	Communication	Consumer education
Human genome related	Interfaces	Data analysis-extraction tools	Disease mgt.	Economics of IT	Continuing education
Human interfaces	Knowledge based systems	Data entry	EPR-CPR-EMR	Ethics	Digital Libraries
Image Processing	Networks		Epidemiological research Hospital IS	Implementation- deployment	E-Business
Mathematical models in medicine	Neural networks	Data policies	Event-based systems	Diffusion of IT	HI/MI education
Pattern recognition	Pen based	Data protection	Evidence based guidelines	Evaluation	Information management-dissemination
	Security		Expert systems	Human Factors	Knowledge bases
	Speech recognition	Database design	Health services research	Legal issues, implementing national laws	Knowledge management
	Standards	Indexing	HIS management	Management	Learning models
	Systems architecture	Syntax	Knowledge-based systems	Managing Change	Online/distance education
	Telehealth			Needs assessment	
	User interfaces	Language representation	Laboratory data	Organizational redesign processes	
		Lexicons		Organizational transformation	
		Linguistics	Image processing	Planning	
		Modeling	Operations / Resource management	Policy Issues	
		Nomenclatures	Outcomes research and measurement	Privacy	
			Quality management	Project Management	
		Standards		Security	
		Terminology-vocabulary	Patient identification	Strategic plans	
			Patient monitoring	Unique identifiers	
		Thesaurus tools	Minimum Data Sets	User-computer interface	
			Supply chain		
			Telematics		
			Telemedicine		

organization, IMIA's goals are: 1) moving theory into practice by linking academic and research informaticians with care givers, consultants, vendors, and vendor-based researchers; 2) leading the international medical and health informatics communities throughout the 22nd century; 3) promoting the cross-fertilization of health informatics information and knowledge across professional and geographical boundaries; 4) serving as the catalyst for ubiquitous worldwide health information infrastructures for patient care and health research. The IMIA family includes a growing number of Working Groups (WG) and Special Interest Group (SIG), which consist of individuals who share common interests in a particular focal field. Current WGs and SIG are as follows: Biomedical Pattern Recognition, Consumer Health Informatics, Dental Informatics Health and Medical Informatics Education, Health Informatics for

Development, Health Information Systems, Human Factors Engineering for Healthcare Informatics, Informatics in Genomic Medicine, Intelligent Data Analysis and Data Mining, Medical Concept Representation, Mental Health Informatics, Open Source Health Informatics, Organizational and Social Issues, Primary Health Care Informatics, Security in Health Information Systems, SIG NI Nursing Informatics, Smart Homes and Ambient Assisted Living, Standards in Health Care Informatics, Technology Assessment & Quality Development in Health Informatics, Telematics in Health Care.

3 Topics in Healthcare Informatics

The pace of change in healthcare information environment has been particularly remarkable in the last decade, spurred on continuous needs to fulfill effectiveness and efficiency as well as equality in healthcare service. Among the advancements, some topics are described.

3.1 Electronic Patient Record (EPR)

In general, healthcare events contain data components pertaining to the three stages (observations, decisions and interventions) of a healthcare (clinical) process cycle. A patient record must describe those events as a function of time as official documents. In 1999, for example, the Japanese Ministry of Welfare authorized EPR in condition that integrity, preservability and readability are simultaneously assured in a clinical information system [3]. Since then, based on billing/accounting system, computerized physicians' order entry (CPOE), EPR systems have been deployed in healthcare facilities. However, there still exist paper-based clinical documents and sheets such as Informed-Consent sheet, referrals from other facilities and so on. As the patient-specific aggregation of digital-born and non-digital born data is so important to maintain healthcare management, a document archiving and communication system (DACS) has been proposed by the author as a new paradigm of healthcare information system. The first DACS was installed in the beginning of 2010 at Osaka University Hospital in Japan, where the total paperless system has been operated [4]. DACS also represent life-long readability and proof of electronic medical record as "Document-centric (electronic) Patient Record (DPR)".

3.2 Electronic Health Record (EHR)

EHR is electronic applications through which individuals can maintain and manage their health information in a secure and confidential environment. There may be two ways for EHR; Top-down and Bottom-up. The former is developed mainly in Nordic countries and United Kingdom. The latter is typically provided by Microsoft Vault and Google Health. In order to make EHRs interoperable and secure, standard bodies such as ISO TC215 should play an important role. It will be further considered for utilization of lifelong data for extracting "evidences" for research, education and management by means of integrated data-warehouse and data-mining methodology.

4 Conclusion

Archiving and sharing healthcare information electronically can improve communications among caregivers and assist diagnosis, treatment and care in comprehensive healthcare delivery systems. Patients/citizens can have more control of their own healthcare. However, increasing access to data through EPR and EHR systems also brings new risks to the privacy and security of health records. Healthcare informaticians, information processing/communication professionals and stakeholders had better collaborate and cooperate to solve the practical problems.

References

1. http://www.imia.org/endorsed/2002_scientific_map.lasso
2. Haux, R.: Aims and tasks of medical informatics. Int. J. Med. Inf. 44(1), 9–20 (1997)
3. Takeda, H., Endoh, E.: Commentary on Health care in the information society. A prognosis for the year 2013. Int. J. Med. Inf. 66(1), 107–111 (2002)
4. Matsumura, Y., et al: A Scheme for Assuring Lifelong Readability in Computer Based Medical Records. In: Proc. MEDINFO 2010, Cape Town (2010) (in press)

The HL7 RIM in the Design and Implementation of an Information System for Clinical Investigations on Medical Devices

Daniela Luzi[1], Mariangela Contenti[2], and Fabrizio Pecoraro[1]

[1] National Research Council, Institute for Research on Population and Social Policy,
Via Palestro, 32, I-00100 Rome, Italy
{d.luzi,f.pecoraro}@irpps.cnr.it
[2] National Research Council, Institute for Biomedical Technologies,
Circonvallazione Nomentana, 496, I-00100 Rome, Italy
m.contenti@itb.cnr.it

Abstract. The paper describes MEDIS (Medical Device Information System), a system developed to support the whole lifecycle of a Clinical Investigation (CI) for Medical Devices, providing details on the approach used in its development. MEDIS is a software system that collects and manages data and documents, exchanged between an applicant and the Italian National Competent Authority during all the phases of the business process, from the CI notification up to the submission of the final results. The development of the MEDIS Domain Analysis Model (DAM) following the HL7 v.3 methodology as well as the approach followed in the system implementation are discussed in relation to the business domain peculiarities.

Keywords: Information Model, HL7, Clinical Investigation, Medical Devices.

1 Introduction

Medical devices (MDs) are becoming ever increasingly used tools in daily clinical practice to diagnose as well as treat or prevent many diseases. Their development and final product commercialization undergo several steps, which generally include their testing and assessment during Clinical Investigations (CIs), where MDs' safety and efficacy are verified under normal condition of use.

European directives [1], national laws as well as a body of international technical norms regulate CIs approval procedures and performances. At European level the aim is to implement a common Member States approach able both to facilitate MD manufacturers to perform international multi-centric investigations, and to improve information exchange among National Competent Authorities (NCA) that evaluate CI proposals and monitor their performance. EUDAMED (European Database for Medical Devices) is following these objectives, currently focusing on information sharing related to MDs placed on the market, while the design of a European registry on CIs of MDs is in its early stage.

H. Takeda (Ed.): E-Health 2010, IFIP AICT 335, pp. 5–14, 2010.

To improve communication, information sharing on MDs has to be based on the identification of a standard set of data able to describe MD characteristics and track them in interoperable information systems. This makes it necessary to develop a common standard language to achieve semantic interoperability among systems and organizations.

In Italy the National Research Council is carrying out a project supported by the Ministry of Health aiming to develop an information system - MEDIS (Medical Device Information System) - that manages the information flows between applicants and the Ministry of Health's Competent Authority. MEDIS plays the role of both a registry of clinical investigation data and a content repository of documents submitted by manufacturers to the NCA to obtain the approval for the clinical investigation start. In particular, MEDIS supports manufacturers in the documentation submission process as well as the NCA evaluators in assessing the data received. It also manages the communication among the different stakeholders and collects the data produced during the whole lifecycle of clinical investigations.

The paper describes the MEDIS system, providing details on the approach used in its development. The adoption of the HL7 v.3 methodology is explained on the basis of the business domain characteristics. After the description of the clinical investigation lifecycle, we analyze standardization initiatives related to clinical investigation for medical devices. Afterwards a concise description of the MEDIS system is given. We describe our approach providing some examples of the MEDIS DAM related to its transformation to a data model.

2   The Clinical Investigation Lifecycle

A high level description of the lifecycle of a CI on MDs is shown in figure 1 using BPMN notation. The business process can be divided into three main sub-processes:

- In the notification sub-process the CI applicant sends the documentation composed by administrative documents (letter of designation of an authorized representative, signed statement, etc.) and technical documentation (clinical protocol, the risk analysis document, etc.) to the NCA.

- In the evaluation sub-process, the NCA activates the administrative procedure assigning the notification to an evaluation team. Its tasks are to verify the formal completeness and consistency of the documentation submitted and to analyze its content in order to assess MD safety requirements as well as the scientific, clinical and ethical fulfillments of the clinical protocol. During this sub-process the NCA can require further information and documents.

- If the CI proposal is approved, the investigation sub-process can begin and its start date is communicated by applicants to the NCA. During this sub-process, the applicant has also to notify amendments in the clinical protocol, if any, and/or report serious adverse events that may have occurred during the CI. In any case, end date of the investigation or eventually its anticipated termination has to be communicated and the final report on CI results provided.

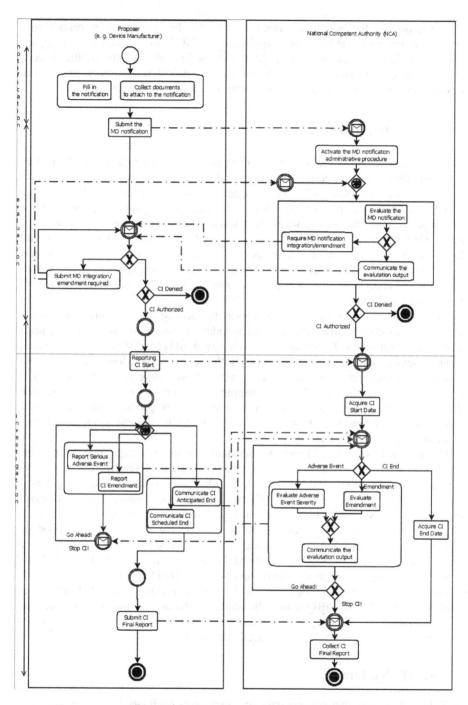

Fig. 1. The clinical investigation lifecycle

The majority of the activities carried out in the business process pertain to a communication exchange between CI applicants and NCA. Moreover, other participants could be included in the messaging flow, such as Ethical Committees, that have to approve the CI verifying its scientific merits and ethical acceptability, and clinical investigators, who could directly report information on Serious Adverse Events.

3 Standardization Initiatives

Even if European Directives provide the main requirements for CI approval, there are still many differences concerning the types of data and documents required by NCAs. In Europe only few countries have developed their own electronic submission system of CIs on MDs, the majority of them still relies on a paper-based information exchange. Among the organizations that develop health care standards, it is worth mentioning Clinical Data Interchange Standard Consortium (CDISC) and Health Level Seven (HL7). These organizations have begun to standardize the description of MDs capturing aspects related to specific points of view and/or sub-processes. However, a comprehensive standardized model pertaining MDs within the CI framework is still missing.

CDISC is developing standards to support the acquisition, exchange, submission and archive of clinical research data and metadata, focusing in particular on clinical trials on pharmaceutical products [2]. Recently a SDTM (Study Data Tabulation Model) Device sub-team has been formed with the aim of developing a domain that describes information (properties and characteristics) usable for different types of devices such as implantable devices, imaging and diagnostic devices. Starting from the SDTM related to clinical trials on pharmaceuticals products, the sub-team is proposing a device property domain, able to capture MDs data and metadata collected by manufacturers during CIs [3].

Health Level Seven (HL7) provides standards for the exchange, management and integration of electronic health care related data. It has released three models focusing on particular aspects of the MD domain [4, 5]. One was created by the "Implantable Device–Cardiac" Project within the Therapeutics Device domain, which comprises models, messages related to cardiac therapy delivery and observations related to implantable medical devices. Another standard concerns the Regulated Product Domain, where MDs are described in the framework of adverse events to be tracked in surveillance processes. Finally, the Regulated Studies Domain describes a part of clinical investigation through the Periodic Reporting of Clinical Trial Laboratory Results.

Also the joint effort carried out by BRIDG (Biomedical research Integrated Domain Group) [6] and caBig (cancer Biomedical Informatics Grid) [7], considers the domain of clinical trial on pharmaceutical products, focusing on the harmonization between HL7 messaging model and CIDSC data model.

4 MEDIS System

MEDIS is a registry that collects data and documents exchanged between applicants and NCA during the whole lifecycle of a CI, from the phase of notification to the phase of collecting the final results. The system supports:

- Applicants in the notification submission process, i.e. the collection and submission of regulatory data and documents to the NCA in order to obtain the approval of the CI start-up as required by national and European Directives;
- NCA evaluators during the assessment of the submitted data and documents in order to authorize or deny the start-up of the proposed CI;
- Both applicants and NCA facilitating their information exchange during the whole lifecycle of a CI (e.g. request for data and/or document integration, reports of amendments and/or serious adverse events).

By collecting the data and documents uploaded throughout the whole CI, the MEDIS systems also supports NCA in scheduling the evaluation activities, as well as monitoring the ongoing CI performance.

From the architectural point of view, MEDIS is a client-server three-tiered system where the front-end is implemented with a mix of server-side and client-side technologies. The business logic layer consists of a set of software modules in charge of:

- Dynamic generation of electronic forms depending on the user, the MD under investigation, and the state reached in the workflow;
- Control of the completeness and consistency of the data and documents uploaded in a single form or in a correlated set of forms;
- Provision of common services (e.g. authentication and authorization, XML and PDF documents generation, digital signature, etc.).

Finally, the MEDIS persistence layer is divided into:

- A content repository in charge of archiving documents uploaded as attachments to the notification or generated by the system starting from the data filled in the electronic forms;
- A relational database that contains data describing MD and CI instances, data tracking the CI lifecycle workflow and metadata related to documents stored in the content repository.

5 MEDIS Domain Analysis Model

HL7 is today mainly applied within health care organizations, where different legacy systems have to interact in order to exchange administrative and clinical data on patients and health care services provided. At the basis of HL7 v.3 messaging there are three main information models:

- The Reference Information Model (RIM), which is a simple abstract framework that addresses wildly heterogeneous clinical data described through six base classes [8];
- The Domain Analysis Model (DAM), which is a specification of the RIM to define information elements for a specific domain;
- The Refined Message Information Model (R-MIM), which is a refined view of the DAM to define the information elements of a specific message or a family of messages.

The advantages of using the HL7 RIM abstract model to define a specific domain model following the further steps to derive encoded messages make the information flows among different information systems homogeneous and sound. Moreover, the agreement reached on the DAM constitutes a common representation shared by the domain stakeholders. Therefore, the development of a MD DAM could foster already at an initial stage a common agreed data model and messaging that facilitate information sharing and seamless integration among different organizations. Following the first step of the HL7 v.3 methodology figure 2 depicts the portion of the MEDIS DAM [9] modeling MD in the framework of CI. This example shows how the HL7 DAM notation (UML class diagram notation) is able to capture important aspects of MD static and dynamic characteristics.

In our interpretation, the HL7 RIM can be decomposed into two parts:

- The static part is captured by the classes Entity and Role, i.e. objects or subjects involved in a process and the role played by them (i.e. a person who has the role of a physician);

- The dynamic part is represented by the classes Participation and Act, which describe actions, performed or scheduled, and how subjects and objects take part in them (i.e. in the activity of performing a clinical investigation a physician participates as a principal investigator).

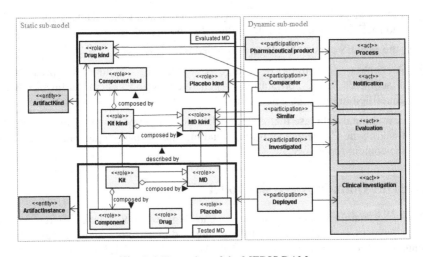

Fig. 2. MD portion of the MEDIS DAM

5.1 MD Static Representation

The regulatory documents submitted for CI approval contain detailed descriptions of the investigational MD, including MD components and their interactions, materials used, methods for its sterilization, etc. This information makes it possible to evaluate MD safety requirements as well as the risk analysis performed by the MD manufacturer.

When a MD is actually used in the investigation, other information become relevant. This is for instance the case when it is necessary to track a specific MD implanted in a specific patient. For this reason in the DAM we model each product under two points of view: *ArtifactKind* and *ArtifactInstance*:

- The former represents an abstract description of any MD as reported in detail in the technical documents submitted to obtain the approval of the clinical investigation start-up;

- The latter models the description of a single tangible MD used in real investigation conditions.

In this way it is possible to manage data representing any medical device artifact as well as data gathered during the investigating process of a specific MD tracked by its lot or serial number. To connect these different aspects of the MD description in MEDIS DAM the attribute Determiner code of the HL7 Entity class is used. The abstract description of any product is represented by the <<entity>> *ArtifactKind* and associated with the relevant Role: *MD kind, Kit kind, Component kind, Drug kind, Placebo kind* (fig. 2).

5.2 MD Dynamic Representation

Many different MDs are involved in the CI lifecycle, other than the one under investigation. Some MDs often represent a technological evolution of already commercialized devices. They are often mentioned in the documentation to prove through the similarity with the investigational product the fulfillments of safety requirements. Moreover, in randomized CIs, a comparator is used to test differences in safety and efficacy between two devices.

In order to distinguish the aim and functions of these different MDs described and/or used during the CI lifecycle, we use the stereotypes *Participation* and *Act*. For instance, the Role *MD kind* participates to the whole CI process either as *Investigated* or *Comparator*. In addition, it could participate to the *Notification* and *Evaluation* activities as *Similar*. Likewise, a drug can participate, as a *Comparator* or as a *Pharmaceutical product* in the whole CI process. Analogously the *Roles* related to *ArtifactInstance* are associated only to the *Clinical Investigation* activity through the Participation *Deployed*.

6 MEDIS Data Model

In the HL7 methodology the construction of a DAM is intended to capture in a formal language both the static and dynamic aspects of a certain domain. The sharing of a common representation of the world facilitates the communication among different parties. Actually when the interaction among parties is modeled through use cases, the HL7 Development Framework provides the methodology and tools to derive the message format through which different information systems could send and receive syntactic and semantic interoperable information. Even if the task of defining a shared format for the messages to be exchanged is simplified, when legacy systems have to interoperate, the mapping between the message format and the internal representation of data could demand a meaningful effort.

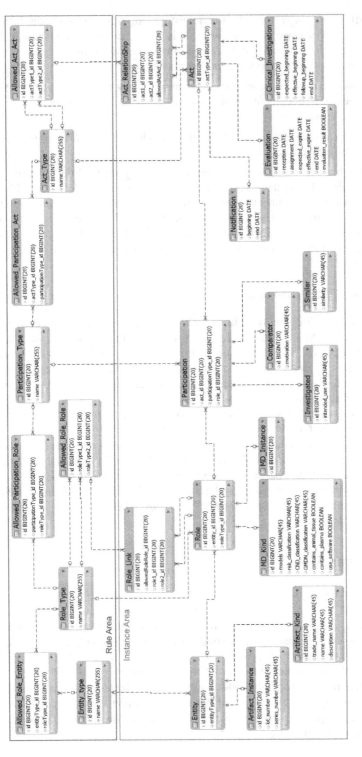

Fig. 3. MEDIS data model

Actually some contributions trying to design and implement automation tools for mapping between DAM classes with relational databases are already available in the literature [10, 11].

In the MD domain there are not so many legacy systems to integrate; large part of the information systems to automate this domain still have to be developed. In this respect, our intention is to propose a normalized data model for a relational database, representative for the MEDIS DAM, in order to make the population of message instances straightforward.

The MEDIS DAM representative data model is depicted in figure 3. It is divided in two different conceptual areas, the instance and the rule areas:

- The instance area matches the MEDIS DAM and is related to the instance of the MD domain. It represents the data collected during the whole clinical investigation process.

- The rule area represents the rules of the business process of the clinical investigation life cycle semi automated by the MEDIS system.

A peculiarity of the presented relational database model is the explicit representation of the six base entities derived from the HL7 RIM meta-model. They are introduced in the instance area as generalizations of more specialized MEDIS DAM entities. They are also used for describing the rules used by the MEDIS system to determine each steps in the evolution of the workflow of any single CI.

Looking at the instance area of the database, the individual activities related to the three clinical investigation sub-processes are stored in the *Notification*, *Evaluation* and *Clinical Investigation* tables. The advances in the business process are described through relationship between these activities and are stored in the Act_*Relationship* table. In this way all the sub-processes of the clinical investigation lifecycle are linked together and in any time it is possible to identify the state reached by each CI instance.

A pre-defined set of CI activities are stored in the table Act_*Type*, tuples representing pre-defined consecutive activities are stored in the table *Allowed_Act_Act*. These rules are used by the business logic layer of the MEDIS system to determine, at any time, the sole active functionalities. This makes it possible for instance to prevent CI applicant to notify any serious adverse event before he/she has communicated the start date of the investigation.

7 Conclusions and Future Works

The paper describes the MEDIS system, providing details on the approach used in its development. The adoption of the HL7 v.3 methodology is explained on the basis of the business domain characteristics.

Interesting aspects of the implemented solution are also described, highlighting the co-presence in the E-R data model of the entities derived from both the specialized DAM and the abstract RIM. In particular, due to the fact that the database collects not only the CI lifecycle instances data but also the rules governing the CI lifecycle workflow, the RIM entities were introduced in order to relate the two datasets.

Currently we are validating the MEDIS system involving real users with the objectives to evaluate the performances of the implemented solution.

In more general terms the results achieved with the development of MEDIS represent an important contribution to foster the debate among Member State on agreed upon standardization initiatives on CIs on MDs. Actually large agreement on the MEDIS DAM could facilitate the development of national registries that need to exchange information on CIs, as well as their interoperability with EUDAMED.

In this respect we are analyzing types of information exchanged between NCAs in order to identify cooperative scenarios as well as an initial set of contents, which need to be exchanged among enrolled parties. The proper modeling of real use cases in order to get the R-MIM and the interoperable message format is in its early stage.

Acknowledgments

This study was supported by the Italian Ministry of Health through the MEDIS project (MdS-CNR collaboration contract n° 1037/2007).

References

1. European Parliament, Directive 2007/47/EC of the European Parliament and of the Council of 5 September 2007 amending Council Directive 90/385/EEC on the approximation of the laws of the Member States relating to active implantable medical devices, Council Directive 93/42/EEC concerning medical devices and Directive 98/8/EC concerning the placing of biocidal products on the market. Official Journal of the European Union, L. 247/21 (21.9.2007)
2. CDISC: Clinical Data Interchange Standards Consortium, http://www.cdisc.org
3. Smoak, C.: CDISC for the Medical Device and Diagnostic Industry: An Update (2009), http://www.wuss.org/proceedings09/09WUSSProceedings/papers/cdi/CDI-Smoak.pdf
4. Health Level Seven v3, http://hl7.org/v3ballot/html/welcome/environment/index.htm
5. Health Level Seven, Inc. HL7 Reference Information Model. Ann Arbor, MI, http://www.hl7.org
6. Fridsma, B.D., Evans, J., Hastak, S., Mead, C.N.: The BRIDG Project: A technical report. JAMIA 15, 130–137 (2007)
7. caBIG: Cancer Biomedical Informatics Grid, http://cabig.nci.nih.gov
8. Schadow, G., Mead, C.N., Walker, D.M.: The HL7 Reference Information Model under scrutiny. SHTI 124, 151–156 (2006)
9. Luzi, D., Pecoraro, F., Mercurio, G., Ricci, F.L.: A medical device domain analysis model based on HL7 RIM. STHI 150, 162–166 (2009)
10. Eggebraaten, T.J., Tenner, J.W., Dubbels, J.C.: A health-care data model based on the HL7 Reference Information Model. IBM Journal of Research and Development 46(1), 5–18 (2007)
11. Umer, S., Afzal, M., Hussain, M., Ahmad, H.F., Latif, K.: Design and implementation of an automation tool for HL7 RIM-To-Relational Database Mapping. In: IHIC Conference, Kyoto, Japan (2009)

Two Human-Centered Approaches to Health Informatics: Cognitive Systems Engineering and Usability

Tania Xiao[1,2], Wendy Broxham[1], Cara Stitzlein[2],
Jasmine Croll[1], and Penelope Sanderson[1,2]

[1] National ICT Australia, St Lucia,
Queensland, Australia
[2] The University of Queensland, St Lucia,
Queensland, Australia
{Penelope.Sanderson,Tania.Xiao,Wendy.Broxham,
Jasmine.Croll,firstname.lastname}@nicta.com.au,
cara.stitzlein@uqconnect.edu.au

Abstract. There is growing recognition among many healthcare researchers that a human-centered approach to the design and evaluation of health information systems is vital for the success of such systems in healthcare. In this paper, we survey the work of two human-centered research communities that have been active in the area of health information systems research but that have not been adequately discussed in past comparative reviews. They are cognitive systems engineering and usability. We briefly consider the origins and contributions of the two research communities and then discuss the similarities and differences between them on several topics relevant to health information systems. Our objective is to clarify the distinction between the two communities and to help future researchers make more informed decisions about the approaches and methods that will meet their needs.

Keywords: health information systems, human-centered technology, cognitive systems engineering, usability, cognitive engineering.

1 Introduction

The Institute of Medicine's report "Crossing the quality chasm" (2001) has generated great interest in the development of health information systems to support safe and effective healthcare. Unfortunately, there has been limited success associated with the introduction of health information systems in healthcare settings [1]. There is growing recognition amongst many healthcare technology researchers that the failure of many health information systems can be attributed to poor understanding of the needs and work practices of the human user and the socio-technical context in which work is done [2].

There is already much research focused on human-machine interaction from a human-centered perspective. For example, Hoffman and Militello [3] identify eight

H. Takeda (Ed.): E-Health 2010, IFIP AICT 335, pp. 15–26, 2010.

'communities of practice' that emerged in the 1980s driven by the common goal to better understand and support human cognitive tasks. In the healthcare context, Greenhalgh et al. [2] classified existing human-centered research into nine meta-narratives which include 'computer supported cooperative work', 'actor-network analyses' and 'critical sociology'.

Greenhalgh et al.'s [2] review offers new insights into human-centered health information systems research. However, because they limited their focus to Electronic Patient Records (EPR), they may have overlooked traditions that have done less research on EPRs and more research on other types of health information systems. In this paper, we extend Greenhalgh et al.'s work by discussing two research communities that have also made important contributions to our understanding of the needs and practices of the human user.

1.1 Current Paper

In this paper we highlight the work of the cognitive systems engineering and usability communities, neither of which was covered in Greenhalgh et al.'s [2] review. Based on our interpretation of the literature and our participation from time to time in these communities, we identify and discuss similarities and differences between them. Our goal is to bring these two communities to the attention of health informatics researchers and to clarify actual or potential confusions that may exist in the literature.

To achieve this aim, first we describe how we identified some key papers that represent the core ideas of the two traditions. Then we discuss each tradition in detail, considering their similarities and differences. Finally we note current and potential contributions of each community to the successful development and implementation of health information systems.

2 Method

We conducted a systematic and comprehensive search of the Web of Science (via ISI Web of Knowledge) between January and May, 2009 to investigate which research communities were involved in health information systems research. Combinations of keywords including patient safety, technology, decision support, usability, health information systems and automation were used to conduct an extensive literature search of technology in healthcare. Three researchers read through the abstracts of 1642 papers and identified four contributing research communities. We focus on two research communities, usability and CSE, for the purposes of this paper.

To refine our search to the key papers in each of the above two communities, we selected papers (1995-2009) with ten or more citations. A focused search of highly-cited papers from 2006 to 2009 ensured we did not miss important recent contributions. This process resulted in approximately 25 papers for each community.

Five group sessions were conducted during which the papers were discussed in terms of their representativeness of a research community and the quality of the empirical research. As a result of the discussions, we chose to exclude certain papers to achieve a more coherent message for our paper. First, we focused on empirical work because we were interested in the application of theoretical ideas to practice.

Second, we limited our scope to hospital-based work because it represented the dominant research context. Third, we excluded all conference papers because we wanted to focus on journal publications in which authors could present more information about their research. For the usability and CSE communities, the above exclusion process yielded a total of 7 and 8 papers respectively that we considered most representative of each area Finally, an examination of the reference lists of these empirical papers and communications with experts in the areas helped us to identify key theoretical papers that define the historical roots and major contributions of the two research communities.

3 Results

3.1 Usability

Background. Usability is defined as "the extent to which a product can be used by specified users to achieve specified goals with effectiveness, efficiency and satisfaction in a specified context of use"[4]. Fundamentally, usability professionals are concerned with enhancing the interactive experience between human users and a piece of technology (usually a computer software interface). Usability emerged as an important property of computers and computer software during the proliferation of computers in the general workplace during the 1960s and 1970s. The launch of the Macintosh in 1984 led to usability being recognized as essential to the development of computer technology [5].

The work of usability practitioners is usually informed by other research traditions including cognitive psychology, human factors and software engineering. Some of the earliest proponents of usability worked for companies such as IBM, Macintosh and Xerox PARC and later shared their experiences with the research community. In the last few decades, the usability profession has acquired a distinct identity. The Usability Professionals Association (UPA) was established in 1991 and it provides resources to support usability research and practice. In addition, the ACM-sponsored Computer Human Interaction (CHI) conference covers some advances in usability research, amongst many other topics. Moreover, publications dedicated to usability research have emerged, such as *Journal of Usability Studies*.

For usability professionals, the usability of a system is determined by five main criteria [6]: its learnability, efficiency, memorability, ease of recovery from errors, and user satisfaction. To achieve these criteria, usability researchers encourage (a) early user participation in terms of setting usability goals and design requirements and (b) early and iterative user testing and redesign of prototypes both in the laboratory and work context. Many sets of principles have been created to guide the development of user-centered designs [7, 8] and many techniques exist for evaluating designs, including heuristic task analysis, cognitive walkthroughs, and benchmark user testing [7, 9]. Figure 1 gives a characterization of user testing.

Usability in healthcare. In recent decades, usability has emerged as a critical issue in healthcare. Many health information systems fail because of poor usability [10]. Allwood and Kalen [11] were amongst the first to report research on health information systems inspired by usability concepts. Following a four-year field investigation of the introduction of a patient administration system in a Swedish hospital, they identified key issues related to the development process (such as failing to identify usability goals, not having user participation) that contributed to the difficulties users experienced when learning and using the system. More recently, many researchers have raised concerns about how poorly-designed technology may make healthcare systems more vulnerable to adverse events [12]. Thus, there is growing urgency among the usability community to use their methods to identify and prevent technology-induced error in healthcare systems [13].

Usability research in healthcare is now quite common – here we highlight some representative examples. First, researchers have used usability methods to identify associations (a) between physician order entry systems and adverse drug events [14] and (b) between handheld prescription writing tools and prescription errors [15]. Second, researchers have applied user-centered and iterative testing and design principles to the development of a health information system interface [16] and a mobile electronic patient record prototype [17]. Third, usability evaluation has been used to assist with decisions about the procurement of hospital equipment such as infusion pumps [18] and patient monitoring systems [19]. Finally, given the wide range of methods used in usability research, some research focuses on making comparisons between different usability methods to determine which method is best suited to certain evaluation needs [20].

Fig. 1. Characterization of a traditional usability method (user testing). Researcher is the gray figure at right looking through a two-way mirror at a participant performing a task under controlled laboratory conditions. Thought clouds indicate representative concerns of researcher and participant.

3.2 Cognitive Systems Engineering

Background. Cognitive systems engineering (CSE) is an approach to the analysis, modeling, design and evaluation of complex socio-technical systems. It emerged in the early 1980s from studies of the human operator's role in process control during the 1960s and 1970s, culminating in analyses of the Three-Mile Island accident in 1979. The first published usage of the term "cognitive systems engineering" was in 1983 by Hollnagel and Woods [21] who argued that 'instead of viewing man-machine systems as decomposable mechanistic principles, CSE introduces the concept of a [joint] cognitive system', where man and machine work together as a team responding adaptively to complex work problems.

Many CSE researchers are human factors specialists and there is a CSE technical group within the Human Factors and Ergonomics Society. There are several journals dedicated to CSE research including the *Journal of Cognitive Engineering and Decision Making* journal and *Cognition, Technology and Work*. In addition to activity within the Human Factors and Ergonomics Society conference, there are also strong CSE communities in Europe.

CSE research is influenced by many disciplines, including systems engineering, cognitive, ecological psychology, work psychology and anthropology, and so is not considered a "discipline" by its adherents [22]. It is specifically concerned with supporting human cognitive performance in complex safety critical industries such as nuclear power, aviation and healthcare. Some CSE analysts focus on identifying constraints that operate in work domains and that shape activity [22, 23]. CSE researchers argue that if people have a good understanding of fundamental constraints in their work environment, they can reason more effectively about how to solve unfamiliar work problems. More recently, many CSE researchers have embraced a proactive approach to risk management called resilience engineering [35]. Resilience engineering focuses on (a) identifying existing work processes that help people achieve robust and adaptive performance and (b) designing systems that support those processes. Figure 2 gives a characterization of field observation with the questions that a cognitive engineer might bring to it.

Fig. 2. Characterization of a cognitive systems engineering method (field observation). Panel in background represents a workplace artefact – a whiteboard. Figures at left are people in their workplace, whereas gray figure at right is the researcher. Thought clouds are representative questions about how work is organized and supported.

CSE in healthcare. Because the 'computerization' of healthcare has been slower compared with other domains such as aviation, CSE research is less well established in healthcare than in other domains. An early CSE-oriented healthcare study was conducted by Gaba who investigated anaesthetists' responses to critical incidents in a simulated operating theatre environment [24]. Following the Institute of Medicine's suggestion that technology could be more effectively used in healthcare [25], CSE researchers have been quick to express concerns that the technology push might result in brittle work practices that make a system more vulnerable to failure [26].

We now highlight some key empirical works that reflect CSE concerns. First, some research [27] [28] has highlighted side effects that technology (e.g. bar code medication administration system, computerised clinical reminders) can have on communication and coordination practices that may, in turn, contribute to adverse patient outcomes.

Second, researchers have explored how the use of non-electronic cognitive artefacts (e.g. schedules and whiteboards) can reveal hidden aspects of the work that can be used to define information and usage requirements for the design of electronic support [29, 30].

Third, a few researchers have applied CSE principles to the design of health information systems including a blood antibody detection decision support system [31] and a cardiac display [32].

Finally, CSE researchers have studied how variability in and adaptation of work practices contribute to resilient and successful performance in contexts with and without technology such as the introduction of new patient monitoring systems in the operating theatre [33] or the management of bed resources in the ICU [34].

3.3 Nuanced Distinctions between Areas

The terms "usability", "cognitive systems engineering" and "cognitive engineering" are increasingly used in healthcare, but are sometimes confused. Here we provide our own perspective on how the terms can be distinguished and the confusions that might occur otherwise.

A term often used interchangeably with "cognitive systems engineering" is "cognitive engineering" (CE) [36]. However, for some practitioners there are important differences between CSE and CE. According to Norman, who introduced the term in 1980 and was the first person to describe CE as a unique discipline [37, 38], CE is the application of cognitive science principles to the design and evaluation of technical tools that enhance human cognitive performance in general. CE is typically concerned with a broader and simpler range of applications than CSE, including educational support tools and the "design of everyday things" [38, 39]. Many methods proposed by early CE researchers were relatively simple user-centered design and evaluation techniques that are now more commonly associated with usability evaluation. More recently, many CE researchers have performed more complex analyses using methods such as cognitive task analysis and computational cognitive modeling [40].

In a recent paper assessing usability of healthcare technology, Liljegren and Osvalder [19] referred to cognitive walkthroughs and usability tests as cognitive engineering methods. Although such methods were described as cognitive engineering methods in 1986 by Norman [8] this description may be less apt now for several reasons. First, cognitive walkthroughs and usability tests are now more closely associated with usability engineering or user-centered design. Second, given that cognitive systems engineering is often referred to as cognitive engineering, if cognitive walkthroughs and usability tests are referred to as cognitive engineering methods, readers might infer that they are central to CSE as well.

Given that the CSE and usability communities differ in their approach to the design and evaluation of technology, Liljegren and Osvalder's usage could conceivably lead to future researchers thinking they have adopted one approach when they are using methodologies that actually better reflect another approach. For that reason it is probably clearer if methods such as usability tests, cognitive walkthroughs, heuristic evaluations, and so on be referred to as usability engineering methods or user-centered design and evaluation methods rather than as cognitive engineering methods.

3.4 Comparisons of CSE and Usability

In their review of different theoretical approaches to examining the impact and effectiveness of EHRs, Greenhalgh et al. [2] presented some themes that highlight tensions among different research meta-narratives. In a similar vein, below we present five themes that show where usability and CSE approaches to healthcare may be most strongly contrasted. The first three themes are inspired by themes in the Greenhalgh et al. paper. The last two are new themes that emerged during our group discussions and that helped us distinguish between the usability and CSE communities. In Table 1 we present the studies reviewed according to which theme we think each study best represents.

Note that we do not say that the two research communities have no connection. Researchers in each community incorporate ideas from the other to strengthen their work. In addition, the two communities share many similarities: both are concerned about user experience, both are empirical in nature, and both draw from the human sciences in different forms and different ways.

The Technology. Greenhalgh et al. [2] noted two different perceptions of technology in healthcare among the human-centered research communities: (a) technology as a 'tool or container' or (b) technology as an artifact that 'acts' in the environment. Usability professionals are more likely to adopt the former view that technology is a tool that processes and communicates information [41]. Their primary concerns are to (a) determine which tasks need to be supported by the technology, and (b) design the technology and test whether it helps users effectively perform the task.

On the other hand, CSE professionals are more likely to adopt the latter view that technology is an artifact that brings new opportunities and challenges into the work environment. The primary concern is to develop new concepts or models that give designers insight into new phenomena that may emerge when new technology is introduced into a workplace (e.g. automation surprises, clumsy automation) [33, 42].

The User. Given that both are human-centered approaches, usability and CSE emphasize the importance of drawing from user experience when designing and evaluating health information systems. However, different aspects of the user are

Table 1. List of reviewed usability and CSE studies organized according to theme comparisons

	Usability	CSE
The Technology	Liljegren & Osvalder (2004) [19] Ginsburg (2005) [18]	Cook & Woods (1996) [33]
The User	Kjeldskov & Slov (2007) [17]	Xiao & Seagull (2006) [30] Saleem (2005) [28]
The Work Context	Kushniruk et al. (2005) [15]	Patterson et al. (2002) [27] Nemeth et al. (2006) [29]
Theory	Johnson et al. (2005) [16] Jaspers (2009) [20]	Effken (2006) [32] Guerlain (1999) [31]
Human Error	Koppel et al. (2005) [14]	Cook (2006) [34]

considered in each case, because of differences in their research goals. Usability researchers focus on physical, perceptual, and cognitive similarities and differences between users in order to design technology that supports all kinds of people. The user is an evaluator of the technology and may also be involved in the design process on a participatory basis. On the other hand, CSE researchers focus on the adaptive and resilient behaviors of users as they tailor their work practices and work environment (including technology) to achieve successful performance. Each design is considered a hypothesis about how technology shapes work behavior and it is the user who completes the design with their workarounds and tailor-made adaptations [43].

The Work Context. Usability and CSE researchers handle work context differently. In much usability evaluation, users are tested on specific tasks in controlled environments [44] where there is a strong focus on measurement. Contextual factors such as time and place, social norms or power structure are only considered later, in terms of how they affect the adoption and use of technology in the workplace. On the other hand, in CSE research there is less separation of work context, work itself and the technology designed to support work. CSE empirical work is usually conducted in the field where researchers explore the so-called 'wrapped package' of dynamic interactions among workers, tools, tasks and structures that make up the cognitive work context [45]. Consequently, CSE researchers may identify more subtle or tacit factors that should also be considered when evaluating designs, even though such factors may be less directly measurable.

Theory. The role of theory also differs across usability and CSE research. Usability and user testing are often embedded in the software engineering process. Designers may draw from various theories in cognitive science, cognitive psychology, and social psychology when developing and testing designs [46]. Similarly, evaluators may draw from theories of human perception and cognition when considering how a user might interact with a system. On the other hand, CSE involves the development of general theories about human interaction with systems, but particularly with technology-intensive and safety-critical systems. CSE research is informed by a broad range of theories such as systems theory, control theory, ecological psychology and cognitive sciences in the quest to gain insight into the interaction between people and technology. Model-development is a key theme.

Human error. Both the usability and CSE communities recognise that accidents conventionally attributed to 'human error' are more often the result of badly designed technology. However, there are differences in the way the two communities approach this problem. Usability researchers focus on how to design technology that reduces the likelihood of user mistakes, slips, and lapses. In contrast, CSE researchers see "error" as emerging from the same work processes that lead to success. People adapt their behavior to respond to workplace pressures towards efficiency or thoroughness [47]. Most of the time such adaptation is successful, but occasionally conditions are hostile and unintended consequences occur.

4 Discussion and Conclusion

The aim of this paper was to review research that demonstrates similarities and differences between CSE and usability—two research communities contributing to the design and evaluation of health information systems. Both communities share the goal of designing technologies that support human cognitive performance, and both encourage active user participation in the design and evaluation of health information systems. Although the review is limited in scope given our exclusion criteria, we hope it provides readers with a better understanding of the type of work carried out in both research communities and, more importantly, of some key distinctions between them.

The design and evaluation of human-centered health information systems is a challenging task. Reviews such as Greenhalgh et al.'s [2], Hoffman and Militello's survey of communities of practice investigating cognitive tasks [3], and the current paper can provide useful information to help healthcare researchers and practitioners make more informed decisions about which theoretical approaches and methods are most appropriate for their needs. Usability techniques can be very effective when practitioners need objective measurements about relatively fine points of interaction. However, researchers may wish to start with CSE methods when a broad perspective on work processes is needed, or if they want to check whether technology affects other work processes that are important for successful performance, but that are removed from the immediate point of interaction. All research communities have their unique strengths and limitations. It is up to the researcher to find the right combination that will help them answer their specific research question.

Acknowledgments

We gratefully acknowledge substantial input and assistance from members of the National Information and Communication Technology Australia (NICTA) Cognitive and Organisational Systems Engineering (COSE) project. NICTA is funded by the

Australian Government as represented by the Department of Broadband, Communications and the Digital Economy and the Australian Research Council through the ICT Centre of Excellence program.

References

1. Wears, R., Berg, M.: Computer Technology and Clinical Work Still Waiting for Godot. Jama-Journal of the American Medical Association 293(10), 1261–1263 (2005)
2. Greenhalgh, T., et al.: Tensions and Paradoxes in Electronic Patient Record Research: A Systematic Literature Review Using the Meta-narrative Method. Milbank Quarterly 87(4), 729–788 (2009)
3. Hoffman, R.R., Militello, L.G.: Perspectives on cognitive task analysis. CRC Press, New York (2008)
4. ISO9241-11, Ergonomic requirements for office work with visual display terminals (VDTs) Part 11: Guidance on Usability (1998)
5. Dumas, J.: The great leap forward: The birth of the usability profession (1988-1993). Journal of Usability Studies 2, 54–60 (2007)
6. Nielsen, J.: Usability Engineering. Morgan Kaufmann, San Diego (1993)
7. Nielsen, J.: Heuristic Evaluation. In: Nielsen, J., Mack, R. (eds.) Usability Inspection Methods. John Wiley & Sons, New York (1994)
8. Norman, D.A., Draper, S.: User-centred system design: New perspective on human-computer interaction. Erlbaum Associates, Hillsdale (1986)
9. Polson, P.G., et al.: Cognitive walkthroughs - A method for theory-based evaluation of user interfaces. International Journal of Man-Machine Studies 36(5), 741–773 (1992)
10. Johnson, C.W.: Why did that happen? Exploring the proliferation of barely usable software in healthcare systems. Quality & Safety in Health Care 15, I76–I81 (2006)
11. Allwood, C.M., Kalen, T.: User-Competence and other Usability Aspects when introducing a Patient Administrative System - A case-study. Interacting with Computers 5(2), 167–191 (1993)
12. Ash, J.S., Berg, M., Coiera, E.: Some unintended consequences of information technology in health care: The nature of patient care information system-related errors. Journal of the American Medical Informatics Association 11(2), 104–112 (2004)
13. Borycki, E., Kushniruk, A.: Identifying and preventing technology-induced error using simulations: Application of usability engineering techniques. Healthcare Quarterly 8, 99–105 (2005)
14. Koppel, R., et al.: Role of Computerized Physician Order Entry Systems in Facilitating Medication Errors. Jama-Journal of the American Medical Association 293(10), 1197–1203 (2005)
15. Kushniruk, A., et al.: Technology induced error and usability: The relationship between usability problems and prescription errors when using a handheld application. International Journal of Medical Informatics 74(7-8), 519–526 (2005)
16. Johnson, C.M., Johnson, T.R., Zhang, J.J.: A user-centered framework for redesigning health care interfaces. Journal of Biomedical Informatics 38(1), 75–87 (2005)
17. Kjeldskov, J., Skov, M.B.: Exploring context-awareness for ubiquitous computing in the healthcare domain. Personal and Ubiquitous Computing 11(7), 549–562 (2007)
18. Ginsburg, G.: Human factors engineering: A tool for medical device evaluation in hospital procurement decision-making. Journal of Biomedical Informatics 38(3), 213–219 (2005)

19. Liljegren, E., Osvalder, A.L.: Cognitive engineering methods as usability evaluation tools for medical equipment. International Journal of Industrial Ergonomics 34(1), 49–62 (2004)
20. Jaspers, M.W.M.: A comparison of usability methods for testing interactive health technologies: Methodological aspects and empirical evidence. International Journal of Medical Informatics 78(5), 340–353 (2009)
21. Hollnagel, E., Woods, D.D.: Cognitive systems engineering - New wine in new bottles. International Journal of Man-Machine Studies 18(6), 583–600 (1983)
22. Rasmussen, J., Pejtersen, A., Goodstein, L.: Cognitive systems engineering. J. Wiley & Sons, New York (1994)
23. Vicente, K.: Cognitive work analysis: Toward safe, productive, and healthy computer-based work. Lawrence Erlbaum Associates, Mahwah (1999)
24. Gaba, D.M., Deanda, A.: The Response of Anesthesia Trainees to Simulated Critical Incidents. Anesthesia and Analgesia 68(4), 444–451 (1989)
25. Institute of Medicine: Crossing the quality chasm: A new health system for the 21st century. National Academy Press, Washington (2001)
26. Vicente, K.J.: Less is (sometimes) more in cognitive engineering: the role of automation technology in improving patient safety. Quality & Safety in Health Care 12(4), 291–294 (2003)
27. Patterson, E.S., Cook, R.I., Render, M.L.: Improving patient safety by identifying side effects from introducing bar coding in medication administration. Journal of the American Medical Informatics Association 9(5), 540–553 (2002)
28. Saleem, J.J., et al.: Exploring barriers and facilitators to the use of computerized clinical reminders. Journal of the American Medical Informatics Association 12(4), 438–447 (2005)
29. Nemeth, C., et al.: Discovering Healthcare cognition: The use of cognitive artifacts to reveal cognitive work. Organization Studies 27(7), 1011–1035 (2006)
30. Xiao, Y., Seagull, F.J.: Emergent CSCW systems: The resolution and bandwidth of workplaces. International Journal of Medical Informatics (2006)
31. Guerlain, S., et al.: Interactive Critiquing as a Form of Decision Support: An Empirical Evaluation. Human Factors 41(1), 72–89 (1999)
32. Effken, J.A.: Improving clinical decision making through ecological interfaces. Ecological Psychology 18(4), 283–318 (2006)
33. Cook, R.I., Woods, D.D.: Implications of automation surprises in aviation for the future of total intravenous anesthesia (TIVA). Journal of Clinical Anesthesia 8, S29–S37 (1996)
34. Cook, R.: Being bumpable: Consequences of resource saturation and near-saturation for cognitive demands on ICU practitioners. In: Woods, D., Hollnagel, E. (eds.) Joint Cognitive Systems: Patterns in Cognitive Systems Engineering, pp. 23–35. Taylor & Francis, London (2006)
35. Hollnagel, E., Woods, D., Leveson, N.: Resilience Engineering: Concepts and Precepts. Ashgate Publishing Company, Aldershot (2006)
36. Vicente, K.: Cognitive Engineering research at Riso from 1962-1979. In: Salas, E. (ed.) Advances in Human Performance and Cognitive Engineering Research, pp. 1–57. Elsevier, New York (2001)
37. Norman, D., Draper, S. (eds.): User Centered System Design - New Perspectives on Human-Computer Interaction. Lawrence Erlbaum Associates, London (1986)
38. Norman, D.A.: Cognitive engineering and education. In: Tum, D., Reif, F. (eds.) Problem Solving and Education: Issues in Teaching and Research, Erlbaum Associates, Hillsdale (1980)
39. Norman, D.: The Psychology of Everyday Things. Basic Books, New York (1988)

40. Gray, W.D.: Cognitive architectures: Choreographing the dance of mental operations with the task environment. Human Factors 50(3), 497–505 (2008)
41. Benyon, D., Turner, P., Turner, S.: Designing interactive systems: People, activities, contexts, and technologies. Person Education Limited, Harlow (2005)
42. Sarter, N., Woods, D., Billings, C.: Automation Surprise. In: Salvendy, G. (ed.) Handbook of Human Factors and Ergonomics. Wiley & Sons, New York (1997)
43. Woods, D.D.: Designs are hypotheses about how artifacts shape cognition and collaboration. Ergonomics 41, 168–173 (1998)
44. Dumas, J., Redish, J.: A practical guide to usability testing. Intellect Books, Exeter (1999)
45. Hoffman, R., Militello, L.: Perspectives on Cognitive Task Analysis: Historical Origins and Modern Communities of Practice. Psychology Press, New York (2008)
46. Carroll, J.: HCI models, theories, and frameworks: toward a multydisciplinary science. Morgan Kaufmann, Amsterdam (2003)
47. Hollnagel, E.: ETTO principle: Efficiency-thoroughness tradeoff - Why things that go right sometimes go wrong. Ashgate Publishing Ltd., Farnham (2009)

A Step towards Medical Ethics Modeling

Miguel Miranda[1], José Machado[1], António Abelha[1],
Gabriel Pontes[2], and José Neves[1]

[1] CCTC, Departamento de Informática, Universidade do Minho
{miranda,jmac,abelha,jneves}@di.uminho.pt
[2] Centro Hospitalar do Alto Ave, Guimarães, Portugal
gabriel.pontes@chaa.min-saude.pt

Abstract. Modeling of ethical reasoning has been a matter of discussion and research among distinct scientific fields, however no definite model has demonstrated undeniable global superiority over the others. However, the context of application of moral reasoning can require one methodology over the other. In areas such as medicine where quality of life and the life itself of a patient may be at stake, the ability to make the reasoning process understandable to staff and to change is of a paramount importance. In this paper we present some of the modeling lines of ethical reasoning applied to medicine, and defend that continuous logic programming presents potential for the development of trustworthy morally aware decision support systems. It is also presented a model of moral decision in two situations that emerge recurrently at the Intensive Care Units, a service where the moral complexity of regular decisions is a motivation for the analyze and development of moral decision support methodologies.

Keywords: Clinical Ethics, Ethical Modeling, Logic Programming, Artificial Intelligence.

1 Introduction

Over viewing the evolution of technology and information systems thematic, a trend of growing pro-activeness and limited intelligence is pushing the role of virtual entities, on a step-by-step basis, higher and higher. Many activities are nowadays performed by automated entities, while supervised by humans. Although most of these virtual entities are still rather limited in learning, adaptation and autonomy, displaying solely reactance to predicted or programmed events, several threads of Artificial Intelligence research methodologies for imbedding further intelligence.

The notion of virtual entity is here used to differentiate entities with higher levels of autonomy, learning, prediction and decision from a mainly reactive and controlled machine. Moreover, considering developments in the area of informatics and Artificial Intelligence (AI) in particular, it must be considered that many of these entities can exist within a single physical machine or even that a single one can be distributed within limitless machines. Therefore, the notion of a virtual entity in this case is similar to the concept of an agent in the area of Multi-Agent Systems.

H. Takeda (Ed.): E-Health 2010, IFIP AICT 335, pp. 27–36, 2010.

As virtual entities become more complex and hold critical functions, a justified doubt and concern regarding the impact of actions performed by these entities arises. From the numerous scenarios where they can interact with their surrounding environment, some carry moral consequences and describe ethically intricate actions from a human point of view. From the need to prevent immoral decisions and ensure confidence regarding these virtual entities, further understanding of the capacity of moral agency, moral modeling and the complexity human moral ethics.

Modeling machine ethics can result in further understanding of human ethics itself, either by defining rules and exceptions, or by knowledge extraction, case classification and patterns search over existing cases and outcomes using different algorithms. One can in fact consider that from the numerous methodologies that exist for the study of moral capacity, for each of them different subsequent potential outcomes can be found. While modeling ethics based on defined moral principles can help defining ethical principles and validate the resulting decision process, using learning algorithms and knowledge extraction over existing moral cases and outcomes can deepen the understanding of the underlying moral rules and patterns that may go unnoticed, but define moral decisions. In other words, theses processes aiming to analyze the essence of morality can be used not only to study their simulation/emulation, but also to deepen and evaluate the moral standards and dilemmas in ethically complex systems. The results from these systems are not limited outcome decisions before an ethical complex problem. Using a perspective of decision support or decision optimization, from a knowledge-base (either by previous studied cases or expert input), bearing in mind a specific scenario, similar cases can be aggregated for human user consideration, rules/principles involved in the decision can be induced with a certain degree of certainty, or conditions can be abduced.

There exists no definite solution for modeling ethical virtual entities, and presently several approaches are being presented and some compared against one another. Studying the present study and investigation in the area, different methodologies for modeling moral capabilities using artificial intelligence techniques can be segmented according to their main characteristics [1]. One of the most definite and important disparity in methodologies is the usage of explicit reasoning versus black-box reasoning. In explicit reasoning, the processes underneath a moral decision are clearly defined as principles, rules, exceptions, or other structure defined for one particular modeling. When analyzing AI techniques derivatives of symbolic, sub-symbolic or statistical approaches, there exist some that are able to represent their "line of though", allowing a transparent view of the moral decision process [2].

One of these techniques is logic programming, in which horn clauses contain the formalisms that mold the reasoning within an existing logical predicate. Current research indicates that non-monotic logic, due to its ability to implement defeasible inference, enabling moral principles to add and still diminish the set of conclusions determined by the knowledge base, is an interesting and promising technique to model moral reasoning [3] [4] [5]. By this mean, principles of benevolence and non-malificience can exist in accordance with other principles that are against their value or state an exception for superseding context principles. Regardless of the use of deductive, inductive or abductive logic, the rules used or attained are explicitly defined. However, the usage of each of these techniques of logic programming varies on the objective and context of application.

On the other hand, while using black-box reasoning, the reasoning behind the moral decision itself cannot be perceived in a clear manner. In other words, within the process of a black-box technique, facing a set of inputs, only a set of outputs can be obtained, not the process or reason behind it. That is the case of neural networks, regardless of the methodologies used to attempt to understand the reasoning behind them, the fact remains that no certainty of the processing underneath the trained neural network exists [2]. Although interesting results can be achieved using neural networks trained on existing moral cases and consequently implementing case based reasoning, the understanding of the moral principles within these black boxes is unknown [6]. Different techniques can be used to reverse-engineer neural network's inner structure and imbedded rules, however, the result is not exactly the rules used but rather an induced or a probabilistic set of them [7]. In the end of this reverse-engineer process, it is attained an induced set of rules of a systems that already uses induction or probabilistic methods to train its processing, revealing a certainty of doubt over the extracted rules.

Another divergence in ethical modeling is the learning process of rules or reasoning methodologies in ethical dilemmas. When considering a specific area such as medicine, most of the existing knowledge essential to model moral reasoning is contained in deontological principles or case studies [8]. In either of these cases the core of this knowledge is based on individuals or panels of experts. In light of these sources, the moral decision model can be developed from existing principles, from learnt principles or from hybridization of both sources. While one can consider existing deontological principles as existing principles, learnt principles are those extracted from existing cases. These machine-learning behaviors applied to ethics are a rather complex theme as principle learning may result in immoral principles and depending of the methodology used it may not be possible to clearly understand the underlying principles (e.g. black-box machine learning). Inductive logic programming has also expressed in existing research potential to induce principles and their relations from experts reasoning.[9]

When modeling moral behavior in virtual entities, researchers must always bare in mind the environment that molds its principles. For research purposes selection of an area and a purpose is of the essence in order to evaluate results and contextualize the used approach. With this in mind, the disparity between ideal and real environments in the medical arena creates a complex set of scenarios, which are pressing and interesting to analyze from an ethical point of view. Therefore, this article will address moral reasoning in medicine, and apply it in clinical context.

2   Medical Ethics Modeling – Analysis and Applications

Clinical ethics is an arena of public interest, where themes such as end of life, abortion and refusal or futility of treatment, among others, are constantly discussed as specific dilemmas occur or opinions and believes change. Although the deontic principles of a physician remain centered in the best practice towards the patient, legislation and court decisions mold the parameters of how physicians should behave in specific cases, which bare moral consequences. In fact, the context in which a morally complex case presents itself may uphold different results. One european study analyzing the frequency and types of withholding and withdraw of life-sustaining therapies within the Intensive Care Units (ICU) of European countries, indicated that different countries and cultures deal in diverse ways with ethical dilemmas arising from these therapies [10]. One can go a step further, and consider the hypothesis that the physicians training and context can as well affect the moral decision making process. In fact, these decisions of withholding and withdraw of therapy, similarly to many other in clinical ethics, are far from an hypothetical situations, they happen frequently in the healthcare arena and allow no time for extensive legal or ethical consulting by the physician responsible for this decision. The moral demanding of clinical staff is overwhelming and can become even more complex and dubious in contexts of intensive and emergency care. Intensivists are constantly presented with new moral dilemmas, which demand for a quick and asserted answer [11]. Medical staff must therefore, be taught and trained to deal with these situations. Studies analyzing moral dilemmas and ethics modeling methodologies can be of help in this mater, to enhance the existing guidelines and understanding of moral decisions.

In the area of medicine, both practice and research activities have been actively overviewed and ultimately limited by existing legislation and court jurisprudence. This legislative effort is deeply connected to the existing moral principles and ethical concerns [11]. However, the existing legal directives can ease a decision concerning a morally complex situation and ethical confrontation, without fear for civil consequences. Some limitations occur on situations, in which decisions that sound ethically sound are limited by law, nevertheless professional conduct codes generally defined the proper conduct within the limits of the law [8].

For centuries, the clinical ethics with roots on Hippocrates principles defined as its main deontological fact, the obligation of the physician to give to the patient all treatments medicine knowledge considered the best fit. Nowadays, the decision is centered on the patients will, moreover, with the development of medical technologies, through their breakthrough and short-comes, physicians have also to take in consideration consequences of physical, mental and financial order [12]. This change of paradigm and the subjacent increment of ethical and civil load to the decisions of clinical staff, is an environment where synergies of medical ethics and AI, in order to understand how moral processing should be designed and how tutoring and decision support systems can be developed and implemented.

One interpretation of the process of learning and practicing clinical ethics is based on a set of corner-stones rules (i.e. moral principles), completed by the interpretation of existing fact in light of the existing numerous case studies. One can therefore consider that the moral behavior of physicians is a complex intertwined system of both rule-based and case based reasoning. Case studies can represent to some extents either rules or specific conditions which classify exceptions. This notion of exception is one of a logical programming point of view, where a context of known and unknown values of an universe can result in an exception to an existing predicate. Case studies can concur with the existing moral principles, alter their relationship, or define a context in which the existing principles were disregarded. When one analysis an ethical case study in medicine, the surrounding context that materializes the moral action defines an example of a decision with moral consequences, where the boundaries of right or wrong are complex to ascertain. The analysis of such cases is complex, however one should always bear in mind that the existing moral rules and principles of medicine are the barebones of clinical ethics and should not be superseded unless valid exceptions are deemed correct.

From the distinct environments within the medical arena, intensive care medicine embodies an environment where moral decisions are usual and complex. In this specific context, decisions must be taken within short time spans while also regard limited resources and patients in critical conditions [11]. This context enables interest in using moral decision modeling in clinical cases appertaining to the ICU.

3   Modeling Clinical Ethics

With respect to the computational paradigm, it was considered Logic Programming in the form of a Continuous Logic Programming (CLP), once the truth values are defined in the range $0...1$, with two kinds of negation, classical negation, $\neg$, and default negation, not. Intuitively, following the close world assumption, not p is true whenever there is no reason to believe p, whereas $\neg$p requires a proof of the negated literal. A continuous logic program (program, for short) is a finite collection of rules and integrity constraints, standing for all their ground instances, and is given in the form:

$$p \leftarrow p_1 \wedge ... \wedge p_n \wedge not\ q_1 \wedge ... \wedge not\ q_m; \text{ and}$$
$$?p_1 \wedge ... \wedge p_n \wedge not\ q_1 \wedge ... \wedge not\ q_m\ (n,m \geq 0)$$

where ? is a domain atom denoting falsity, the p_i, q_j, and p are classical ground literals, i.e. either positive atoms or atoms preceded by the classical negation sign $\neg$. Every program is associated with a set of abducibles. Abducibles may be seen as hypotheses that provide possible solutions or explanations of given queries, being given here in the form of exceptions to the extensions of the predicates that make the program.

Therefore, being Γ a program in CLP and $g(X)$ a question where X contains variables $X_1 \wedge ... \wedge X_n\ (n \geq 0)$, one gets as an answer:

The answer of Γ to $g(X)$ is true iff
$$g(X) \rightarrow demo(\Gamma, g(X), true)$$
The answer of Γ to $g(X)$ is false iff
$$\neg g(X) \rightarrow demo(\Gamma, g(X), false)$$
The answer of Γ to $g(X)$ is unknown iff
$$not\ \neg g(X) \wedge not\ g(X) \rightarrow demo(\Gamma, g(X), unknown)$$

where unknown stands for a truth value in the interval $]0...1[$. Being Γ a Program, it is possible to define the Minimal Answer Set of Γ (MAS(Γ)):

$$\Gamma \vdash s \text{ iff } s \in MAS(\Gamma)$$

where $\Gamma \vdash s$ denotes that s is a logical consequence or conclusion for Γ.

Being now AS_i and AS_j two different answer sets of Γ, being E_{ASi} and E_{ASj}, respectively, the extensions of predicates p in AS_i and AS_j, it is defined that AS_i is morally preferable to AS_j ($AS_i < AS_j$) where $<$ denotes the morally preferable relation, denoting that for each predicate p_1 there exists a predicate p_2 such that $p_1 < p_2$ and E_{ASi} \ E_{ASj} is not empty (\ denotes the difference set operator).

In our approach, the morally preferable relation is based on evolution and it is built on a quantification process of the quality-of-information that stems from a continuous logic program. Indeed, let p_i ($i \in \{1,...,m\}$) denotes the predicates whose extensions make a continuous logic program that models the universe of discourse, in terms of the extensions of predicates and let a_j ($j \in \{1,...,n\}$) stands for the attributes for those predicates. Let $x_j \in [min_j,max_j]$ be a value for attribute a_j. To each predicate it is also associated a scoring function $V^i_j [min_j, max_j] \rightarrow 0...1$, that gives the score of predicate p_i assigned to a value of attribute a_j in the range of its acceptable values, i.e. its domain (for sake of simplicity, scores are kept in the continuous interval $[0,...,1]$). The quality-of-information with respect to a generic predicate it is therefore given by

$Q_i = \dfrac{1}{Card}$, where Card denotes the cardinality of the exception set for the predicate pi, if the exception set is not disjoint. If the exception set is disjoint, the quality of

information is given by $Q_i = \dfrac{1}{C_1^{card} +...+ C_{card}^{card}}$ where C_k^{card} is a k-combination

subset, with card elements. The relative importance that a predicate assigns to each of its attributes under observation, w^i_j, stands for the relevance of a_j for the predicate p_i and it is given by $V^i(x) = \sum w^i jV^i j(x)$, for all p_i. On the other hand, the predicate scoring function, when associated to a value $x = (x_1,...,x_n)$ in a multi-dimensional space defined by the attribute domains, is given in the form

$V^i(x) = \sum w^i jV^i j(x)$.

Therefore, it is now possible to measure the quality-of-information that stems from a continuous logic program, by posting Qi values into a multi- dimensional space, whose axes denote the program predicates with a numbering ranging from 0 (at the center) to 1. The area delimited by the arcs gives a measure of the quality-of-information carried out by each problem solution that may be under consideration, therefore defining the process of quantification of the morally preferable relation, as it is stated above in formal terms.

4   Model Behavior

Case 1
Mr. PD is a man with 81 years, a long background of cardiopathy and diabetes is admitted in an ICU with fever, hypertension and dyspnea. The thorax radiography is compatible with Acute Respiratory Distress Syndrome (ARDS) and the arterial partial oxygen tension (PaO2) is of 50 mmHg. This condition is often fatal, usually requiring mechanical ventilation and although the short-time mortality in these cases has been

decreasing, the probability of mortality is considerably high and moreover this procedure results in a low quality-adjusted survival in the first year after ARDS [8, 13]. At the noon service meeting, while analyzing the current cases, the assistant physician asks the interns whether in light of the survival rates, treatment costs and probable low quality of life, should the ICU resources be used with this 81 years old men.

Case 2

During this meeting Mrs. GB, a woman with 36 years interned at the same hospital due to a car accident and diagnosed with sepsis, Acute Lung Injury (ALI) and Glasgow coma scale of 3, shows breathing complications and needs to be admitted an ICU. The level of its PaO2 and the severity of the ALI indicated a pressing need for mechanical ventilation and intensive care. However the number of beds in the ICU is limited and for this matter Mr. PD would have to be changed to another service. Due to the fragile state of Mr. PD this procedure is problematical, but considering his clinical status, complications and age with Mrs. GB, the greater probability of her to full recover with better quality of life tends to tip the balance from a critical point of view. In light of this context, how should the assistant physician act?

The continuous logic program for the extension of the predicate survival-rate:

```
{
¬survival-rate(X, Y) ← not survival-rate(X, Y ) and
    not exception(survival-rate(X, Y)),
exception(survival-rate(X, Y)) ← survival-rate(X,
unknown-survival-rate),
survival-rate(X, Y) ← ards(X) and pao2(X, low) and
evaluate(X,Y),
exception(survival-rate(gb, 0.5)),
?((exception(survival-rate(X,Y)) or
exception(survival-rate(X,Z))) and ¬(exception(survival-
rate(X,Y)) and exception(survival-rate(X, Z)))
/This invariant states that the exceptions to the
predicate survival-rate follow an exclusive or/
}agsurvival-rate
```

The continuous logic program for the extension of predicate survival-quality:

```
{
¬survival-quality(X, Y) ← not survival-quality(X, Y )
and not exception(survival-quality(X, Y)),
exception(survival-quality(X, Y)) ← survival-rate(X,
unknown-survival-quality),
survival-quality(gb, 0.8),
exception(survival-quality(pd, 0.1)),
?((exception(survival-quality(X,Y)) or
exception(survival-quality(X,Z))) and
¬(exception(survival-quality(X,Y)) and
exception(survival-quality(X, Z)))
  }agsurvival-quality
```

The continous logic program for the extension of predicate cost:

```
{
¬cost(X, Y) ← not cost(X, Y ) and
     not exception(cost(X, Y)),
exception(cost(X, Y)) ← cost(X, unknown-cost),
cost(gb, unknown-cost),
cost(pd, unknown-cost),
?((exception(cost(X,Y)) or exception(cost(X,Z))) and
¬(exception(cost(X,Y)) and exception(cost(X, Z)))
  }agcost
```

In this specific case we assume that the costs are unknown, so they will be considered as null values for the calculi.

5 Discussion

The extensions of the predicates that make the universe of discourse have to generated and considered in the CLP program construction, in order to have a basis for decision making. This is a bi-directional process because beyond the organizational, functional, technical and scientific requisites, one may have also to attend the ethical and the legal ones, as well as data quality, information security, access control and privacy. This generation is made from the nosocomial Electronic Health Records (EHR). EHR is a core application which covers horizontally the health care unit and makes possible a transverse analysis of medical records along the several services, units or treated pathologies, bringing to healthcare units new computational models, technologies and tools, based on data warehouses, agents, multi-agent systems and ambient intelligence. An EHR is an assembly of standardized documents, ordered and concise, directed to the register of actions and medical procedures; a set of information compiled by physicians and others health professionals; a register of integral facts, containing all the information regarding patient health data; and a follow up of the risk values and clinical profile. The main goal is to replace hard documents by electronic ones, increasing data processing and reducing time and costs. The patient assistance will be more effective, faster and quality will be improved.

Whatever form of an information society related to healthcare we can imagine, it will be based on three basic components, namely raw medical data, reconstructed medical data and derived medical data. Indeed, clinical research and practice involve a process to collect data to systematize knowledge about patients, their health status and the motives of the health care admittance. At the same time, data has to be registered in a structured and organized way, making effective automation and supporting using Information Technologies. For example, from an information repository, one may have collected patient data, which are registered in an efficient, consistent, clear and structured way to improve disease knowledge and therapy; the medical processes for registering data are complemented with the information interchange between the different physicians that work around the patient; and the clinical data recording are guaranteed in the EHR application and procedural context. Interoperability will allow for sharing information among several information systems.

The process to collect data comes from Problem Oriented Medical Record (POMR) method. This is a format for clinical recording consisting of a problem list; a database including the patient history with physical examination and clinical findings; diagnostic, therapeutic and educational plans; and a daily SOAP (Subjective, Objective, Assessment and Plan) progress note. The problem list serves as an index for the reader, each problem being followed through until resolution. This system widely influences note keeping by recognizing the four different phases of the decision making process: data collection; formulation of problems; and devising a management plan; and reviewing the situation and revising the plan if necessary.

6 Conclusion

Different methodologies for problem solving based on the AI paradigm have been proposed to model ethical reasoning, however we consider that continuous logic programming expresses characteristics that overcome the main shortcomings of other techniques such as black-box techniques. One of the main advantages of using CLP concern the context of ethical modeling itself, as most of the trustworthy knowledge is based on deontological principles and is oriented towards experts consideration. The principle and exception modeling demonstrated presents a modeling clearly understandable by experts, traceable through proof trees and which processing is clearly identifiable, predictable and updatable.

The ultimate goal of using CLP is not to simulate moral reasoning itself, but rather enable decision support architectures, which take into account moral context. That is the reason why the possibility to justify moral decision and doubt on real-time to clinical staff is of the essence. Using such modeling principles, this staff could recur to moral decision support on real time and understand the line of reasoning implicit in the decision advised by the system.

Although a long path has to be walked before such moral aware decision support systems are implemented, this study of moral modeling and representation is of the essence to set the basilar structure in which morality can be imbedded in future systems.

References

1. Tonkens, R.: A Challenge for Machine Ethics. Minds and Machines 19(3), 421–438 (2009)
2. Nugent, C., Cunningham, P.: A Case-Based Explanation System for Black-Box Systems. Artificial Intelligence Review 24(2), 163–178 (2005)
3. Horty, J.F.: Moral Dilemmas and Nonmonotonic Logic. Journal of Philosophical Logic 23(1), 35–65 (1994)
4. Powers, T.M.: Prospects for a kantian machine. IEEE Intelligent Systems 21(4), 46–51 (2006)
5. Machado, J., et al.: Modeling Medical Ethics through Intelligent Agents. I3E, 112–122 (2009)
6. Guarini, M.: Particularism and the classification and reclassification of moral cases. IEEE Intell. Syst. 21(4), 7 (2006)
7. Floares, A.G.: A reverse engineering algorithm for neural networks, applied to the subthalamopallidal network of basal ganglia. Neural Networks 21(2-3), 379–386

8. Jonsen, A.R., Siegler, M., Winslade, W.J.: Clinical Ethics, 4th edn. McGraw-Hill, New York (1997)
9. Anderson, M., Anderson, S.L., Armen, C.: An approach to computing ethics. IEEE Intelligent Systems 21(4), 56–63 (2006)
10. Sprung, C.L., et al.: End-of-Life Practices in European Intensive Care Units: The Ethicus Study. Journal Of the American Medical Association 290(6), 790–797 (2003)
11. Danbury, C.M., Waldmann, C.S.: Ethics and law in the intensive care unit. Best Practice & Research Clinical Anaesthesiology 20(4), 589–603 (2006)
12. Serrão, D., Nunes, R.: Ética em Cuidados de Saúde. Porto Editora (1998)
13. Angus, D.C., et al.: Quality-adjusted Survival in the First Year after the Acute Respiratory Distress Syndrome. Am. J. Respir. Crit. Care Med. 163(6), 1389–1394 (2001)

Overview of the Health Informatics Research Field: A Bibliometric Approach

Hai-Ning Liang

National ICT Australia (NICTA),
Queensland Research Lab, Brisbane, Australia
hai-ning.liang@nicta.com.au

Abstract. Health informatics is a relatively new research area. Over the last decade or so, research in health information has been growing at a very rapid rate, as evidenced by the large number of publications. While this growth has been beneficial to the field, it has also made understanding the scope of the field more difficult. Consequently, it is difficult to answer questions such as how the research field has evolved over time, what the landmark publications are, what impact these publications have had, and who are the most prolific and high impact researchers. The purpose of this paper is to provide an overview of the research field of health informatics and, in doing so, attempt to answer some of the questions just mentioned. To this end, we make use of two bibliometric tools: HistCite and CiteSpace II. Because these tools offer complementary bibliometric methods, their use together provides results that are more robust. In this paper, we report some general findings of our bibliometric analysis using these two tools.

Keywords: Health informatics; medical informatics; e-health; bibliometrics; literature review; research field; citation and co-citation analysis.

1 Introduction and Background

The term 'health informatics' came into existence around 1973 [1]. For the last decade or so health informatics research has been growing at a rapid rate, partly fuelled by advances in information technologies and partly by an urgent need to improve quality of care and patient safety [2, 3]. Although there are several definitions for health informatics, Coiera [3] suggests that it is "the study of information and communication systems in healthcare" (p.xxii). Health informatics is thought to be situated at the crossroad of information science, computer science, medicine, and healthcare, with a wide range of application areas including nursing, clinical care, public health, and biomedicine [3, 4].

Because of its multidisciplinary foundations and diverse application areas, health informatics has captured the interest of researchers from numerous areas. Engagement from these researchers has been beneficial to the field as it has led to the development of a rich research literature appearing in many journals. Consequently, because the corpus of literature has become so complex, it is difficult for newcomers to the area to grasp its foundations and main themes, and even for those versed in the area to stay abreast of new developments.

H. Takeda (Ed.): E-Health 2010, IFIP AICT 335, pp. 37–48, 2010.

As research in health informatics continues to grow, it may be useful to have a clearer understanding of its major themes. Perhaps only then will it be possible to answer questions such as how the field has evolved over time, what its landmark publications are, what impact these landmark publications have had, and who have been the most prolific and high impact researchers.

The purpose of this paper is to provide an overview of research field of health informatics. We use bibliometric methods [5-8], which are formal, quantifiable techniques for analysing research activities and output, such as publications and patents. Bibliometric methods are becoming more popular; for example, the UK government is looking into the possibility of using such methods to assess the quality of research publications of UK universities [see 9]. These methods require an aggregation of publications, and when bibliometric methods are applied to the aggregation, it is possible to identify statistical and structural properties of citation, co-citation, or co-author networks and patterns.

There are currently several computer-based biblimetric tools such as Bibexel [10], CiteSpace II [11], HistCite [12], and Sitkis [13], each of which operationalizes certain bibliometric methods. These tools allow for a more automated analysis of research output in order to determine the impact of a field, of a set of researchers, or of a specific publication.

We selected two bibliometric tools, CiteSpace II [11, 14] and HistCite [15, 16], to assist in the analysis of the research field of health informatics, and in doing so, we attempt to find answers to the questions noted above.

2   Method

2.1   CiteSpace II and HistCite

An important step of this research was to survey the available bibliometric tools. Four potential tools were identified: Bibexel [10], CiteSpace II [11], HistCite [12], and Sitkis [13] [1]. Broadly speaking, these tools can be classified as visualization-based or text-based. Visualization-based tools emphasize the use of graphical means in the exploration and analysis of patterns in research productivity. These tools provide their output as visual representations through which patterns and trends can be detected by visual inspection. One attractive feature of visualization-based tools is that their visual representations are often interactive and so are directly responsive to analysts' needs [17]. Text-based tools, on the other hand, give more primacy to the use of tables and charts as outputs for inspection and analysis.

We selected one tool from each group: CiteSpace II and HistCite. CiteSpace II is visualization-based whereas HistCite is text-based. Another criterion for the choice was that each offers features not available in the other. CiteSpace II bases its analysis on co-citation counts. HistCite, on the other hand, bases its analysis on citation counts. Because the tools are complementary, using them together may add to the validity of our analysis.

---

[1] HistCite is the only commercial tool.

2.2 Data Collection

We conducted a literature search on the ISI Web of Knowledge, Web of Science databases [18], which include Science Citation Index Expanded, Social Sciences Citation Index, Arts & Humanities Citation Index, and Conference Proceedings Citation Index—both Science, and Social Science & Humanities. We intentionally made our search as broad as possible using the terms "medical informatics", "health informatics", "eHealth", and "e-Health". Overall, our search returned 3708 results[2]. The search results were entered into both CiteSpace II and HistCite for analysis.

3 Results

3.1 Descriptive Results

Figure 1 shows the growth of research output since 1973 within the scope of our query, and Table 1 displays the output per year since 1973. Several important observations can be made. First, the first publications appeared in the early seventies. The first World Congress on Medical Informatics took place during this time [19]. Second, growth in the number of publications in the seventies, eighties, and early nineties was slow. Third, there were five key years in which publications jumped in numbers: 1992-1993, 1996-1997, 2000-2001, 2003-2004, and 2006-2007 (highlighted in Table 1). In short, if this trend continues, we will expect to see the number of publications in the next few years to be around 400-500, if not higher.

The search collection contains 8472 authors and co-authors. Table 2 shows the most productive authors—those who have published at least fifteen papers. The most productive author is R. Haux with 73 papers, having more than twice the number of publications than the next author, E. Ammenwerth, who is closely followed by P. Knaup, and A. Hasman. As discussed further down, the work of these researchers, especially of R. Haux, seems to have had great impact in the field, particularly in laying its initial foundations.

Table 1. Yearly output of publications (adapted from HistCite)

1973	1	1986	11	1998	177
1974	1	1987	10	1999	119
1976	1	1988	5	2000	145
1977	1	1989	25	**2001**	**205**
1978	1	1990	13	2002	184
1979	2	1991	48	2003	159
1980	5	1992	18	**2004**	**246**
1981	3	**1993**	**58**	2005	291
1982	5	1994	72	2006	342
1983	4	1995	78	**2007**	**450**
1984	8	1996	67	2008	420
1985	8	**1997**	**128**	2009	371

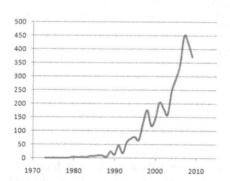

Fig. 1. Growth of publications in the collection

---

[2] Search was in January, 2010.

Table 3 presents the list of top research institutions based on output. The Harvard School of Medicine is ranked first with 42 publications. The National Library of Medicine is next with 30 publications, followed by the School of Health Information Science at the University of Victoria with 28 publications. The papers in the collection have come predominantly from research institutions in the US (9 out of 14), followed by institutions in Germany (3 out of 14).

Table 2. Authors with at least fifteen papers in the collection (adapted from HistCite)

Rank	# Papers	Authors
1	73	Haux, R.
2	34	Ammenwerth, E.
3	30	Knaup, P.
4	28	Hasman, A.
5	21	Wyatt, J.C.
6	20	Moehr, J.R.
7	20	Shortliffe, E.H.
8	19	Blobel, B.
9	19	Maojo, V.
10	18	Cimino, J.J.
11	18	Timpka, T.
12	17	Ball, M.J.
13	17	Eysenbach, G.
14	17	Gardner, R.M.
15	17	Patel, V.L.
16	16	Rigby, M.
17	16	Sullivan, F.
18	15	Leven, F.J.
19	15	Martin-Sanchez, F.

Table 3. List of top research institutions (adapted from HistCite)

Rank	# Papers	Institutions/Subdivision	Country
1	42	Harvard University, School of Medicine	USA
2	30	National Library of Medicine	USA
3	28	University of Victoria, School of Health Information Science	Canada
4	25	University of Heidelberg, Department of Medical Information	Germany
5	24	Tech Univ Carolo Wilhelmina Braunschweig, Inst Med Informat	Germany
6	20	Univ Amsterdam, Acad Med Ctr	Holland
7	19	Yale Univ, Sch Med	USA
8	19	Rutgers State Univ, Dept Comp Sci	USA
9	19	Univ Heidelberg, Inst Med Biometry & Informat	Germany
10	19	Vanderbilt Univ, Med Ctr	USA
11	17	Indiana Univ, Sch Med	USA
12	17	Stanford Univ, Sch Med	USA
13	17	Univ Utah, Sch Med	USA
14	15	Univ Texas, Hlth Sci Ctr	USA

Finally, Table 4 shows the most important journals according to how many publications described by our search terms were found in the journal. The three top journals are *Methods of Information in Medicine*, *International Journal of Medical Informatics*, and *Journal of the American Medical Informatics Association*, with 295, 271, and 233 publications respectively.

Table 4. Top journals based on publication output (adapted from HistCite)

Rank	# Papers	Journals	Impact Factor[3]
1	295	Methods of Information in Medicine	1.1
2	271	International Journal of Medical Informatics	2.8
3	233	Journal of the American Medical Informatics Association	3.4
4	79	Telemedicine Journal and E-Health	1.4
5	54	Journal of Medical Internet Research	3.6
6	52	Journal of Telemedicine and Telecare	0.9
7	42	Connecting Medical Informatics and Bio-Informatics	NA
8	42	Journal of Biomedical Informatics	1.9
9	35	Computer Methods and Programs in Biomedicine	1.2
10	35	M D Computing	NA
11	30	British Medical Journal	12.9

3.2 Results from Citation Analysis

3.2.1 Citation Analysis

As noted earlier, HistCite uses citation counts for its bibliometric calculations. It relies on two main measures: (1) Local Citation Score (LCS) which indicates the count of citations to a paper within the collection; and, (2) Global Citation Score (GCS) which represents the total number of citations to a paper in the Web of Science, regardless of the whether citing papers belong to the collection or not. Using GCS, LCS, and other measures, HistCite calculates the impact of a particular publication or author [12]. The output of HistCite can be "used to help the searcher quickly identify the most significant work on a topic and trace its year-by-year historical development" [12 , p.119].

Table 5. Publication ranking based on Local Citation Score (Adapted from HistCite)

Articles	LCS	Rank (LCS)	GCL	Rank (GCL)
Greenes & Shortliffe [20]	83	1	157	5
Haux & Knaup [22]	41	2	50	43
Eysenbach [23]	32	3	126	6
Kaplan [24]	32	4	88	16
Gustafson et al. [25]	30	5	161	4
Ammenwerth et al. [26]	30	6	48	47
vanBemmel [27]	27	7	38	74
Kaplan [28]	24	8	68	24
Martin-Sanchez [29]	24	9	40	66
Sittig [30]	22	10	38	72
Haux [31]	22	11	25	146
Lorenzi et al. [32]	22	12	69	23
Kulikowski [33]	22	13	24	160
Collen [21]	21	14	26	>200
Stead et al. [34]	21	15	51	41
Heathfield & Wyatt [35]	21	16	24	156

Table 5 shows the ranking of articles based on LCS and GCS measures. It seems that the LCS measure provides a more accurate representation of the relevance of

---

[3] Numbers were obtained from each journal's website (visited on February 2010).

publications to the search terms than the GCS measure. When using the GCS measure as the main criterion, in contrast, some high-ranking articles are not so relevant to health informatics. The publications from Table 5 include articles that seem to have provided the foundations and created the initial momentum for health informatics as a research discipline.

One of the most useful features of HistCite is its ability to produce a *historiograph* of the most-cited articles in the collection (see Figure 2). The nodes represent publications and the links between them depict citations. An arrow pointing from one node back to another indicates that the article at the origin of the arrow cites the article at the end of the arrow. For example, article 99 [20] cites article 50 [21]. The size of the node at the end of the arrow is proportional to how often it is cited.

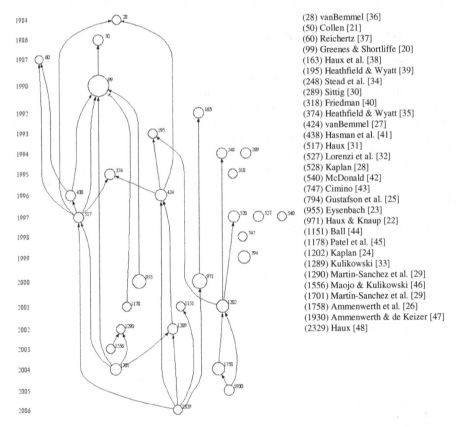

(28) vanBemmel [36]
(50) Collen [21]
(60) Reichertz [37]
(99) Greenes & Shortliffe [20]
(163) Haux et al. [38]
(195) Heathfield & Wyatt [39]
(248) Stead et al. [34]
(289) Sittig [30]
(318) Friedman [40]
(374) Heathfield & Wyatt [35]
(424) vanBemmel [27]
(438) Hasman et al. [41]
(517) Haux [31]
(527) Lorenzi et al. [32]
(528) Kaplan [28]
(540) McDonald [42]
(747) Cimino [43]
(794) Gustafson et al. [25]
(955) Eysenbach [23]
(971) Haux & Knaup [22]
(1151) Ball [44]
(1178) Patel et al. [45]
(1202) Kaplan [24]
(1289) Kulikowski [33]
(1290) Martin-Sanchez et al. [29]
(1556) Maojo & Kulikowski [46]
(1701) Martin-Sanchez et al. [29]
(1758) Ammenwerth et al. [26]
(1930) Ammenwerth & de Keizer [47]
(2329) Haux [48]

Fig. 2. *Historiograph* of the 30 most cited publications (based on LCS) in the collection (adapted from HistCite)

The threshold number is user-defined; and the user can choose to use either LCS or GLS as the main criterion. Figure 2 shows the 30 most-cited articles in terms of LCS—i.e., citation made from the articles within the collection. Greenes and Shortliffe's article [20] (node 99; published in 1990) is the most dominant node in the collection, followed by articles from Eysenbach [23] (node 955; published in 2000) and Haux and Knaup [22] (node 971; also published in 2000). These three articles are the top three items of Table 5. What Table 5 does not show, but which Figure 2 does, is how the most cited articles are related. A closer look at these articles indicates that they are conceptual in nature, and attempt to provide the foundations for health informatics as a field. For example, Greenes and Shortliffe [20] make a strong case for health informatics to be an academic discipline by describing its scope, some basic research problems, and potential career paths for graduates. In general, most of the articles in Figure 2 are conceptual and endeavor to define the aims and tasks of medical informatics [31]; to describe its origins [21]; to provide a systematic view [31]; to delineate its grand challenges [20]; point out its structure [36]; to provide some direction for future research [26, 48].

In term of how the articles are related, according to Figure 2, one of the key articles is by vanBemmel [36], published in 1984, which has been cited by Haux [31] and self-cited by another of vanBemmel's articles [27]. The next two important articles are from Collen [21] and [37]. Greenes and Shortliffe's [20] seminal article comes next, citing Collen's 1986 article and it is cited by several important articles in the collection [23, 29, 31, 41, 45]. The influence of Greenes and Shortliffe's article trickles down to a recent article in the collection from Haux [48], where the past, present, and future of health information systems is described. Further relationships can be discerned from Figure 2. A deeper analysis of the content of the articles is needed to ascertain the degree of the influence of the different articles. This level of analysis is beyond the scope of this paper.

3.2.2 Co-citation Analysis

The above analysis is based mainly on the output of HistCite, which relies primarily on citation counts. To complement this analysis, another bibliometric tool, CiteSpace II [11], is used to analyze the same collection of search results. Unlike HistCite, CiteSpace II relies on both citation and co-citation counts. In addition, with the exception of the historiograph, HistCite provides outputs that are text-based; whereas CiteSpace II's main outputs are visualizations, which are intended to support the detection of trends and patterns in a body of literature. CiteSpace II's visualizations are interactive, and include illustrations of co-citation networks. By specifying different threshold levels, e.g., for citation and co-citation counts, it may be possible to (1) determine influential publications for a particular period; and (2) observe trends and patterns within the body of literature.

In CiteSpace II, the entire time interval is divided into equal segments (e.g., 1-year, 2-year, 3-year, and so on). For each segment, CiteSpace II creates a co-citation network, and integrates all the networks into one single synthesized visualization network. The publications in the collection extend from the early 1970s to the present. Because of the large number of publications, the resulting network of all years included as one continuous interval is very complex. Therefore, we divided the analysis into three intervals: 1970-2000, 2001-2005, and 2006-2009.

Figure 3 shows the resulting network of co-citations for the first interval (1970-2000). Nodes in the network depict publications. The nodes are represented as concentric rings, where the thickness of a ring is proportional to the number of citations in a given time slice. The size of the outermost ring and the size of the font are proportional to the centrality of the publication. The links depict co-citations, and their color represent the year of the first co-citation of the publication. As can be observed from Figure 3, the main articles that are also the most influential articles are: Greenes [20], Heathfield [35], vanBemmel [27], and Lorenzi [32]. The dominant color of the links is orange and corresponds to co-citations which were first made during the 1990-2000 timeframe. The other salient colors, yellow and green, depict co-citations first made prior to 1990.

Fig. 3. Co-citation network of publications for 1970-2000 (5-year slice, parameters c, cc, ccv: 3, 3, 25) (output from CiteSpace II)

A different pattern emerges in Figure 4, which shows a co-citation network of publications for 2001-2005. No longer is Greenes' 1996 article the most dominant; instead in terms of co-citations made to the article. It appears that Hunt's article [49] and Eysenbach's article [23] are the most co-cited in this period. It is interesting to note that, whereas for the 1970-2000 period the most important articles were theoretically-based, for the 2001-2005 period there seems to be a switch on emphasis to empirical and evidence-based research, as exemplified by Hunt's article. This observation is corroborated by a closer examination at other highly co-cited articles.

The rapid growth in publications and the switch from a theoretical to an empirical focus suggests that health informatics, as a discipline, has grown and developed in multiple ways, leading to a divergence in research themes and priorities. In addition, from Figure 4, it is possible to detect some clusters of publications. The group of publications connected by yellow links (top-left corner), whose co-citations began in 2004, seem much influenced by articles by Haux and Knaup [22] and Kulikowski [33] (see black highlighted oval). The Haux and Knaup article provided recommendations on health informatics education; whereas, Kulikowski has described some challenges of health informatics, at both micro and macro levels and from multiple perspectives. Both articles are the linkage articles between the yellow cluster and light blue cluster. It is interesting to note that the two most influential articles by Hunt and Eysenbach have direct connections with the orange, green, blue, and light blue clusters, but not with the yellow cluster.

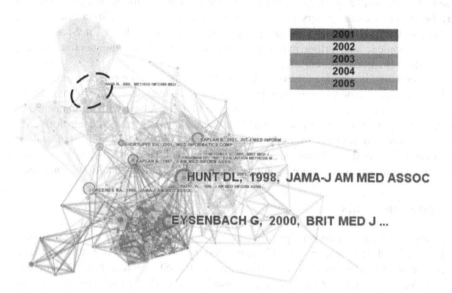

Fig. 4. Co-citation network of publications for 2001-2005 (1-year slice, parameters c, cc, ccv: 3, 3, 25) (output from CiteSpace II)

Similar patterns can be observed from the 2006-2009 period, where a greater number of articles seem to be empirically orientated—an observation confirmed by a rapid survey of the articles first co-cited during this period. The co-citation network is more complex than the one for 2001-2005 because of the large number of publications (see Table 1) and of co-citations. It is difficult to locate patterns within such complex visualization.

4   Summary, Limitations, and Future Work

In this paper, we have used two bibliometric tools to provide an overview of the research field of health informatics. A broad literature search was conducted on Web of Science database, producing a large number of results. The results were analyzed using the bibliometric tools HistCite and CiteSpace II. The analysis lead to the identification of patterns of growth, some of the most influential articles, the most prolific authors and research institutions, the most important publication venues, and some recent patterns of emphasis.

One limitation of the approach taken is that it excludes articles not found on the Web of Science database. In addition, the approach relies on the output from two bibliometric tools, both of which depend on citation or co-citation counts. Consequently, it does not take into account publications with low citation and co-citation counts, a common property with recent publications. A further limitation is that the approach can only hint at the reasons for the citation patterns because it does not examine in detail the content of the articles. Content analysis is required to infer reasons for citation patterns. Some reasons for citation are profound, but other reasons may be trivial because papers often are cited in a perfunctory fashion and are not essential to the goals of the citing paper. In addition, the output from CiteSpace II can be quite complex, and further exploration is required to determine specific patterns and trends in the body of literature.

An interesting avenue for future work would be to conduct a more detailed content analysis to discern how the important publications have shaped or still are shaping the field. Furthermore, a more detailed analysis could be conducted with CiteSpace II to locate emerging "research fronts" and "intellectual bases" in medical informatics research—where a research front is the state-of-the-art of a research area and an intellectual base is the publications cited by the research front. This analysis would allow us to understand the future evolution and research trends in health informatics.

Acknowledgments

The author gratefully acknowledges the valuable input and assistance from members of the National Information and Communication Technology Australia (NICTA) Cognitive and Organisational Systems Engineering (COSE) project. NICTA is funded by the Australian Government as represented by the Department of Broadband, Communications and the Digital Economy and the Australian Research Council through the ICT Centre of Excellence program.

References

1. Protti, D.: The synergism of health/medical informatics revisited. Methods of Information in Medicine (34), 441–445 (1995)
2. Deloitte: Queesnland Health: eHeatlh Strategy (2006)
3. Coiera, E.: Guide to Health Informatics, 2nd edn. Hodder Headline Group, London (2003)
4. Shortliffe, E.H., Cimino, J.J. (eds.): Biomedical Informatics: Computer Applications in Health Care and Biomedicine, 3rd edn. Springer, Heidelberg (2006)
5. De Bellis, N.: Bibliometrics and citation analysis: From the science citation index to cybermetrics. The Scarecrow Press, Inc., Lanham (2009)
6. Van Leeuwen, T.N., Visser, M.S., Moed, H.F., Nederhof, T.J., Van Raan, A.F.J.: The Holy Grail of science policy: Exploring and combining bibliometric tools in search of scientific excellence. Scientometrics 57(2), 257–280 (2003)
7. Bordons, M., Morillo, F., Gómez, I.: Analysis of cross-disciplinary research through bibliometric tools. In: Moed, H., Glänzel, W., Schmoch, U. (eds.) Handbook of Quantitative Science and Technology Research: The Use of Publication and Patent Statistics in Studies of S&T Systems, pp. 437–456. Kluwer Academic Publishers, New York (2004)
8. Nederhof, A.J., Meijer, R.F.: Development of bibliometric indicators for utility of research to users in society: Measurement of external knowledge transfer via publications in trade journals. Scientometrics 32(1), 37–48 (1995)
9. Higher Education Funding Council for England. HEFCE: Research: REF: Bibliometrics (2010)

10. Persson, O.: BIBEXCEL, Umeå, Sweden. BIBEXCEL A tool-box developed by Olle Persson (2010)

11. Chen, C.: CiteSpace II: Detecting and visualizing emergent trends and transient patterns in scientific literature. Journal of the American Society for Information Science and Technology 57(3), 359–377 (2006)

12. Garfield, E.: Historiographic mapping of knowledge domains literature. Journal of Information Science 30(2), 119–145 (2004)

13. Schildt, H.A., Mattsson, J.T.: A dense network sub-grouping algorithm for co-citation analysis and its implementation in the software tool Sitkis. Scientometrics 67(1), 143–163 (2006)

14. Chen, C.: CiteSpace: Visualizing patterns and trends in scientific literature (2010)

15. Garfield, E., Pudovkin, A.I., Istomin, V.I.: Mapping the Output of Topical Searches in the Web of Knowledge and the case of Watson-Crick. Information Technology and Libraries 22(4), 183–187 (2003)

16. HistCite Software LLC. HistCite, Bala Cynwyd, PA (2010)

17. Chen, C.: Information visualization: Beyond the horizon, 2nd edn. Springer, London (2006)

18. Reuters, T.: Web of Science - Science - Thomas Reuters (2010)

19. Dem, T.: MEDINFO 1974: First World Conference on Medical Informatics. Biomedical Engineering 9(11), 524–525 (1974)

20. Greenes, R.A., Shortliffe, E.H.: Medical informatics: an emerging academic discipline and institutional priority. Journal of the American Medical Association 263(8), 1114–1120 (1990)

21. Collen, M.F.: Origins of medical informatics. Western Journal of Medicine 145(6), 778–785 (1986)

22. Haux, R., Knaup, P.: Recommendations of the International Medical Informatics Association on education in health and medical informatics. Methods of Information in Medicine 39(3), 267–277 (2000)

23. Eysenbach, G.: Recent advances: Consumer health informatics. British Medical Journal 320(7251), 1713–1716 (2000)

24. Kaplan, B.: Evaluating informatics applications–some alternative approaches: theory, social interactionism, and call for methodological pluralism. International Journal of Medical Informatics 64(1), 39–55 (2001)

25. Gustafson, D.H., Hawkins, R., Boberg, E., Pingree, S., Serlin, R.E., Graziano, F., Chan, C.L.: Impact of a Patient-Centered, Computer-Based Health Information/Support System. American Journal of Preventive Medicine 16(1), 1–9 (1999)

26. Ammenwerth, E., Brender, J., Nykanen, P., Prokosch, H.U., Rigby, M., Talmon, J.: Visions and strategies to improve evaluation of health information systems - Reflections and lessons based on the HIS-EVAL workshop in Innsbruck. International Journal of Medical Informatics 73(6), 479–491 (2004)

27. van Bemmel, J.H.: Medical informatics, art or science? Methods of Information in Medicine 35(3), 157–172 (1996)

28. Kaplan, B.: Addressing organizational issues into the evaluation of medical systems. Journal of the American Medical Association 4(2), 94–101 (1997)

29. Martin-Sanchez, F., Iakovidis, I., Noraer, S., et al.: Synergy between medical informatics and facilitating genomic medicine for future bioinformatics: health care. Journal of Biomedical Informatics 37(1), 30–42 (2004)

30. Sittig, D.F.: Grand challenges in medical informatics. Journal of the American Medical Association 1(5), 412–413 (1994)

31. Haux, R.: Aims and tasks of medical informatics. International Journal of Medical Informatics 44(1), 9–20 (1997)

32. Lorenzi, N.M., Riley, R.T., Blyth, A.J.C., Southon, G., Dixon, B.J.: Antecedents of the people and organizational aspects of medical informatics: Review of the literature. Journal of the American Medical Association 4(2), 79–93 (1997)

33. Kulikowski, C.A.: The micro-macro spectrum of medical informatics challenges: From molecular medicine to transforming health care in a globalizing society. Methods of Information in Medicine 41(1), 20–24 (2002)

34. Stead, W.W., Haynes, R.B., Fuller, S., et al.: Designing medical informatics research and library-resource projects to increase what is learned. Journal of the American Medical Association 1(1), 28–33 (1994)

35. Heathfield, H.A., Wyatt, J.: The road to professionalism in medical informatics: A proposal for debate Methods of Information in Medicine 34(5), 426–433 (1995)

36. van Bemmel, J.H.: The structure of medical informatics. Medical Informatics 9(3-4), 175–180 (1984)

37. Reichertz, P.L.: Preparing for change: Concepts and education in medical informatics. Computer Methods and Programs in Biomedicine 25(2), 89–101 (1987)

38. Haux, R., Dudeck, J., Gaus, W., et al.: Recommendations of the German association for medical informatics, biometry and epidemiology for education and training in medical informatics. Methods of Information in Medicine 31(1) (1992)

39. Heathfield, H.A., Wyatt, J.: Philosophies for the design and development of clinical decision-support systems. Methods of Information in Medicine 32(1), 1–8 (1993)

40. Friedman, C.P.: Where's the science in medical informatics? Journal of the American Medical Association 2(1), 65–67 (1995)

41. Hasman, A., Haux, R., Albert, A.: A systematic view on medical informatics. Computer Methods and Programs in Biomedicine 51(3), 131–139 (1996)

42. McDonald, C.J.: The barriers to electronic medical record systems and how to overcome them. Journal of the American Medical Informatics Association 4(3), 213–221 (1997)

43. Cimino, J.J.: Desiderata for controlled medical vocabularies in the twenty-first century. Methods of Information in Medicine 37(4-5), 394–403 (1998)

44. Ball, M.J., Lillis, J.: E-health: transforming the physician/patient relationship. International Journal of Medical Informatics 61(1), 1–10 (2001)

45. Patel, V., Arocha, J., Kaufman, D.: Review? A primer on aspects of cognition for medical informatics. Journal of the American Medical Informatics Association 8(4), 324–343 (2001)

46. Maojo, V., Kulikowski, C.: Bioinformatics and medical informatics: Collaborations on the road to genomic medicine? Journal of the American Medical Informatics Association 10(6), 515–522 (2003)

47. Ammenwerth, E., de Keizer, N.: An inventory of evaluation studies of information technology in health care - Trends in evaluation research 1982-2002. Methods of Information in Medicine 44(1), 44–56 (2005)

48. Haux, R.: Health information systems - past, present, future. International Journal of Medical Informatics 75(3-4), 268–281 (2006)

49. Hunt, D.L., Haynes, R.B., Hanna, S.E., Smith, K.: Effects of Computer-Based Clinical Decision Support Systems on Physician Performance and Patient Outcomes: A Systematic Review. Journal of the American Medical Association 280(15), 1339–1346 (1998)

Testing for Usability Is Not Enough: Why Clinician Acceptance of Health Information Systems Is also Crucial for Successful Implementation

Jasmine Croll

National ICT Australia, St Lucia,
Queensland, Australia
jasmine.croll@nicta.com.au

Abstract. Health Information Systems (HIS) are being implemented in all aspects of healthcare; from administration to clinical decision support systems. Usability testing is an important aspect of any HIS implementation with much done to deliver highly usable systems. However, evidence shows that having a highly usable system is not enough. Acceptance by the clinician users is critical to ensure that the HIS implemented is used fully and correctly. A longitudinal case study of the implementation of the Community Health Information Management Enterprise System (CHIME) in NSW is used to illustrate the importance of ensuring clinician acceptance of a HIS. A mixed methods approach was used that drew on both qualitative and quantitative research methods. The implementation of CHIME was followed from the early pre-implementation stage to the post implementation stage. The usability of CHIME was tested using expert heuristic evaluation and a usability test with clinician users. Clinician acceptance of CHIME was determined using the Technology Acceptance Model (TAM). The clinician users were drawn from different community health service departments with distinctly different attitudes to information and communication technology (ICT) in healthcare. The results of this research identified that a successful implementation of a HIS is not a measure of its quality, capability and usability, but is influenced by the user's acceptance of the HIS.

Keywords: health information systems, acceptance, usability, information and communication technology.

1 Introduction

Health information systems are used in all aspects of healthcare from administration to prescriptions to clinical care [1]. ICT, via Health Information Systems (HIS), is used to manage this ever-growing health information generated by healthcare providers [2]. The different stakeholders in healthcare have a mixed reaction to the use of HIS, with some welcoming the many benefits in their drive towards increased safety and quality in healthcare. ICT in healthcare can bring increased accuracy, speed of access, portability, remote access, location awareness, access to more information

H. Takeda (Ed.): E-Health 2010, IFIP AICT 335, pp. 49–60, 2010.

resources, higher precision, and management of large data masses [3, 4, 5, 6, 7, 8]. However, these stakeholders, who include health managers, administrators, technicians, clinicians and nurses, can also be concerned about the detrimental aspects of health ICT. HIS can disrupt work practice, is expensive, could result in poorer quality of health care and make the users more inefficient. The confidentiality, security and privacy of health information can also be compromised. Poor usability and system failure of HIS can also result in many of these systems not being accepted or fully used [9, 10, 11]. Kushniruk et al [12] claimed that the ultimate acceptance or rejection of a HIS depended on the usability of that system.

Usability is defined as extent to which a product can be used by specified users to achieve specified goals with effectiveness, efficiency and satisfaction in a specified context of use [13]. Usability of HIS is a growing area with much research highlighting the importance of having highly usable systems. Poor usability can lead to failure of HIS. The increasing complexity and cross-platform operability of health information systems make it critical to ensure that the usability of these systems has been evaluated. The myriad changes in the healthcare environment require the development of information systems that are well designed and usable. Usability evaluation is a well researched area with many tried and tested methods including analytic, expert, observational, survey and experimental evaluations [14]. However, even well designed and usable systems can result in lack of acceptance by its users.

HIS clinician users can be unwilling to learn new routines and are uninvolved with the process of implementation. The negative impacts on the clinician-patient relationship that may result from use of a health information system while the patient is present can be of concern [5]. Clinician users are also unwilling to change their traditional long-standing practice patterns. Disruption to their established work roles results in resistance [11]. Some clinicians are computer illiterate and have low expertise in using the system. They may also have had to learn how to use Information and Communication Technology (ICT) without the benefit of formal study. Johnson [9] identified the lack of ICT training as a major barrier to the acceptance by clinicians and hence to the implementation of health information systems. Clinicians had fears concerning the effects of the system and had no intimate knowledge of it or responsibility for decisions relating to its implementation [6].

Johnson [9] stated that even a technically best system can be brought to its knees by users who have low psychological ownership in the system and who vigorously resist its implementation. Some clinicians simply do not bother to use it either fully or even partially [11]. They have a lack of insight about the benefits and are concerned about the sheer magnitude of the change caused by the health information system. Clinicians are also ambivalent about the changes that the health information system is designed to improve and are uninformed about its capabilities in that they actively discourage having the system or fail to support its use [9]. Clinicians are also burdened by the stress of anxiety about the new system, and ICT in general, resulting in high levels of stress and feelings of vulnerability in a profession which is already engulfed by enormous pressure and strain [7].

This paper presents a case study which illustrates why having a usable and well-designed HIS is not enough without ascertaining clinician acceptance.

2 Method

A mixed methods approach was used with both qualitative and quantitative research methods with an emphasis on the qualitative. It was a longitudinal (over the course of six months of a health information system implementation) case study. A community health information system, the Community Health Information Management Enterprise (CHIME) was implemented in two separate community health services in the Illawarra in New South Wales, namely, the Child Assessment Intervention Team (CA) in November, 2002, and the Aged Care Assessment Team (AC). CHIME is part of the Electronic Health Record Network or EHR *Net which provided web-enabled access to the personal clinical information held by the NSW public health system. CHIME is an amalgam of the Patient Administration System, the fundamental information infrastructure for all patient information systems, and the Point of Care Clinical Systems, which provides critical fundamental clinical data, in a community setting.

The two case studies comprised clinicians who were given training before the system was implemented. They were then interviewed over a series of stages: before the system was implemented and training given, after the training, after three months, and after six months. The usability of CHIME was also assessed by a variety of tests including heuristic evaluation and usability testing of the efficiency, effectiveness and satisfaction of the system. Clinician acceptance of CHIME was then examined using the Technology Acceptance Model to determine any relationship with the usability of CHIME.

There were 21 participants from Child Assessment (CA) and 10 participants from Aged Care (AC). These participants were clinicians in the two community health services. These two services (part of Community Health in the Illawarra Area Health Service) were selected by New South Wales Health to be the pilot sites for the implementation of a community health information system CHIME.

These services offered a range of specialists including nurse audiometrists, audiologists, psychologists, social workers, speech pathologists, occupational therapists, physiotherapists, nurse-clinicians (including enrolled and registered nurses) and clinical nurse consultants, occupational therapists, social workers, physiotherapists and dementia specialists.

The following table shows the stages, timing and type of data collection.

Table 1. The Stages, Timing and Type of Data Collection

Stage	Timing	Data Collection
1	2 weeks before implementation	Interviews, User Profile Quetionnaire
2	After 4 days of training	Interviews, TAM Questionnaire
3	After 3 months	TAM Questionnaire, Interviews, Heuristic Evaluation
4	After 6 months	Usability Test

The multi-methods approach in usability and acceptance evaluation resulted in the use of a variety of instruments to collect the data in this research. The instruments used included semi-structured interviews, questionnaires, checklists and testing. All the instruments were planned and used at specified times. For Stage 1, there was a User Profile questionnaire, and individual semi-structured interviews. Stage 2 and Stage 3 utilized the Technology Acceptance Model questionnaire and semi-structured interviews, and the heuristic evaluation checklist and for Stage 4, a usability test was done. For the purposes of this paper, only the TAM questionnaire and usability evaluations will be considered.

2.1 Usability Evaluation of CHIME

The usability of CHIME was evaluated using two standard methods; heuristic evaluation and a usability test. Heuristic evaluation is a usability engineering method used for finding the usability problems in a user interface design [15]. A small set of experts examine the CHIME interface and judged its compliance with recognised usability principles (the heuristics). These heuristics are:

1.   Visibility of System Status
2.   Match Between System and the Real World
3.   User Control and Freedom
4.   Consistency and Standards
5.   Help Users Recognize, Diagnose, and Recover From Errors
6.   Error Prevention
7.   Recognition Rather Than Recall
8.   Flexibility and Minimalist Design
9.   Aesthetic and Minimalist Design
10. Help and Documentation
11. Skills
12. Pleasurable and Respectful Interaction with the User
13. Privacy [16]

A usability test was also used to evaluate CHIME with specific tests to measure the interactions between the system and the users for efficiency, effectiveness and satisfaction. Satisfaction was measured using the QUIS. Five significant tasks in a performance test were undertaken by the clinicians. These were: Application Basics; Client Notes; Diary; Service Request Folder and Episode Service Request. Software called Camtasia was used to record the clinicians' efficiency and effectiveness of CHIME by measuring the time taken to complete tasks, counting the number of mouse clicks, the observation of errors, and observing how the clinicians used CHIME. Satisfaction of CHIME was tested using the Questionnaire for User Interaction Satisfaction (QUIS), a tool developed by a multi-disciplinary team of researchers at the University of Maryland. This tool was designed to assess users' subjective satisfaction with specific aspects of the human-computer interface including: Overall User Reaction; Screen; Terminology and System Information; Learning; System Capabilities; Technical Manuals and Online Help; Online Tutorials;

Multimedia; Teleconferencing and Software Installations. The interviews conducted at the different stages of the CHIME implementation also gave rich information about the usability of CHIME.

2.2 Acceptance Evaluation of CHIME

Acceptance of CHIME was measured using the Technology Acceptance Model [17]. The Technology Acceptance Model (TAM) [17] is based on Ajzen and Fishbein's Theory of Reasoned Action [18,19] which was developed to explain human behaviour that is under voluntary control.

Davis [17] adapted the Technology Acceptance Model and designed it specifically to model user acceptance of information systems. The model suggests that when users are presented with new technology, a number of factors influence their decision about how and when they will use it.

The two main factors are the perceived usefulness (PU) and the perceived ease of use (PEOU). Davis [17] defined PU as "the degree to which a person believes that using a particular system would enhance his or her job performance" (p. 320). PEOU is defined as "the degree to which a person believes that using a particular system would be free from effort" (p.320). In other words, PU and PEOU would be able to predict computer systems users' acceptance behaviours [20]. The Technology Acceptance Model asserts that the influence of external variables upon user behaviour is mediated through user beliefs and attitudes (see Figure 1).

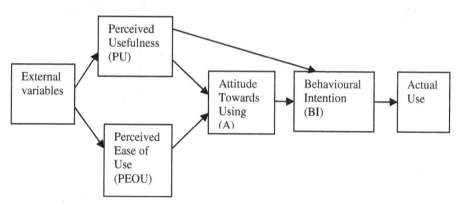

Fig. 1. Technology Acceptance Model (TAM)

3   Results

3.1   Usability Evaluation Results

The results of the heuristic evaluation are presented in Table 2. These show the heuristics, the percentage of problems identified by the three experts and a description of the usability problems of CHIME. None of the experts found more than 35% of usability problems with CHIME. Nielsen (2003) stated that this is an acceptable percentage which would evaluate a system as usable. The usability problems identified

Table 2. Results of Expert Usability Testing

Heuristics	Expert1	Expert2	Expert3	Description of usability problems
Visibility of System Status	28%	21%	21%	No header or title that described the screen. The error messages did not allow the user to see the field in error. The response time was inappropriate to the task (it took too long) in the organisation unit diary. The menu naming terminology was not consistent with the user's task domain as it was not logical and the term service provider should have read health worker instead
Match between System and the Real World	4%	17%	8%	As seen in the diary, the language was not in line with the real world. The numbered codes (ICDT10) should have be omitted, if possible
User Control and Freedom	25%	28%	22%	Users could not rearrange window on the screen. Users could not switch between windows when using overlapping windows. Users could not type ahead. Once saved, users could not reverse their actions
Consistency and Standards	30%	25%	32%	The method for moving the cursor to the next or previous field was not consistent. Pages in multi-page data entry screens did not have the same title. In multi-page data entry screens, pages did not have a sequential page number.
Help Users Recognize, Diagnose, and Recover From Errors	4%	4%	4%	The prompts needed to be brief and use simpler language.
Error Prevention	34%	30%	30%	Users had to enter one group of data at a time. When the system displayed multiple windows, navigation between windows was tedious. In the service request wizard for issues and diagnosis comment field, the number of characters available was not indicated.
Recognition Rather Than Recall	0%	0%	0%	None
Flexibility and Minimalist Design	N.A.	N.A.	N.A.	Not Applicable (N.A.)
Aesthetic and Minimalist Design	6%	10%	13%	All information not just the essential was displayed on the screen. The data entry screens did not have a short, simple, clear, distinctive title.
Help and Documentation	0%	0%	0%	None
Skills	N.A.	N.A.	N.A.	Not Applicable (N.A.)
Pleasurable and Respectful Interaction with the User	4%	8%	4%	The amount of window housekeeping when linking activities in the diary to phase in tree-view needed to be kept to a minimum.
Privacy	0%	0%	0%	None

by the expert evaluators were, in general, minor. This uncovering of minor problems is one of the results of doing heuristic evaluation [21]. Based on the results, CHIME addressed many of the concerns that would have affected its usability. It kept users informed via appropriate feedback and used language that was pertinent although some of the medical terminology needed changing. Users were able to select and sequence tasks freely. However, CHIME did not cater to a wide range of users as a certain level of skill and competence was expected. This was expected as this system had been specifically designed to bring community health information into the electronic health record. The help and documentation was user-centred with easy to search information. It was also aesthetically pleasing.

The results according to the experts were that, overall, CHIME was a usable system. Any usability problems identified were minor compared to what the system could achieve in terms of managing the community health data. Such a usable system should therefore have no problems being accepted by its users.

The second usability evaluation was the usability test where the three determinants of usability; efficiency, effectiveness and satisfaction, were measured separately.

The efficiency of CHIME was measured by the time it took the clinicians to perform the five tasks. The results indicated that the clinicians performed slower at some of the tasks than the others. There were a variety of reasons for this including, the complexity of the tasks, the production of and the care with which some clinicians performed the tasks. Compared against the benchmark times, the clinicians appeared not to have performed as efficiently. A compelling explanation for the poorer performance by the clinicians is that the benchmark times by the expert user was because he was working with information from the training sessions as he was not a clinician. He had no qualms about making errors or keying in incorrect details. The clinicians, on the other hand, were working with real data in real time. They were exercising the same level of professional care with the tasks as they would in their normal work practice. Their concern was not to achieve the fastest times but to ensure that they performed the tasks as accurately as possible.

It must be noted that the expert user used client information from the training sessions as he was not an actual clinician. The clinicians, however, were working with real data in real time situations. The overall results could imply that as a system, CHIME is not as efficient as it is effective. However, the type of client information used in the tests must be taken into account.

The ISO 9241-11 Standard for Usability [13] stated that effectiveness, as a determinant of usability, is measured in terms of the accuracy and completeness with which users achieve specified goals. CHIME's effectiveness was tested in terms of accuracy, that is, whether errors were produced, and completeness, that is, finishing all the steps of the tasks.

In terms of accuracy, the number of errors made both simple recoverable and critical irrecoverable was small; not higher than four per task. The clinicians had to perform a large number of steps in completing the tasks, some of which were complex. Although the critical errors were not able to be removed from the permanent record, they consisted of typographical errors not errors of diagnosis or outcomes. The simple errors were mostly that of mistyped passwords and failure to click or follow navigational direction on the system. These errors did not stop the clinicians from completing the tasks.

The results of the tests for the effectiveness of CHIME in terms of completeness indicate how more than 70% of the clinicians managed to finish all of the steps of the tasks. The unsuccessful clinicians did not complete all the steps of the tasks because they made mistakes, stopped to check details or stopped doing the task. The tasks ranged from simple to complex and involved a series of steps. A high majority of the clinicians were able to navigate successfully through the steps of the tasks. A low rate of error production and a high rate of completion indicate that, CHIME is an effective and, therefore, usable system.

The satisfaction of CHIME was measured using QUIS. The results indicated that the clinicians found the system to be neither satisfying nor unsatisfying. Examination of the different sections indicated that the clinicians did find certain aspects of the system to be positive, for example, the quietness of the system, the ease of operation and their own abilities to respond to commands. However, the majority of the responses were negative, in particular the undoing of operations and the number of steps for each task. Many of the responses were at the neutral midpoint value of 5 indicating that the clinicians did not have a strong opinion on whether or not CHIME, as a system, was satisfying to use.

CHIME, in terms of the third determinant of usability, neither satisfied nor unsatisfied its users.

Table 3. Stage 2 Perceived Usefulness

Perceived Usefulness	AC Clinicians	CA Clinicians
Using Chime would improve my job performance	30% would not at all 20% would slightly not at all 40% neutral 10% would slightly	75% would not at all 19% neutral 6% would slightly
Using Chime would make it easier to do my job	90% would not 10% would slightly	63% would not 38% neutral
Using Chime would enhance my effectiveness on the job	70% would not 30% neutral	69% would not 25% neutral 6% would slightly
Using CHIME in my job would increase my productivity	70% would not 20% neutral 10% would slightly	75% would not 25% neutral
Using CHIME in my job would enable me to accomplish tasks more quickly	60% would not 30% neutral 10% would slightly	69% would not 19% neutral 13% would slightly
I would find CHIME useful in my job	70% would not 20% neutral 10% would definitely	56% would not 25% neutral 19% would slightly

3.2 Acceptance Evaluation Results

The clinician acceptance of CHIME was evaluated in Stage 2 after the 4 days of training, and Stage 3 after three months of use. The results of the Perceived Usefulness and Perceived East of Use in the TAM are seen in the tables below.

Table 4. Stage 2 Perceived Ease of Use

Perceived Ease of Use	AC Clinicians	CA Clinicians
Learning to operate CHIME would be easy for me	10% not at all 20% neutral 40% slightly 30% definitely	25% not at all 44% neutral 13% slightly 19% definitely
My interaction with CHIME would be clear and understandable	20% not at all 50% neutral 30% slightly	38% not at all 31% neutral 18% slightly 13% definitely
It would be easy for me to become skilful at using CHIME	10% would not 20% neutral 40% slightly 30% definitely	13% would not 25% neutral 44% slightly 19% definitely
I would find it easy to get CHIME to do what I want	30% did not 40% neutral 30% slightly	69% did not 19% neutral 6% slightly 6% definitely
I would find CHIME to be flexible to interact with	100% did not	81% did not 13% neutral 6 % slightly
I would find CHIME easy to use	30% did not 30% neutral 30% slightly 10% definitely	50% did not 19% neutral 19% slightly 13% definitely

The overall finding at this stage is that clinicians at both health services did not perceive CHIME to be useful. From these results it is clear that the clinicians from both services find CHIME to be the problem rather than their own skills at learning to use it.

After three months of usage, the results of the TAM is represented in Tables 5 and 6

Again, as in Stage 2, the overall finding at this stage is that clinicians at both health services did not accept CHIME after using the system for three months.

Table 5. Stage 3 Perceived Usefulness

Perceived Usefulness	AC Clinicians	CA Clinicians
Using CHIME has improved my job performance	90% had not at all 10% neutral	95% had not at all 5% neutral
Using CHIME has made it easier to do my job	90% had not 10% would slightly	95% had not at all 5% slightly
Using CHIME has enhanced my effectiveness on the job	90% had not at all 10% neutral	95% had not at all 5% slightly
Using CHIME in my job has increased my productivity	90% had not 10% would slightly	95% had not at all 5% slightly
Using CHIME in my job has enabled me to accomplish tasks more quickly	60% had not 30% neutral 10% would slightly	95% had not at all 5% slightly
I have found CHIME useful in my job	50% had not 20% neutral 30% had slightly	71% had not 14% neutral 10% had slightly 5% had definitely

Table 6. Stage 3 Perceived Ease of Use

Perceived Ease of Use	AC Clinicians	CA Clinicians
Learning to operate CHIME was easy for me	30% not at all 10% neutral 50% slightly 10% definitely	24% not at all 38% neutral 29 % slightly 10% definitely
My interaction with CHIME was clear and understandable	30% not at all 20% neutral 40% slightly 10% definitely	39% not at all 17% neutral 44% slightly
I have become skilful at using CHIME	40% had not 20% neutral 20% slightly 20% definitely	5% had not 33 % neutral 38% slightly 24% definitely
I have found it easy to get CHIME to do what I want	80% did not 20% neutral	76% did not 24% neutral
I have found CHIME to be flexible to interact with	100% did not	100% did not
I have found CHIME easy to use	50% did not 40% neutral 10% definitely	40% did not 40% neutral 20% slightly

4 Conclusion

The main result in this research was that having the most usable system is not the crux; it is having a system that is accepted by its users that is important. The findings from this research confirmed that usability of a system was indeed focused on the users. The CHIME system was evaluated by the expert heuristic evaluation and found to be a usable system; however, the users did not accept it and therefore it became unusable. The key finding in the literature review for this research was Kushniruk et al. [12] who asserted that the ultimate acceptance or rejection of a health information system depended to a large extent on the degree of the usability of the health information system. This implied that if a system was usable then the users would accept it; if it were not usable, then the users would reject it. The results of the research indicated otherwise. CHIME was a usable system; it was easy to use, efficient and effective. It facilitated the clinicians to manage all aspects of their clinical work, from basic record keeping, access, to collection and collation of statistics. However, the clinicians were not satisfied with it and did not accept it.

The clinician acceptance of any HIS needs to be evaluated along with the system's usability. The large costs involved in the implementation of HIS and the political implications of such costs in healthcare cannot allow for systems that are not accepted or used fully. More research needs to be done in this area.

References

1. NSW Health. NSW Health Strategy for the EHR NSW EHR* NET. (Report of the Health Information Management Implementation Coordination Group). NSW Health Department (2002)
2. Wickramasinghe, N., Sharma, S., Reddy, H.: Evidence-Based Medicine: A New Approach in the Practice of Medicine. In: Wickramasinghe, N., Gupta, J., Sharma, S. (eds.) Creating Knowledge-Based Healthcare Organizations, pp. 125–135. Idea Group Publishing, London (2005)
3. Safran, C., EMR: A Decade of Experience. Journal of the American Medical Informatics Association 285(13), 1766 (2001)
4. Spaziano, K.: EMR. Radiologic Technology 72(3), 287 (2001)
5. Gadd, C.: Dichotomy between Physicians and Patients Attitudes Regarding EMR Use During Outpatient Encounters. American Medical Information Association (2000)
6. Anderson, J.: Clearing the way for physicians use of clinical information systems. Communications of the ACM 40(8), 83–90 (1997)
7. Nielsen, A.C.: Attitudes towards IT in Australian General Practice (Qualitative Research Report, Computerisation in GP), vol. 2. Commonwealth Department of Health and Family Services, Canberra(1998)
8. DHAC. The Benefits and Difficulties of Introducing a National Approach to Electronic Health Records in Australia, Commonwealth Department of Health and Aged Care (2000)
9. Johnson, K.: Barriers that impede the adoption of pediatric IT. Archives of Pediatrics and Adolescent Medicine 155(12), 1374–1380 (2001)
10. Smith, A.: Human-Computer Factors: A Study of Users and Information Systems. McGraw-Hill, London (1997)

11. Laerum, H., Ellingsen, G., Faxvaag, A.: Doctors use of electronic medical records systems in hospitals: cross sectional survey. British Medical Journal 323(7325), 1344–1349 (2001)
12. Kushniruk, A., Patel, V., Cimino, J.: Usability Testing in Medical Informatics: Cognitive Approaches to Evaluation of Information Systems and User Interfaces. In: Proceediings of 1997 AMIA Annual Fall Symposium, pp. 22–26 (1997)
13. ISO 9241-11 Ergonomic requirements for office work with visual display terminals (VDTs), Part 11: Guidance on Usability. ISO (1998)
14. Preece, J., Rogers, Y., Sharp, H., Benyon, D., Holland, S., Carey, T.: Human-Computer Interaction. Addison-Wesley, Harlow (1994)
15. Molich, R., Bevan, N., Butler, S., Curson, I., Kindlund, E., Kirakowski, J., Miller, D.: Comparative Evaluation of Usability Tests. In: Proceedings of the Usability Professionals Association Conference, pp. 189–200. UPA, Washington (1998)
16. Barnum, C.: Usability Testing and Research. Longman, New York (2002)
17. Davis, F.: Perceived Usefulness, Perceived Ease of Use and User Acceptance of IT. MIS Quarterly, 319–340 (1989)
18. Ajzen, I., Fishbein, M.: Understanding Attitudes and Predicting Social Behaviours. Prentice-Hall, Englewood Cliffs (1980)
19. Fishbein, M., Ajzen, I.: Belief, Attitude, Intention and Behaviour: An Introduction to Theory and Research. Addison-Wesley, Reading (1975)
20. Hubona, G., Geitz, S.: External Variables, Beliefs, Attitudes and IT Usage Behavior. In: Proceedings of the Thirtieth Annual Hawaii International Conference on System Sciences. IEEE, Los Alamitos (1997)
21. Dumas, J., Redish, J.: A Practical Guide to Usability Testing. Intellect Books, Exeter (1999)

Towards Characteristics of Lifelong Health Records

Eldridge van der Westhuizen and Dalenca Pottas

Nelson Mandela Metropolitan University, Summerstrand, Port Elizabeth, South Africa

Abstract. Since the beginning of this century, the view has developed that high quality health care can be delivered only when all the pertinent data about the health of a patient is available to the clinician. This viewpoint brings forth the notion of a lifelong health record. Various types of health records have emerged to serve the needs of healthcare providers and more recently, patients or consumers. The purpose of this paper is to present a set of characteristics or best practices for lifelong health records which are seen independently from implementation constraints such as technology and operational context. The characteristics, comprised by four core characteristics and nine dimensions, are synthesized from the characteristics of various types of health records used by healthcare providers and consumers. Examples are provided of evaluation measures that give an indication of compliance to the broadly stated characteristics of lifelong health records.

Keywords: Lifelong Health Record, Personal Health Record, Electronic Health Record, Electronic Medical Record.

1 Introduction

For as long as healthcare has existed, there has been health information stored in some kind of record. The earliest such records were kept in the paper files of the provider, whereas currently, a combination of paper and computer media for recording health information is used. For a variety of reasons, these individual health records have become fragmented into multiple information systems and dispersed across the planet. At the same time, the information inside the records has become more complex, and is required on a regular basis by an increasing number of commercial, educational, and governmental information systems [1]. Factors like these, have led the quest to create a single lifelong health record that is easily accessible, comprehensive and complete.

A health record or medical record is a chronological written account of examination and treatment of the patient that includes their medical history and complaints, the physical findings of the physician, the results of diagnostic tests and procedures, and medications and therapeutic procedures [2]. A degree of interaction is required between both the doctor and patient for this health record to be complete. For many years, the doctor/patient relationship has been asymmetric, with the doctor traditionally seen as holding the balance of power and the patient as being dependent. There are many reasons for this and one of the most important is the asymmetry of knowledge; the doctor controlled almost all the information and often shared it sparingly.

H. Takeda (Ed.): E-Health 2010, IFIP AICT 335, pp. 61–70, 2010.

Technology has developed along the same lines. The need for administrative and clinical e-health systems originated from healthcare providers. Electronic Medical Records (EMRs) and Electronic Health Records (EHRs) were created to address the needs of healthcare providers and to provide them with a tool that enables them to be more competent in their daily activities. Over the past years, a dramatic shift in the amount of information available to the patient has been witnessed. This shift has contributed to a noticeable increase in patient autonomy and choice in medical care. Information is more easily available due to major advances in technology. This led to the development of consumer-focused e-health systems.

The developments in healthcare provider versus consumer-directed e-health systems have resulted in two main types of electronic health records, based on the ownership of the record. These include healthcare provider-owned health records, for example, EMR/EHRs and consumer- or patient-owned health records, for example, Personal Health Records or PHRs. Hybrids between these two types are common. Operationally, each of the health record types can satisfy the need of being a truly lifelong health record to a greater or lesser extent [3].

The purpose of this paper is to present a set of characteristics or best practices for lifelong health records which are seen independently from the implementation constraints such as technology, operational context and similar. The characteristics, comprised by four core characteristics and nine dimensions, are synthesized from the characteristics of the various types of health records used by healthcare providers and consumers. Examples are provided of evaluation measures that give an indication of compliance to the broadly stated characteristics of lifelong health records.

2 The Case for Lifelong Health Records

It is apparent when viewing the medical error statistics of only the United States of America (US), that the importance of lifelong health records cannot be underestimated. The total number of medical errors and deaths in the US is equivalent to six 747 aircraft crashes daily for a year. Specific statistics in this regard include [4]:

- 7,000 patients die annually because of careless handwriting;
- 7.5 million unnecessary medical and surgical procedures are performed annually;
- More than half of the U.S. population has received unnecessary medical treatment which equates to 50,000 people per day;
- 42% of people have been directly affected by a medical mistake, procedure or drug;
- 84% of the population personally know someone who has been a victim of a medical error;
- Preventable medication mistakes affect 1.5 million patients yearly;
- Nearly 14% of doctor visits were missing test results and other documentation resulting in 44% of patients being adversely affected;
- Over 59% of patients have received delayed care or duplicate services with doctor visits; and
- 160,000 lab misidentification errors occur each year.

These figures raise serious concerns. An accurate, complete lifelong health record could reduce these medical errors by providing the healthcare provider with the opportunity to correctly diagnose a condition by viewing the *complete* "picture".

This leads to the question of what precisely constitutes a lifelong health record. It is important to conceptualize the core intentions of the various health record types to characterize the true essence of lifelong health records, as seen from a generic point of view.

3   The True Essence of Lifelong Health Records

Various authors have defined the characteristics of the different types of health records [5],[6],[7],[8],[9],[1]. This paper synthesizes these characteristics into four core characteristics and nine associated dimensions of generic *lifelong* health records. These broadly stated core characteristics and dimensions are taken to represent the characteristics of lifelong health records. These are summarized in Table 1 and discussed thereafter.

Table 1. Characteristics of Lifelong Health Records

CHARACTERISTICS OF LIFELONG HEALTH RECORDS	
Core Characteristics	**Dimension**
Interoperability	Standardization
Comprehensiveness	Integrity Accuracy Completeness Apomediation
Legal Value	Privacy Confidentiality Auditability
Availability	Accessibility

3.1   Interoperability

Interoperability refers to the interconnectedness of multiple healthcare organizations or systems using a model that enables the full interchange of healthcare information. An overwhelming majority of people, currently, receive their care from more than one caregiver or provider. A lack of integration means that choice leads to fragmentation of the health care experience of the patient. Fragmentation, in turn, results in errors, duplication, lack of coordination, and many other problems [10] as confirmed by the statistics provided in Section 2.   Health information will remain in proprietary silos without both interoperability and health information exchange.

Standardization is the main dimension of Interoperability. Standardization, in the field of health informatics, strives to achieve compatibility and interoperability between independent information systems and devices, and to reduce the duplication of effort and redundancies. Healthcare Information Technology (HIT) standards are developed, adopted, or adapted by standards development organizations, government agencies, professional associations, and care providers [11]. The creation of a lifelong health record will be unattainable without standards which facilitate proper interoperability between the different types of health records.

3.2 Comprehensiveness

Comprehensiveness can be subdivided into four dimensions, namely *Integrity, Accuracy, Completeness* and *Apomediation.*

A lifelong health record must provide information to improve care quality. The healthcare provider must trust that the information provided in the health record is correct for this to be considered true. The general principle of *Integrity* implies that no unauthorized person is able to add, remove, or change any data in the health record.

Accuracy implies that the information captured in the lifelong health record, reflects exactly the original meaning of the paper copy or diagnosis made by the healthcare provider. This maps closely to the garbage in, garbage out (GIGO) concept. Valuable output is attained from the lifelong health record when the information that is captured is both accurate and correct.

Completeness implies that all the latest relevant information about the health of the patient is contained in the health record for it to be considered lifelong. There should be no significant delay between when the data is entered into the record and when it becomes available to the different healthcare providers [3].

There has been much discussion about what data or information belongs in a lifelong health record. Advances in data storage devices and their related capacity have made this a less pressing issue. A lifelong health record should contain any information relevant to the health of the patient. Examples of information to be captured include the following [12]:

- Personal identification, including name and birth date;
- People to contact in case of emergency;
- Names, addresses, and phone numbers of the physicians, dentists, and specialists of the patient;
- Health insurance information;
- Living wills, advance directives, or medical power of attorney;
- Organ donor authorization;
- A list and dates of significant illnesses and surgical procedures;
- Current medications and dosages;
- Immunizations and their dates;
- Allergies or sensitivities to drugs or materials, such as latex;
- Important events, dates, and hereditary conditions that occur in the history of the family;
- Results from recent physical examinations;

- Opinions and notes of clinical specialists;
- Important tests results; eye and dental records;
- Correspondence between an individual and his or her healthcare provider;
- Diet and exercise logs, in addition to a list of over-the-counter (OTC) medications.

Apomediation - The term apomediation was defined by Dr. Gunther Eysenbach, a Health Policy and eHealth professor at the University of Toronto. This newly coined term is best explained by Dr. Eysenbach who states that: "Apomediation is a new scholarly socio-technological term that characterizes the process of disintermediation (intermediaries are middlemen or gatekeepers, e.g. health professionals giving relevant information to a patient, and disintermediation means to bypass them), whereby the former intermediaries are functionally replaced by apomediaries, i.e. network/group/collaborative filtering processes. The difference between an intermediary and an apomediary is that an intermediary stands in between the consumer and information/service, i.e. is absolutely necessary to get a specific information/service. In contrast, apomediation means that there are agents (people, tools) which stand by to guide a consumer to high quality information /services/experiences, without being a prerequisite to obtain that information/service in the first place" [13].

Apomediation is affected in the lifelong health record through current advances in technology. The contents of a lifelong health record can be enriched with collaborative filtering and recommender systems like bookmarking, blogs, wikis and communication tools. These networked/collaborative systems enable the creators of lifelong health records, to better capture information contained in scripts, the notes written by healthcare providers and general written information contained in the paper-based patient file. Certain terminology and abbreviations are meaningless to a non-medical person, but through having access to these blogs, wikis and other tools, it is possible to capture the record accurately and have a sense of understanding while doing so.

3.3 Legal Value

The addition of legal regulations and amendments to current regulations, with the intention of increasing security pertaining to HIT, is a norm in the modern day society [14]. This underscores the importance of the *Legal Value* core characteristic. The three main dimensions of this core characteristic are *Privacy, Confidentiality* and *Auditability*.

Privacy implies that the patient gives consent for other parties to access their personal health information. Patients can allow or deny sharing their information with other healthcare workers. Consent is either implied or explicitly given before the act of sharing. Implicit consent assumes the patient to have consented by default unless they specifically state otherwise. This is referred to as opt-out. Explicit consent or opt-in is the reverse, where the access to the information is prohibited unless the patient gives consent [9].

Confidentiality requires that proof is given that the information has not been made available or disclosed to unauthorized entities, whether persons or systems. This can be implemented in two ways. Either information is tagged with metadata about its confidentiality status or confidentiality is enforced through access rules. The use of access rules to enforce confidentiality relies on audit logs to verify that confidentiality has not been breached.

Auditability refers to the ability of the lifelong health record to be used for the following [9]:

- The monitoring of access to and possible misuse of the record, preferably in real-time;
- Review purposes to keep track of previous versions;
- Legal disputes to verify claims about what information was available and whether it was accessed.

One auditability technique is to use audit logs which document all the actions performed on the information and the users who perform those actions to enable the restoration of the past state of the data. The logging should include all events and not be restricted to the information handled. This leads to a huge amount of audit data that should be kept secure for future analyses. For best security, audit logs should be kept and stored separate from the lifelong health record.

3.4 Availability

A lifelong health record must be available when the healthcare provider needs it. It is necessary to make the system housing this lifelong record robust. Failure of the lifelong health record device is not an option, because human lives are at risk. A health record is deemed lifelong when it is continuously available. The main dimension of this characteristic is *Accessibility*.

Accessibility of the health record can be contentious. Ease of accessibility increases the risk that the record can be compromised. Alternately, a record that is too secure and cannot be accessed in case of emergency, nullifies the creation of a lifelong health record. Any access control mechanism that protects the healthcare data needs to be relatively simple and fast. These mechanisms should protect the privacy of the patient by disclosing information only in those situations when it is needed. This latter requirement requires a highly complex mechanism and is hard to combine with the first requirement of a simple mechanism. A middle way needs to be found that addresses the problem of availability versus confidentiality.

This concludes the discussion on the core characteristics and dimensions of a lifelong health record. The next section provides examples of measures towards evaluating compliance with the characteristics. The strengths and weaknesses inherent to the various health record types can be identified by applying the evaluation measures, while taking cognizance of the implementation constraints of technology, social context and similar. For example, an EHR might be weak in the area of *apomediation* because when it was designed, the intent was not to allow for user collaboration and patient interaction. Alternately, the PHR developments by Microsoft and Google do not satisfy *integrity* and *legal value* when measured against these characteristics [3].

4 Evaluation Measures

The evaluation measures listed in Table 2 can be used to determine whether a particular health record type satisfies the dimension that the measure represents. The list is not exhaustive and can be supplemented if required. Each evaluation measure must be used to quantify the extent of achievement of the relevant dimension.

Table 2. Evaluation Measures

CHARACTERISTICS OF LIFELONG HEALTH RECORDS		
Core Characteristics	**Dimension**	**Evaluation Measures**
Interoperability	Standardization	• Does the record support (secure) two-way data exchange? • Does the record use common standards, like XML and PDF/H? • Does the record have the ability to store non-text data such as x-rays, scans and MRI's?
Comprehensiveness	Integrity	• Is this record in a state of entirety and free from corrupting influences or motives?
	Accuracy	• Is this record up-to-date? • Do the data values in the record correspond to the real world objects or events? • Does the data entry application provide for drop-down boxes and checklists to eliminate possible errors?
	Completeness	• Is this record complete, i.e. does it contain the entire health history and all health providers seen?
	Apomediation	• Does the online record provide education about condition, surgeries, medications, etc of the patient and the ability to interact with patients with similar illness to achieve a more complete and correct health record? (Health Information Portal)

Table 2. (*continued*)

Legal Value	Privacy	▪ Does the record bridge language and cultural divides by providing skills to increase the health literacy of the patient and therefore supporting the accuracy of the record? ▪ Does the patient have the facility to grant and/or revoke access or consent to his online record?
	Confidentiality	▪ Can the online record be accessed by unauthorized parties? ▪ Can changes to the record be limited to authorized parties?
	Auditability	▪ Does the online record contain access logs? ▪ Does the health record support non-repudiation (one cannot deny making an entry)? ▪ Does the record provide full auditing features, like tracking of all changes, additions, deletions, etc? ▪ Can the record be restored to a past state? ▪ Are audit logs stored separately from the lifelong health record?
Availability	Accessibility	▪ Can the online record be accessed from any place at any time by patient and health care providers? ▪ Is the system housing the health record robust? ▪ Can emergency access be enabled for health professionals? ▪ Does the capturing frontend provide an offline mode to capture and synchronize later when online?

From Table 2 it is clear that the health record by itself (i.e. the *data*) is not the only contributor to the success or failure of satisfying a particular dimension. Kaelber et.al. [15] state that three primary components of a health record can be identified, viz. *data*, *infrastructure*, and *applications*. For example, the *accuracy* of the record can be improved if the *application* supports data entry through the use of drop-down boxes and checklists. Other obvious examples include provision for educational material and sensitivity to cultural divides, which must be supported through HIT applications. Again, the role of implementation constraints, in this case technology, comes to the fore in the "performance" of the lifelong health record.

5 Conclusion

The main output of this paper comprises a set of characteristics of lifelong health records, which are expanded to include associated dimensions and examples of relevant measures. The set is not necessarily complete, but represents a first attempt at providing such a guideline for lifelong health records. The conceptual nature of the characteristics precludes the consideration of technological, legal, social or economic aspects that relate to the implementation of lifelong health records. However, when evaluating compliance with the characteristics, operational realities tend to determine the extent of achievement of particular health record types. For example, the integrity value of the patient-owned PHR is debatable, given the right of patients who are not health professionals, to update their health records.

While this paper proposes a set of characteristics of lifelong health records, no single solution exists to satisfy all of the stated requirements. As proposed in Wainer [3], it seems that the most one can do is to prioritize and accept that not all the core characteristics and associated dimensions will be achieved. The solution will be geared to the socio-technical, economic and medico-legal requirements of the operational context, while the goal will always be to improve healthcare costs, quality, and efficiency.

References

1. Christopher, J., Feahr, O.D.: The Electronic Health Record – A Fresh Perspective. OptiServ Consulting (2003)
2. The American Heritage® Medical Dictionary. Health Record - Definition of Health Record in Medical Dictionary (January 1, 2007), The Free Dictionary's Medical dictionary, http://medical-dictionary.thefreedictionary.com/ Health+record (retrieved January 18, 2010)
3. Wainer, J.: Security Requirements for a Lifelong Electronic Health Record System: An Opinion. The Open Medical Informatics Journal, 160–165 (2008)
4. BIBLIOGRAPHY \l 7177 Answer My Health Question, Medical Error Statistics. Answer my Health Question (2006), http://www.answer-my-health-question.info/medical-error-statistics.html (retrieved January 5, 2010)
5. Kahn, J.S., Aulakh, V., Bosworth, A.: What It Takes: Characteristics of The Ideal Personal Health Record. Health Affairs, 369–376 (2009)
6. BMC Medical Informatics and Decision Making. Integrated personal health records: Transformative tools for consumer-centric care. BioMed. Central, 8–45 (2008)
7. Heinold, J., Stone, D., MacClary, M.: PHR Consumer Guide (May 14, 2009), http://www.stoneandheinold.com/consumers/consumers2.pdf (retrieved November 12, 2009)

8. Early experiences with Personal Health Records. JAMIA Journal of the American Medical Informatics Association, 1–7 (2008)

9. van der Linden, H.: Inter-organizational future proof EHR systems - A review of the security and privacy related issues. International Journal of Medical Informatics, 141–160 (2009)

10. Brailer, D.J.: Interoperability: The Key To The Future Health Care System (January 19, 2005), Healt Affairs from, `http://content.healthaffairs.org/cgi/content/full/hlthaff.w5.19/DC1` (retrieved January 31, 2010)

11. Health Informatics. Health Informatics TC215 (2009), Transforming Healthcare Through IT from, `http://www.himss.org/ASP/topics_ISO.asp` (retrieved January 3, 2010)

12. Groen, P.J.: Personal Health Record (PHR) Systems: An Evolving Challenge to EHR Systems (July 22, 2007), Virtual Medical Worlds from, `http://www.hoise.com/vmw/07/articles/vmw/LV-VM-08-07-26.html` (retrieved February 4, 2010)

13. P2PFoundation. Apomediation (August 30, 2008), P2PFoundation from, `http://p2pfoundation.net/Apomediation` (retrieved November 16, 2009)

14. Zacharias, E.: Penalties for HIPAA Violations Increase Significantly (November 23, 2009), Health Care Law Reform from, `http://www.healthcarelawreform.com/articles/health-it/` (retrieved February 9, 2010)

15. A Research Agenda for Personal Health Records (PHRs). JAMIA Journal of the American Medical Informatics Association, 729–736 (2008)

Physicians' Concept of Time Usage – A Key Concern in EPR Deployment

Rebecka Janols, Bengt Göransson, Erik Borälv, and Bengt Sandblad

Uppsala University, Department of Information Technology, Human-Computer Interaction,
Box 337, SE-751 05 Uppsala, Sweden

Abstract. This paper is based on an interview study with 19 resident, specialist and senior physicians. The study was initiated by a Swedish Hospital management to investigate physicians' attitude towards their EPR (Electronic Patient Records) and give recommendations for improvement in organization, development, deployment and training. The management had experienced that the physicians were unwilling to take part in the EPR deployment process and simultaneously complained about the low usability and potential safety risks of the systems. The study shows that the EPR must be considered a shared responsibility within the whole organization and not just a property of the IT department. The physicians must consider, and really experience, EPR as efficient support in their daily work rather than something they are forced to use. This includes considering work with the EPR as an important part of their work with patients.

Keywords: EPR, Physicians, Usability, Hospital Information Systems, Organizational Change, Deployment, Qualitative research, Management, Education.

1 Introduction

When implementing IT in health care it is important to have all potential users and management onboard. A large Swedish university hospital started to replace a paper-based record system with an EPR (Electronic Patient Record) system seven years ago. The system covers the whole care process, from primary care to specialized care at the hospital with totally 10 000 employees. The EPR system makes it possible for all care professionals in the county, to track the patients through all health care activities, regardless of treatment unit. The system is modular and the deployment process has been step wise, with modules implemented successively.

In 2001, the county council started a process of investigating the needs of an EPR system for all their care units. One of the visions was to have *one* medical record per patient. This would enable shared care, meaning that all health care providers can access and register information related to a specific patient in the same record. In the process of choosing an EPR system, technical issues, safety and users' requirements were considered. Physicians, nurses, medical secretaries and other care professionals took part in the process as representatives from their professions. They had the opportunity to communicate their needs and requirements and evaluate the different

H. Takeda (Ed.): E-Health 2010, IFIP AICT 335, pp. 71–81, 2010.
© IFIP International Federation for Information Processing 2010

systems. In 2003 the county council decided on a relatively new system from a Swedish company. They assumed that the system easily could be changed upon request and modified according to new needs and practices. Now, seven years after the first pilot deployment, the list of desired modifications has grown. Some of the users' requests have been implemented but there are still a lot to modify until the care professionals are satisfied with the system. Several other Swedish counties use the same EPR system and they all want their say in the development of the system. Therefore the process of modifying it is long and cumbersome. The systems customers are working together in a user group that negotiate with the company about future features and modifications to the system.

2 Research Background

Our research group conducts research in cooperation with several health care units of a Swedish University hospital since a couple of years. The overall method of the research project is action research, which means that we as researchers have dual aim with the research: *"practical problem solving and generation of new knowledge"* [1] . This paper describes a study where the purpose was to analyze the physician's attitudes toward EPR systems and the deployment process. It is the first interview study in a series with different care professions. The next study will be with nurses that work at the same units as the physicians. The result from these studies will later on be used as a basis for changes in the deployment activities.

3 Purpose and Justification

The hospital's EPR deployment group, the EPR support organization, the organizational system owner and other professions have expressed concerns with physicians not participating in the deployment process. Common remarks were that the physicians were not willing to participate in deployment activities, they were often complaining about the quality of the EPR systems and they seldom attended training sessions. The management described the physicians as a dominant profession and explained that the physicians' attitude was one of the reasons for the deployment process being cumbersome and the use of the EPR being inefficient. They tried to solve the problem by forcing them to take part in education sessions and other deployment activities. In order to investigate the reasons behind the experienced problems, we decided to make an interview study with physicians. The main purpose with the study was to clarify the physicians' attitude towards the EPR system, the deployment of the EPR and IT usage in general. Factors as the usability of the EPR were not in focus, although it is important that the EPR is intuitive, effective and supporting their needs.

4 Related Research on Deployment of EPR and Physicians' Use of EPR

A few studies have been made about physicians' use of and attitudes towards electronic medical records [2-7]. We have found some of them particularly relevant for our study.

Marc Berg has done several studies on implementing information systems in health care organizations, e.g. [8].

Nancy Lorenzi et al. have studied organizational changes in health care organizations. Introducing systems in complex organizations requires more than technical skills. The challenges are often more behavioral than technical [9]

Robert H Miller and Ida Sims paper *Physicians' use of electronic medical records: Barriers and solutions* [4] is based on a qualitative study with physicians. They identify barriers such as high initial physician time costs, technology, difficult complementary changes, inadequate support, inadequate electronic data exchange and attitudes.

M.J. Van der Meijden et al. [7] have studied the users' role in design and implementation of an EPR system. Their methods were questionnaires and interviews. They came to the conclusion that both experienced and inexperienced users have little definite expectations regarding the effects of computers in health care. The only important aspects that the users mentioned were accessibility and reliability. Their conclusion is that *"future users had no clear view of what could be expected after introducing computers into their daily work"*.

Ann-Britt Krog [10] has written a thesis on how care professionals negotiate with each other about how to use EPR systems. The thesis is based on qualitative studies at a Danish hospital. Krog mentions three common assumptions about EPR; better overview, less hazard and less time consumption. The studied users think that the EPR system gives them increased accessibility, increased communication and a better insight into each other's work between the professions. Her conclusion in the thesis is that the three mentioned visions have not been met in practice. As in the case above, we found these results interesting. The Danish and Swedish healthcare environment is comparable and the EPR used in Krog's study is actually the same that is used at the hospital we have studied.

5 Method

The main purpose of the study was to clarify the physicians' attitudes towards the EPR system, the deployment of the system and IT usage in general. To reach that purpose we decided to perform 19 semi-structured interviews with physicians with different level of expertise, age, and gender. The interviews were organized into the following six themes:

  - *Background information*
  - *How EPR and other IT systems are being used*
  - *Experience of the education and training process*
  - *Participation in IT-development*
  - *Experience of the IT-support in general*
  - *The relationship between the physicians and the management*

For each theme, the researchers started with a question and then continued with follow-up questions, more in a conversational style than as a formal interview.

The University hospital is divided into seven divisions with different specialties. The physicians were chosen from two of the divisions: Children and Women care and

Emergency and Rehabilitation care. The selected physicians represented different levels of expertise, age and gender.

Two researchers performed the interviews during one month. The physicians were told that the purpose of the study was for the management to learn about the physicians' attitudes and experiences with regard to EPR and IT systems. The researchers explained that the interview was based on different themes and that the interview was going to last for 20-30 minutes. 12 of these were in this time slot, 3 become shorter and 4 became longer. The interviews were audio recorded and the researchers took notes in parallel.

5.1 Analysis Method

The interviews were planned and performed by the two researchers. All interviews were transcribed by one of the interviewing researchers. In the analysis phase a third researcher was introduced into the project. The researcher transcribing the interviews conducted the analysis together with this third researcher. The analysis method was affinity diagramming [11] with three iterations. The total amount of transcribed material was 160 pages. Each transcribed interview was marked with level of expertise, department, age and gender to enable deeper analysis. In the first iteration one third of the interviews were analyzed on paper. Interesting quotes were cut out of the paper, put on a wall and sorted into different categories without any predefined themes. (Figure 1)

Fig. 1. The findings put on a wall in an affinity diagram

The quotes were then rearranged into named categories. In the second iteration the next third of the interviews were placed into the categories and then rearranged into new headlines. After that the last third of the interviews were analyzed and sorted into the named categories.

At this point we wanted to go deeper into the material. As the different groups of physicians have different responsibilities and work tasks, they also seemed to use the EPR system in slightly different ways and had mixed opinions about the usage of the system. The notes in each category were then rearranged according to three distinct groups, *senior physicians, specialist physicians and resident physicians*. We also gender marked physicians *within* the groups. But in our analysis, the expertise was far more significant than gender, so we decided not to go deeper into that analysis, although an interesting analysis might have been to look at *all* the material also with gender glasses.

5.2 The Three Physician Groups

The physician community is divided into different groups based on education level, research degree and expertise areas. There is a hierarchical difference between the groups that influence their status among physicians and other professions. (Table 1)

Table 1. The physicians divided into the groups with number of respondents, age and gender

Group	Number of resp.	Age	Gender
Resident	5	27-34	2 men 3 women
Specialist	8	34-55	5 men 3 women
Senior	6	46-64	5 men 1 woman

After basic education, the physicians do their residency at a hospital. They are called *resident physicians* and have been working at the hospital for 0-5 years. They work in one care unit for a longer time and they use the EPR for searching different kind of patient data that they use later on in the medical rounds. Their usage pattern is longer sessions with the EPR.

The second group is the *specialists*. They are specialists in different areas e.g. infection diseases, internal medicine or neonatology. They function as experts within their specialty and are doing a lot of different work tasks. They are moving between different care units within their medical specialty and are also working as consultant in different parts of the hospital. They are using the EPR for searching, writing, ordering tests and referrals and answering referrals. Their usage pattern is many short sessions with the EPR. Some of them are doing PhD research and others are doing their second specialty education.

The third group is *senior physician*. They all have a specialty and often a PhD degree. Most of the senior physicians in this group have management responsibilities, for a medical area or for other physicians. The seniors use the EPR system mainly for searching and not very frequently. They are concerned about that the EPR contains too much information, and consider it hard to find the important information.

6 Findings and Analysis

6.1 Attitudes Toward IT and EPR

Among the physicians there is a positive attitude towards IT and EPR systems in general. They are all quite used to computers and use them both at work and privately.

The physicians have huge expectations on how the EPR should help them and believe that the EPR systems give them benefits that the paper records could not give.

For example, access to more patient information than before, quicker response on referral, possibility to have one complete record for a patient instead of several separate paper records. Despite the possibilities, the physicians are frustrated about the usability of the systems. The users feel that they are not in control because the system does not give a good overview, is not intuitive, requires a lot of "clicks" and involves many steps to perform the work tasks.

A senior physician expressed a view on the usability of the EPR that well shows the common attitude towards the EPR:

Interviewer:
"Would it be meaningful to modify the education sessions to be more tailored to your needs?"

Senior physician:
"No, the meaningful thing would be to make the EPR tailored to the users..."

Most of the physicians compare the electronic records with paper records but come to different conclusions. The senior physicians express that the EPR is much easier to use and talk about the differences between paper-based records and computer-based records. The paper records used to "disappear" and were not always readily available when needed. They believe that all systems have positive and negative aspects. They think that they are more positive towards EPR than other, younger physicians because they remember and compare it to the paper based systems.

A general attitude among the specialists is that the EPR system gives them some positive effects but it is not time efficient because of bad usability. They express their frustration, and some of them even claim that it is better to have some information on paper until they have an EPR that is fully supporting them in their work. The resident physicians come to the conclusion that computer records are safer than paper records. They too are frustrated with the system, but even if the systems are not fully usable they prefer the computer records over of a mix of paper and computer records, as it is today.

6.2 Use of Time

In general, the physicians seem to be continuously short of time. When they refer to time they use different conceptions of time e.g. *patient time* and *administration time*. The interviewed physicians argue that their time is more precious than other care professionals'. Medical knowledge, longer education and higher costs are arguments used. They argue that it is important that physicians not do tasks that other professions can do, otherwise it is a waste of time and money.

The physicians consider their time as split into two parts: patient time and administrative time. A general opinion is that their main work is done when they have direct patient contact. Other tasks, such as documenting, reading, ordering referrals and tests, are tasks that they consider to be done in administrative time. One specialist said:

"The drug module takes a lot of time from the patient time"

The main problem with this separation is that what they refer to as real "physician work" is only the tasks done during patient time. The tasks done in administrative time they refer to as tasks that they want to spend less time on.

"A lot of time [with the EPR] compared to the time I spend with the patients"

The physicians on an average estimated their time in front of computers as 50% of their total time. According to their opinions they spend half of their time with tasks that they do not see as part of their "real work". If they would think of documenting, writing and reading referrals as a part of their "real physician work", it would probably affect their attitude towards EPR.

6.3   Participation in Deployment Activities

As mentioned above, the physicians refer to EPR and IT as something that is not a part of their "real work". Even though they are positive to IT in general, they are not motivated enough to participate in the deployment activities. A consequence of this is that other professions and the management experience that the physicians are unwilling to participate in optimizing EPR work. The senior physicians have all participated in different EPR development, requirement analyses, and taken part in formal groups or smaller informal groups, where they have discussed EPR and other IT questions. A common opinion is that they do not have the power to change anything in the systems. Some senior and specialists try to communicate their requests and thoughts but they express that the hospital management have created a structure that puts a distance between the care professionals and the IT organization. The specialists use lack of time/interests as well as lack of computer knowledge, as arguments for not participating. Some of them have taken part in EPR development activities, but they think that their participation was not valued highly enough. One specialist commented on her lack of participation:

"Yes, if you get time for it. I often think that they ask if you want to participate, but you need to participate instead of taking care of your patients or you have to postpone your consultations. And I don't think that is ok..."

On the other hand, some of the specialists say that when they express complaints about the systems, they are being listened to. But, changes to the systems take a long time to implement, and decreases their willingness to participate. When it comes to resident physicians they are not in such a position that they talk about participating in different EPR activities. They are often moving around between different departments and feel like they cannot educate older, more experienced colleagues. On the other hand, they think that they would have a lot to contribute because they are more used to computers.

To get improved participation, we think that the physicians need to find the EPR as "their" system, not as the IT organizations property.

Lorenzi [9] argue that it is a difference between implementing smaller systems and more complex systems into the organization. *"It has become apparent in recent years that successfully introducing major information systems into complex health care organizations requires an effective blend of good technical and good organizational skills"*. Today the care staff and management in the health care organization consider the EPR as a technical system that is the IT organizations responsibility. We argue that the organization needs to change their attitude toward EPR, and look at EPR as the health care organization responsibility. This is of course not true for the technical infrastructure, but the implementation into the organization and how the system is used as a part of the care process. The IT organization shall be a support and IT expertise organization. If the EPR is the care organizations property, not the IT organizations, participation will be more appreciated and seen as more important.

6.4 About the Education and Training Process

When introducing new IT systems or EPR modules, the hospital uses an education model where representatives from each health care unit educate and teach their colleagues. A common opinion is that this education method is good because it gives an introduction to the systems.

"It is absolutely good that you have the possibility to go to education. But it is hard because the education-hour must be squeezed into the normal physician work. I know a lot of colleagues that missed the education because of lack of time, so they have had to learn the systems by themselves and in real- life situations."

The quote points out some main thoughts that are generally expressed by the physicians. The opinion is that the introduction is not supposed to be longer than 2 hours. Some even express that a 20 minutes briefing is enough. Longer education is considered a waste of time. The rationales for short intensive introduction differ between the groups. Here is a quote from a senior physician that is representative for their opinion:

"I always go to education sessions. But it cost too much to have one whole day for all physicians. I think that the system should be so good that you don't need any education at all, because everybody is using so many other IT systems. I had 20 minutes education at a physician meeting, you don't need any more. You need to know the system's possibilities and then learn to use it by yourself"

The quote indicates that the senior physicians prefer shorter education sessions because otherwise it would take up much too of a physician's time. It also illustrate that they think of education as an introduction to the system, not a session where they learn to use the system. The specialists think it will take too much of their own time. They will not be able to use that time for the usual patient and administrative work. Instead they have to deal with that later. The resident physicians' opinions can be summarized by this quote;

"Sometimes I think that the education sessions can be too basic and simple. They teach you things that you already know."

None of the physicians see any consequences from missing an education session. They all learn to use the system by using it in real-life situations, not at the education session.

Today the management handles the physicians' "negative attitude" by forcing them to go to education sessions and try to teach them how to use the EPR in the "right way". We think that today's point-and-click education session or viewing-the-system education is not the right way to achieve an attitude change toward the EPR. According to Berg, *"In health care, however, the 'core business process' consists of highly knowledge-intensive, professional work, typified by a complexity that defies the predictability and standardization required for simple reengineering. Moreover, the professionals ultimately responsible for this process are powerful actors in the organization, and cannot be simply told to change their work patterns by senior management."* [8] Therefore we considered the education ought to be role-based according to the different physicians work environment, needs and knowledge. The education should focus on how the EPR will support them in their work and not everything that is technically possible to do in the system. It is important that the education gives a critical perspective towards what the EPR can do for them [12], otherwise they get false expectations of what the EPR can support them in.

7   Discussion

The starting point for the study was to find out why physicians do not want to participate in the education sessions and other deployment activities. We conclude that this problem is more like the symptom than the diagnosis of the problem. The real problem is why the care professionals, physicians in this case, do not look at IT as a possibility to perform a better work. Why don't the physicians love their EPR system? The answer is complex. The separation between the EPR and the health care organization confirms the physicians' attitude that using the EPR is an administrative task, not something they want to spend time with. This attitude towards use of IT, which is one of their most important work tools, is not something we have seen in other professional areas. The EPR system is also something that the health care organization does not own and has the power and mandate to change to fit its needs.

Among the physicians, there is a mixed opinion about to which extent the EPR support their work, but the physicians agree on that accessibility is the best feature of an EPR. Beyond that the picture is unclear. We found some similarities with the Miller & Sims study [4], for example difficulties with complementary changes, inadequate support and attitude. Differences between the studies are that Miller & Sims focus on solo/small groups, while we focus on resident, specialists and senior physicians.

7.1   The Differences between the Groups

Residents have often worked with other EPR systems and are used to learn new IT systems. Their opinion is that the EPR has more advantages then disadvantages, but they are not expressing that the EPR is supporting them as much as it could. A general opinion among both specialists and senior physicians is that the system can be much more intuitive, usable and better in supporting them in their patient work. The difference between their opinions is that specialists are more disappointed and frustrated with the EPR, while the seniors understand that the EPR cannot be perfect in the beginning but have high hopes that the system will be better in the future. According to M.J. Van der Meijden et al. both experienced and inexperienced users have little defined expectations regarding the effects of computers in health care. The only important aspects that the users mention are accessibility and reliability. Meijdens' conclusion is that "*future users had no clear view of what could be expected after introducing computers into their daily work*" [7]. Our study indicates that the different physicians have different expectations concerning the benefits of an EPR. We believe that age, education, work tasks, work environment and responsibility are important aspects that explain the differences between the groups' attitudes. None of the physicians express that the EPR support them fully, but the specialists are most expressive and skeptical, because of their dependency of the EPR. The respondents in Meijdens' study expect that "*an EPR should give them more overview than paper records and should release them from copying data from one sheet to the other*" [7]. The respondents in our study do not think that the EPR gives better overview. In fact the specialists point out that using only paper records instead of a mix of papers and computers is better. Using mixed systems means lack of control, which makes them insecure about their ability to perform a great work, and that the EPR is too immature to be used without any complementary papers.

7.2 Conception of Time Usage

The groups have different work tasks and use their time differently. The residents are still learning to become physicians and are not conceptually separating EPR time and patient time as much as the specialists. The senior physicians have much more administrative tasks and are not using the EPR as much as the specialists. The conclusion is that the specialists are more protective about the patient time and hesitant to regard the EPR as a part of that time. We believe that the physicians, especially the specialists, ought to change their attitude toward EPR and should consider EPR usage as an integrated part of the total care work. Changing both the physicians and the health care organizations way of looking at EPR will support this.

8 Summary

The result of the analysis of the interviews, and our preliminary suggestions for improvements of organization and processes, can be summarized as follows.

The physicians have huge expectations on how the EPR should help them and believe that the EPR systems give them benefits that the paper records could not give. Despite the possibilities, the physicians are frustrated about the systems usability. The physicians consider their time as split into two parts: patient time and administrative time. A general opinion is that their main work is done when they have direct patient contact, they consider working in the EPR and other IT systems as administrative tasks. Their own estimation is that they spend 50% of their time in front of the computers.

The physician groups have different work tasks and different experiences with the system. They all have the possibility to participate in education sessions and find it useful as an introduction to the system. The residents think the systems are easy to use and think that the education sessions are too simple and basic. The specialists, on the other hand think that the systems have bad usability and find it better to keep some paper records until the EPR is safer and more intuitive. The seniors do not use the EPR as frequently as the other physicians. They are concerned that the EPR contains too much information, and consider it hard to find the important information.

The seniors, and some of the specialists have participated in different development project but do not think that the hospital management listens to their opinions. We argue that it is important that the physicians participate in education sessions and deployment activities. *If* they do not participate in the education and training they will not learn to use their computer systems in an appropriate way and *if* they are not engaged in the development and deployment process they do not see the full potential of using EPR and other IT-systems to improve organization and work processes.

To solve this problematic situation, several changes must be made. Physicians' participation in development and deployment must be prioritized, given enough resources and be rewarded. They must see EPR and other IT-systems as the responsibility of the care organization and not of the IT department. Education and training procedures must be tailored to each target group and must be focused on learning the new way of working, not on how to handle the new technological artifact.

Acknowledgements. We would like to thank the county Council, hospital management and especially the physicians that managed to squeeze the interview into their tight schedule.

References

1. McKay, J., Marshall, P.: The dual imperatives of action research. Information Technology & People 14, 46–59 (2001)
2. Likourezos, A., Chalfin, D.B., Murphy, D.G., Sommer, B., Darcy, K., Davidson, S.J.: Physician and nurse satisfaction with an electronic medical record system. The Journal of Emergency Medicine 27, 419–424 (2004)
3. Lærum, H., Ellingsen, G., Faxvaag, A.: Doctors' use of electronic medical records systems in hospitals: cross sectional survey. BMJ Journals 323 (2001)
4. Miller, H.R., Sim, I.: Physicians' use of electronic medical records: Barriers and solutions. Health Affairs 23(2), 116–126 (2004)
5. Varpio, L., Schryer, C.F., Lehoux, P., Lingard, L.: Working Off the Record: Physicians' and Nurses' Transformations of Electronic Patient Record-Based Patient Information. Academic Medicine 81 (2006)
6. Brown, S.H., Coney, R.D.: Changes in Physicians' Computer Anxiety and Attitudes Related to Clinical Information System Use. The Journal of the American Medical Informatics Association, 381–394 (1994)
7. Meijden, M.J.v.d., Tange, H., Troost, J., Hasman, A.: Development and implementation of an EPR: how to encurage the user. International Journal of Medical Informatics 64, 173–185 (2001)
8. Berg, M.: Implementing information systems in health care organizations: myths and challenges. International Journal of Medical Informatics 64, 143–156 (2001)
9. Lorenzi, N., Riley, R.T.: Managing Change: An Overview. Journal of the American Medical Informatics Association 7, 116–124 (2000)
10. Krog, A.-B.: Forhandlinger om patienten: den elektroniske patientjournal som kommunikationsmedie. Syddansk Universitet. Det Humanistiske Fakultet, Vol. PhD. Syddansk Universitet, 204 (2009)
11. Beyer, H., Holtzblatt, K.: Contextual Design Defining Customer-Centered Systems (1998)
12. Ash, J.S., Berg, M., Coiera, E.: Some Unintended Consequences of Information Technology in Health Care: The Nature of Patient Care Information System-related Errors. Journal of the American Medical Informatics Association 11, 104–112 (2004)

Oshidori-Net: Connecting Regional EPR Systems to Achieve Secure Mutual Reference with Thin-Client Computing Technology

Shigeki Kuwata[1], Koji Toda[2], Kei Teramoto[1], Hiroshi Kondoh[1], Hiroshige Nakamura[1], Hirohiko Murata[2], Noriaki Tamura[2], and Masahide Ikeguchi[1]

[1] Tottori University Hospital,
36-1 Nishi-cho, Yonago, Tottori, 683-8504, Japan
[2] Saihaku Municipal Hospital,
397 Yamato, Nanbu, Saihaku, Tottori, 683-0323, Japan
{shig,kei,kondoh,hnaka,masaike}@med.tottori-u.ac.jp,
{toda.k,tamura.n}@town.nanbu.tottori.jp

Abstract. A mutual reference system developed by the authors, Oshidori-Net, facilitated medical professionals to remotely access to the existing electronic patient record systems. The system was technically oriented based on the thin-client technology in terms of security enhancement and cost reduction. Formerly a small portion of the patient healthcare information was provided for the counterpart, whereas, by introducing the system, all the electronically formatted information stored in the systems was shared with the professionals so that reduction of duplicated health examinations and improvement of healthcare service in both hospitals were anticipated. The regional medical association with the system would form an ideal model in next generation to achieve virtual full-functioned hospitals providing the best quality of medical services.

Keywords: Electronic Patient Records, Thin-client Computing, Regional Healthcare Service.

1 Introduction

A Newly developed service, Oshidori-Net, providing medical workers with remote access to electronic patient record systems (EPR) of regional hospitals mutually connected using the thin-client computing technology, has been in operation with the participation of a university-affiliated hospital with 697 beds (Tottori University Hospital; TUH) and a regional medical center with 198 beds (Saihaku Municipal Hospital; SMH) in a rural district of Japan since July, 2009. The system was designed based on the thin-client computing (TCC) architecture that TUH had adopted for its intranet system [1] [2], achieving higher security at a low cost with the least modification to the existing hospital information systems.

H. Takeda (Ed.): E-Health 2010, IFIP AICT 335, pp. 82–89, 2010.

1.1 Introduction of Thin-Client Computing Technology in Tottori University Hospital

TUH introduced physician's order entry and EPR to the hospital information system in 2003. As approximately 900 medical specialists with 1,000 client PCs at TUH had used the system for over five years, they were gradually dependant upon the system environment and considered it to be an essential infrastructure for their daily work. The trend caused a growing need of many client PCs by the users: they needed workstation PCs to input orders and to check the results of tests wherever they worked. In response to the requirement, it was of urgent necessity for information managers of the hospital to supply additional client PCs without increasing the risk related to cost and security. TUH introduced models of thin-client computing to the system, also known as server-based computing (SBC), to solve the problem [1].

1.2 Potentiality and Effectiveness of the Thin-Client Computing Technology

As a characteristic of TCC technology, middleware servers (TCC servers) installed between PC clients and database servers of the system are able to process multiple users' applications and to behave themselves as virtual clients providing each PC client with only their screen information without transferring real data (Fig.1).

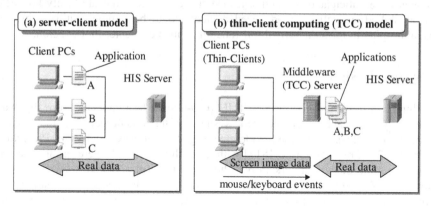

Fig. 1. Difference on a system configuration and a data transferring method between (a) a server-client model and (b) a thin-client computing (TCC) model [1]

This technology drew an attention of hospital information managers in term of its superiority with regard to cost reduction and privacy protection, accordingly its implementation to the hospital information system was carried out in several medical facilities though its application tended to be limited to relatively small domains, *e.g.*, medical telemetry for monitoring sleep-related disorders [3], remote access to the laboratory system [4] and simulation systems for dentistry [5].

As assistance for implementing TCC in large-scale facilities, the authors developed a design model under real hospital settings [2]. In the major replacement of the hospital information system at TUH in 2008, TCC was implemented according to the design model [6]. Consequently about 1,100 client PCs in cooperation with 70 middleware TCC servers worked successfully on the TCC system. The implementation was the first attempt in large hospital settings in Japan.

The authors also evaluated the effectiveness of the system after the implementation. The introduction of thin-clients contributed to the reduction of PC failure rates: the hospital logged 39 failures in the past ten month, while 77 failure cases occurred per year before the implementation. Electric energy consumption was also reduced: the electric power consumed by client PCs averaged 40.5 KW, while that by TCC servers and client PCs averaged 36.1 KW for the new system [1].

2 Purpose of the System

Oshidori-Net allowed medical professionals working for the hospitals to refer to the existing EPRs (CIS-MR by IBM Corp. [7] at TUH and HOPE/EGMAIN-FX by Fujitsu Limited [8] at SMH) for healthcare information of patients who had consented to the mutual referral by the professionals. Formerly a small portion of the patient healthcare information, e.g., referral letters with X-ray films, was provided for the counterpart, whereas, by introducing the system, all the electronically-formatted information stored in the systems was shared with the professionals so that reduction of duplicated health examinations and improvement of healthcare service in both hospitals were anticipated. In addition, medical resources in the university hospital, such as skilled specialists or advanced devices, could be remotely utilized by the general hospital to form the virtual full-functioned medical center in the region.

3 System Design

The thin-client computing system at TUH (GO-Global by GraphOn Corp. [9]) was successfully extended to the network system of the counterpart via the Tottori Information Highway, a closed wide-area giga-bit network in Tottori Prefecture region (Fig.2). Firewalls (Cisco 1812J with Cisco IOS Firewall) were installed at the connection node of the network in both hospitals to form a shared-network domain (namely DMZ) and protect the intranet where the patient healthcare information was stored. Desktop virtualization servers (DVSs), as TCC servers providing the thin-client computing, were installed in the shared-network to play a role as proxy servers to retrieve the information and transfer it to remote clients. The specification of DVSs was composed of a single CPU of Quad Core X-E5405 with a clock frequency of 2GHz, 5GB RAM, four 36GB-HDDs with RAID-5 configuration having a hot spare disk and Windows Server Standard 2003 operating system (Hewlett Packard ProLiant DL360 G5). Thin-client computing middleware, GO-Global, was installed in the DVSs to make every application for EPR and PACS run on the DVSs for multiple login users, with its screen information compressed, encrypted and transferred to the client PCs of the users by the Rapid-X protocol over TCP/IP network. The designed architecture yielded great advantage of the security aspects that frequently aroused concern in people involved; the patient healthcare information transferred to the users was composed of a series of screen images without containing its original data. The innovative architecture was able to minimize the risk that an enormous amount of data might be divulged in a very short moment. In an attempt to further enhance the security protection, use of printers and clipboard functions on DVSs was not allowed to the remote users.

To maintain stable and secure system operation, roles of the system administrators were defined as follows: (1) to conduct a mutual audit on the system utilization of the counterpart users, and (2) to provide an instruction course with the users on privacy protection, precedent to the permission granted to the users.

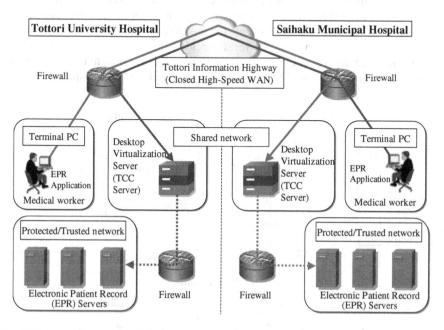

Fig. 2. Conceptual system configuration model of the electronic patient record systems connected with thin-client technology to achieve secure mutual reference

4 Operational Workflow of the System

4.1 User Registration

All users in TUH and SMH were qualified to use the system after they completed an educational course on the system operation and its security provided upon registration. The course was provided by a system administrator at TUH in a classroom style on a regular basis and an e-learning (online) style available anytime on the Internet. User registration was conducted manually and asynchronously at two hospitals: When new users were registered or any attributes (*e.g.* name, position and department) on existent users were altered at one hospital, the system administrator of the hospital sent the users' information to a system administrator of the other hospital in some secure ways (via facsimile or via encrypted email transmission), followed by the user registration at the latter hospital.

4.2 Patient Registration (Fig.3)

An informed consent form should be submitted to one of the hospitals prior to the patient registration into the system. The consent form was first sent to an office administrator of the hospital, to which the patient submitted the form, subsequently to a system administrator to grant read-only permission of the patient information in EPR from the other hospital. The permission would last up to three years without exceptional circumstances. Users of the other hospital were only able to refer to the information of the patients with the permission. Upon completion of the registration, the form was stored in a department of the hospital (*e.g.* health information management center) according to rules decided by the hospital. The office administrator sent the patient's information to an office administrator of the other hospital via facsimile, followed by the same procedures at the latter hospital.

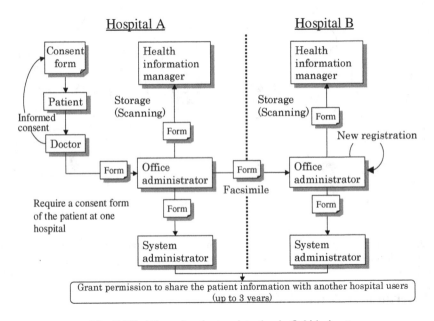

Fig. 3. Workflow of patient registration in Oshidori-net

5 Results

As of January 20, 2010, 66 patients and 245 medical professionals, including 194 for TUH 51 for SMH, were registered for the mutual reference system. The frequency of the patient registration, compared with the observed patient referrals in 2008, corresponded to approximately a half of all the referrals.

Fig.4 shows the frequency of data access to the counterpart system. The fact that access from SMH to TUH was considerably dominant was caused by the imbalance of the need requiring the patient information between the hospitals: TUH as a university hospital tended to provide more advanced medical service than SMH resulting in a growing need of the professionals at SMH for the information unavailable on site. On the other hand, the doctors at TUH tended to retrieve the information stored at SMH only upon referral.

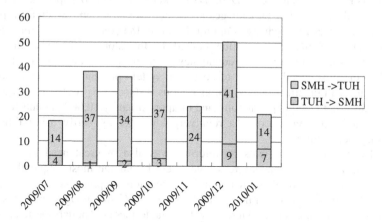

Fig. 4. Frequency of data access to the counterpart system. Consecutive transactions with its duration within 20 minutes were counted once.
SMH: Saihaku Municipal Hospital, TUH: Tottori University Hospital.

Frequency of referred information stored at TUH was presented in Fig.5. The most frequent reference occurred in progress note (37%), followed by blood test (7%), radiology image (5%), prescription (4%) and so forth. Preliminary brief interviews with the doctors at SMH revealed their affirmative impression that the system facilitated the access to the detailed information to know the background or progress on the patient treatment.

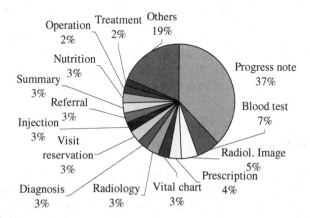

Fig. 5. Ratios of frequency of data access from Saihaku Municipal Hospital (SMH) to Tottori University Hospital (TUH) grouped by sorts of referenced data.
Consecutive transactions to the same referred information with its duration within 10 minutes were counted once. The counted transactions from SMH to TUH were 528 in total.

6 Discussion

Introduction of the system has altered the way of referrals between the hospitals; formerly portable media, e.g., CD or DVD, were attached to paper-based referral letters to send massive DICOM images and accompanied reports, whereas at present only brief messages are exchanged upon referral. In the conventional offline method, provided DICOM images are often copied to the storage server again at the counterpart resulting in excessive redundancy of the images among regional hospitals leading to the unsolicited increase of cost. The system presents an efficient solution for the issue with practical tactics. An analogous instance was found in a large-scale system, Ajisai-net [10] [11], that consisted of approximately 10,000 patients and more than 120 hospitals registered at a relatively low cost by partly using thin-client computing architecture.

Detail description of patients on referrals was also of great need to doctors as illustrated in Fig.5 in which progress notes were by far the most frequently viewed resources. The result implied that detail information in progress notes would be utilized effectively on referrals in addition to DICOM images and discharge summaries that were often transferred with portable media. Though the necessity of such information has been recognized so far, delays in establishing standards would have reduced the possibility to exchange such complicatedly structured and often non-structured information in progress notes. The system, Oshidori-net, simply provided mutual reference of all information in EPR for users, but it would be one of effective solutions in practical use for medical professionals until applicable and feasible standards become widespread for medical data exchange between hospitals.

Some issues were still to be solved in further development of the system. One instance was that professionals registered in the system, specifically doctors, often insisted that the system be more convenient for the users, even allowing for some violations of the policies for privacy protection (e.g. capturing screen information of the other hospital's EMR to duplicate the data which would lead to privacy infringement). The demand obviously stemmed from the strict security implementation enforced in the system operation, therefore the modification would be considered in terms of the usability enhancement. Another issue was on scalability of the system that would be required, as the participation of hospitals would be increased. Some features of the IHE technical frameworks, e.g., PIX or XUA, should be incorporated into the system in further development to maintain the operability and consistency of the system.

7 Conclusion

The mutual reference system developed by the authors facilitated medical professionals to access to the EMR data from a remote site. The system was technically oriented based on the thin-client technology in terms of security enhancement and cost reduction. The regional medical association with the system would form an ideal model in next generation to achieve the advanced virtual hospital providing the best quality of medical services.

References

1. Kuwata, S., Teramoto, K., Matsumura, Y., Kushniruk, A.W., Borycki, E.M., Kondoh, H.: Effective solutions in introducing server-based computing into hospital information system. Stud. Health. Technol. Inform. 143, 435–440 (2009)
2. Teramoto, K., Kuwata, S., Nishimura, M., Kumagai, T., Saigo, T., Kondoh, H.: Development of a design model of Hospital Information System based on Server-Based Computing. Japan Journal of Medical Informatics 27(suppl.), 666–668 (2007)
3. Astaras, A., Arvanitidou, M., Chouvarda, I., Kilintzis, V., Koutkias, V., Sanchez, E.M., et al.: An integrated biomedical telemetry system for sleep monitoring employing a portable body area network of sensors (SENSATION). In: Conf. Proc. IEEE Eng. Med. Biol. Soc., pp. 5254–5257 (2008)
4. Ulma, W., Schlabach, D.M.: Technical Considerations in Remote LIMS Access via the World Wide Web. J. Autom. Methods Manag. Chem., 217–222 (2005)
5. Taylor, D., Valenza, J.A., Spence, J.M., Baber, R.H.: Integrating electronic patient records into a multi-media clinic-based simulation center using a PC blade platform: a foundation for a new pedagogy in dentistry. In: AMIA Annu. Symp. Proc., pp. 11–29 (2007)
6. Teramoto, K., Kuwata, S., Kawai, T., Imai, Y., Fujii, K., Nishimura, M., Kondo, H.: Evaluation of a design model of Hospital Information System based on Server-Based Computing (SBC). Japan Journal of Medical Informatics 28(suppl.), 376–379 (2008)
7. CIS-MR (Medical Record), IBM Corporation (in Japanese),
   http://www-06.ibm.com/industries/jp/healthcare/
   solution/cismr.html (accessed May 1, 2010)
8. HOPE/EGMAIN-FX, Fujitsu Limited (in Japanese),
   http://segroup.fujitsu.com/medical/products/egmainfx
   (accessed May 1, 2010)
9. Graph on Corporation, http://www.graphon.com (accessed May 1, 2010)
10. Matsumoto, T., Honda, M.: The actual status and problems of the development of IT in community medicine Ajisai network at Nagasaki. Japan Journal of Medical Informatics 27(suppl.), 164–165 (2007)
11. Kimura, H., Nakahara, K., Yonekura, M.: The operative experience of five years of the regional medicine cooperation system (Ajisai net). Japan Journal of Medical Informatics 29(suppl.), 530–531 (2009)

Information Security Sharing of Networked Medical Organizations: Case Study of Remote Diagnostic Imaging

Masayo Fujimoto[1], Koji Takeda[1], Tae Honma[1], Toshiaki Kawazoe[2], Noriko Aida[3], Hiroaki Hagiwara[4], and Hideharu Sugimoto[5]

[1] Fuji Xerox Co., Ltd.
[2] Fujifilm Medical Co., Ltd.
[3] Kanagawa Children's Medical Center
[4] Yokohama City University Hospital
[5] Jichi Medical University and Hospital
Fuji Xerox Co., Ltd. Roppongi T-CUBE 15F,
Minato-ku, Tokyo 106-0032 Japan

Abstract. Increasing usage of ICT in medical organizations raises the issue of information security. This research study focuses on, and analyzes technology and management aspects for, information security of networked medical organizations through a teleradiology case study. A 'workshop' to gauge risk assessment was also established in which stakeholders, such as patients and radiologists, discussed the risk threat inherent in teleradiology. Based on this discussion, technological, organizational, physical, and personal security countermeasures were developed and organizational rules for networked organizations created. We conducted a step-by-step approach in which the second medical organization referred to the first medical organization's process and rules, and found that this approach was both efficient and effective. However, we also discovered that many internal and external adjustment works for each medical organization exist. To solve these issues we proposed two societal functions for audit and supportive institutions to handle such issues as compliance and education.

Keywords: Teleradiology, Remote Diagnostics Imaging, Information Security, Personal Information Protection, Risk Management, Cooperation of Medical Organizations.

1 Introduction

According to the OECD health data 2009, the number of CT/MRI per million people is 96.1/42.7 in Japan. This number is quite large in comparison to other OECD member countries. However, this fact alone does not necessarily explain the higher quality of medical service provision. The reason for this is the shortage in number of Diagnostic Radiologists in Japan. We might be able to solve this issue by increasing the number of Diagnostic Radiologists. Although this approach is effective, current diagnostic imaging raises another issue. Because of enlargement and deepening of expertise in this field, together with the evolution of technology, it is difficult for every medical organization

H. Takeda (Ed.): E-Health 2010, IFIP AICT 335, pp. 90–101, 2010.

to employ specialists. Therefore, medical doctors, organizations, and government have been challenging diagnostic imaging by using information and communication technologies (teleradiology). Some services have been introduced to market on a commercial basis, but we still have many medical doctors and organizations that hesitate to use teleradiology because of information security concerns, especially in protection of personal data. In order to further promote use of teleradiology, we need to develop effective information security procedures in order to reduce teleradiology accidents that arise from improper technology usage and management. It is important to encourage teleradiology usages that meet societal safety requirement. Based on the recognition of these problems, we performed an experimental study in which two medical institutions exchanged diagnostic images via an information network. In particular, we focused on the information security management aspect in this study.

2 Settings and Focuses of This Study

In the first section we introduce the three organizations that join this experimental study, in the second section we explain the information and communication technologies that are used in this project, in the third section we show the scope of this study, and the final section we describe the focus of this study.

2.1 Three Organizations

This case study involved the following three organizations, 1) Yokohama City University Hospital (YCUH), department of radiology, 2) Kanagawa Children's Medical Center, department of radiology (KCMC), and 3) information processing providers. Yokohama City University Hospital, department of radiology employs nine radiologists and has CT, MRI, PET/CT, and PACS facilities. Regarding information system management and other operations that relate to this study, the medical information and business administration departments also have responsibilities for whole organizational management. Kanagawa Children's Medical Center is a Kanagawa prefectural hospital and also has CT and MRI facilities. The department of radiology employs three radiologists, two of which are specialist in pediatrics diagnostic imaging. A person employed in the business administration department also joined this study. Information processing providers include three organizations. The first organization is a telecommunication company that provides network infrastructure, the second organization is a PACS provider, and the third organization provides mainly services and advice on internal network designs, system operations, and management.

2.2 Explanation of the Remote Diagnostic Imaging Systems and Operations

In general, diagnostic imaging for single organizations usually goes through the following steps,

(1) A radiological technologist stores medical images in a PACS system.
(2) A diagnostic radiologist diagnoses images and makes a report.
(3) A primary doctor decides on a treatment policy based on the images and the report form provided by the diagnostic radiologist.

In this study of the remote diagnostic imaging, we granted the assigned remote diagnostic radiologist permission to access to the PACS system to review permitted images for a defined period of time. Only the client diagnostic radiologist was able to grant access codes to the remote diagnostic radiologist and set the accessible period. The remote radiologist input the diagnostic report directly into the client diagnostic radiologist's PACS system. Diagnostic images were stored and displayed on the remote machine temporarily, but were deleted each time the remote diagnostic radiologist logged off the machine. The system account of the remote diagnostic radiologist expires after the defined period of time that the client diagnostic radiologist input initially.

2.3   Scope and Focus of This Study as an Information Security Management Case Model

The scope of this case model is described as follows,

(1) Two medical organizations that use the same network and computer systems.
(2) The intended information for this study specifically focuses on medical images and their related diagnostic reports.
(3) Each organization is managed independently.

The dot-line in the figure 1 outlines the scope of this study.

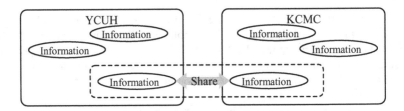

Fig. 1. Scope of this study

This study focuses on information security for remote diagnostic imaging. We can divide the information security into two types of countermeasures. The first is a technological countermeasure, while the second is a management countermeasure. Information security is constructed by combining these actions. In order to select the appropriate countermeasures we need to employ a risk management process. This study covers not only the technological countermeasures, but also management countermeasures. In the case of remote diagnostic imaging where more than one organization provides services, we face more complex management challenges than in the management of a single medical organization. Participants may agree on the same technological security countermeasures, but the management approaches differ depending upon each organization. Participants may need to agree to each other's different management systems. Therefore, in this study, we focused on security management and clarified the discussion points, aiming to discover an effective implementation method to solve the problems.

2.4 Past Studies and Relevant Legal Frameworks

Past Studies. In Japan, a number of studies that focused on organizational information security management have been conducted. For example, Hori discussed both technological security countermeasures as well as organizational countermeasures [1]. A number of books about information security have also been published. For instance, Doi et al. published a book to educate information security managers. The contents of the book also included sections on security management countermeasures [2]. In medical field applications, Tanaka studied personal data protection, and included organizational management countermeasures based on her findings drawn from meetings with medical organizations [3]. There was also study performed on information security incidents in medical institutions [4]. In the case of information security technology, many studies have been performed. In particular, a number of studies on network security have also been performed, as well as many other studies on the methodology of information security management and personal information protection. We also found documents that pointed out the importance of these studies and practices. Some similar studies in medical institutions were also performed. However, there are few studies conducted on management methods for sharing medical information and diagnostics with multiple medical institutions.

Relevant Legal Frameworks. The legislation relating to remote diagnostic imaging is complex and diversified in Japan. For example, we have the Medical Service Act, the Medical Practitioners Act, and the Personal Information Protection Law related guidelines. Because we want to focus on the practice of the remote diagnostic imaging and information securities in this paper, we would like to briefly outline the Personal Information Protection Law and discuss their relationship to management practices in this section. The Japanese Personal Information Protection Law went into effect in April 2005. The law is constructed in four parts. The first is the basic law that is applicable to both public and private sectors. The second is the general law and it is divided into the laws for both the public and private sectors. The third is the law established specifically for priority areas, such as medical, finance, and information and communication fields. The final law is a set of guidelines that each state minister in charge establishes accordingly. This legal framework makes the participating organizations' operations very complicated. For example, in this case study, the YCUH is owned by the city of Yokohama, while Kanagawa Prefecture owns the KCMC. Thus, different regulations of local governments are applied to each. This type of complexity may happen in international situations arising from difference among legislations and societal institutions in each country. We examined the method that medical institutions can enforce to secure remote diagnostic imaging under such a complicated environment.

3 Case Study

In this chapter, we explain the development procedure for the information security management system that we conducted in this study. In section 3.1, we will outline the work flows and explained the four phases(section 3.2 to the section 3.5).

3.1 Process Carried Out in This Study

In this study, we mainly focus on risk management of information security for remote diagnostic imaging. Risk management here means the process of risk assessment and risk treatment. Risk treatment includes technological, organizational, physical, and personnel countermeasures. We practiced these risk management process and PDCA cycle. In the early days of this study, we discussed security with medical institutions connected in a network as a single group. We were going to build one management rule for all related organizations. However, we changed this approach because of their differing sizes and management methodology and decided to follow the measures described in table 1 and figure 2.

Table 1. Procedures in this study

Actions	Description	
1	Risk assessment by workshop	1st-phase
2	Information system design (include technological countermeasures)	
3	Information security management system design for YCUH	2nd-phase
4	Information security management system design for KCMC	3rd-phase
5	Agreement of two organizations	4th-phase

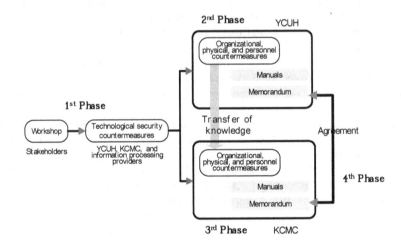

Fig. 2. Overview of four-phase process

3.2 Risk Assessment and Security Technology Selections (1st Phase)

In the September of 2006, the YCUH and the KCMC began discussions on the availability of remote diagnostic imaging. In February of 2007, diagnostic radiologists and information system engineers formed a project team. Through these discussions members shared their perceptions that information security is one of the most important requirements for the project.

Workshop. In June of 2007, the project members held a workshop and invited stakeholders to discussed risk factors. These stakeholders include the following people.

Diagnostic Radiologists, Patients, Hospital Directors, Practitioners, Clinicians, Radiological Technologist, Doctors from medical Information Science Department, Members of Administrative Department, Government Representatives, and System Vendors.

Thirteen stakeholders and one facilitator joined the workshop during two days, and pointed out 152 threats. Redundancies were extracted and the remainder aggregated into 76 threats that we decided to set countermeasures for [5].

Technological Countermeasures. Based on these threats we decided on technological countermeasures. In this experiment, the project members in the medical organizations and system vendors discussed these countermeasures. As examples of these technological countermeasures, we would like to explain the following two technologies that we selected.

(1) Technologies to deal with wiretapping threats to networks
(2) Technologies to deal with spoofing threats from fake remote radiologists

Firstly, for technologies to deal with wiretapping threats to networks, we employed VPN and SSL. We also compared IP-Sec, but selected VPN because in consideration of maintenance costs and compatibility to the spoofing threat countermeasures we employed. We assumed it would be a suitable countermeasure to spoofing attacks, and it had the lowest maintenance costs and higher compatibility than IP-Sec. Secondly, for technologies to deal with spoofing threats, we selected a client certification function of SSL. In normal client certification, a secret key is stored on a PC, but with this method, if malicious persons can successfully access the PC, they can pretend to be the legal owner of that key. In order to solve this problem, we stored the secret key to a biometric device. As a result, we were able to build a structure that gives permission to access the PACS server only to the person who succeeded in passing all device possession certification, biometrics authentication, and client certification of SSL. This certification scheme required some additional operations such as the publication management of the certificates and distribution management of the certification devices. However, system vendors could operate the systems as a part of their PACS maintenances functions. We carefully chose low-cost, widely available technologies, and by combining these technologies, achieved a higher level of security.

3.3 Risk Management in Yokohama City University Hospital (2ⁿᵈ Phase)

Having decided upon the technological countermeasures, we discussed organizational, physical, and personnel countermeasures with Yokohama City University Hospital (YCUH). In order to make these security countermeasures practical, we finalized the organization system and devised official regulations (figure 3).

Fig. 3. Information Security Management Process in the Yokohama City University Hospital (YCUH)

Establish the Organization and the Committee. We developed the organization system and established an internal committee for decision-making. The organization system and the committee were both located in the department of radiology, and we invited members from both the medical information department that manages the information and communication system of the hospital and the business administration department that manages personal information protection for the hospital to attend. In the case of the YCUH, we successfully obtained the cooperation of other sections, and assumed that the workload for adjusting the different rules and manuals required would take considerable time to complete.

Research the Influential Factors. We investigated influential factors both outside and inside the YCUH in the following three categories. Firstly, we researched the legal requirements. We found out that the guidelines published by the Ministry of Hearth, Labor and Welfare related deeply to our project. One guideline focused on information security of medical information systems [6]. The other guideline covers personal data protection for medical and care organizations [7]. In addition to these, the city of Yokohama also published guidelines for city-owned public organizations that the YCUH must also comply with [8]. Secondly, we researched internal existing rules and manuals. We found that the personal data protection manual and information security policy had already been defined. In particular, the information security policy included system security countermeasures. We had to confirm that consistency existed between our technological countermeasures for remote diagnostic imaging and the hospital's information security policy (figure 4). Thirdly, we researched current operations for diagnostic imaging through interviews with diagnostic radiologists, including the physical environment and the movement of patients in the Radiology Department.

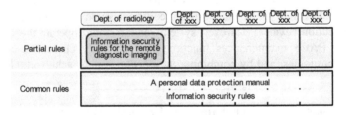

Fig. 4. Organize the relationship of hospital rules

Develop the Policy, Appropriate Countermeasures, and Rules. Firstly, we formulated a basic security policy for this remote diagnostic imaging, and then discussed and adopted appropriate countermeasures. Secondly, we implemented countermeasures and prepared manuals for organizational operations. Through this process we found that it was difficult to work on developing a risk management system based on both risk assessment and legal requirements at the same time. Therefore, we developed our information security management system first, and then we checked its adaptability to both the legal demands and the required guidelines. Through this process we were able to appropriately develop the manual to suit the process.

3.4   Risk Management in Kanagawa Children Medical Center (3rd Phase)

The KCMC adopted same technological countermeasures by collaborating with the YCUH. Therefore, we needed to define organizational, physical, and personnel countermeasures. Two members from the KCMC participated in the discussion. One participant was a diagnostic radiologist and the other was a radiological technologist. At a comparatively early stage, we decided to develop two types of manuals, one for personal data protection and the other for information system security. The reason for this was that the radiological technologist has been taking care of information system security and then we thought that it was effective to maintain consistency between both the person in charge and the charge domain. In comparison to the YCUH, the KCMC was quite small in terms of the number of people who could work for remote diagnostic imaging. Therefore, we employed a different organization system. For example, we reduced the hierarchy for management and, as a result, we could also simplify the approval processes.

Like the YCUH, the KCMC had a higher-level of official rules for handling personal data protection. We drew up a correlation diagram of relating rules (figure5).

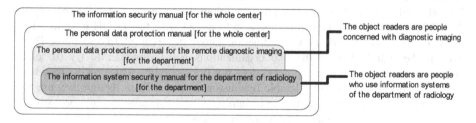

Fig. 5. Correlation diagram of rules

In this diagram, "the personal data protection manual for the remote diagnostic imaging" had been newly developed. "The information system operation manual for the department of radiology" had been revised to respond to operational changes by adding these remote diagnostic imaging activities. Discussion meetings had been held several times. For example, we discussed whether or not to develop a new system operation manual specifically for the remote diagnostic imaging, but we decided to revise the existing system operation manual for the system in the Radiology Department. Because the same radiological technologist mainly took care of both operations, there was no reason to make two manuals. The participating radiologist and radiological technologist carefully checked the usability of the manuals. When creating these manuals, we paid specific attention to developing the contents in accordance with everyday activities.

3.5 The Exchange of the Memorandum (4th Phase)

Through the discussions, we gradually clarified requirements for each organization. Following this, members from both organizations discussed together and drafted a memorandum that included the following contents.

> Organization Systems, Personal Data Protection, Access Control
> Facility Management, Education, and Audit

4 Discussions and Suggestions

In this section, we explain the results of this experiment, and also discuss problems in the practices that became clear as a result of the experiment. In the case of the problems, we would like to give some suggestions on how to solve them.

4.1 The Effect of the Approach Observed in This Experiment

In this experiment, we tried to find a useful methodology to establish a total security management system to use when we connect organizations together via networks and share information. Rather than first lay down a set of common security management countermeasures, we adopted a sequential method. The result showed that this method is useful at least for connecting two organizations.

In this case study, the two organizations are quite different in terms of organizational sizes and management cultures. For example, six people from three different sections attended the discussion meetings to make the manuals in the YCUH, while only two people from the Radiology Department joined the meeting in the KCMC. This reveals that in comparison to the KCMC, the YCUH have to select countermeasures under complex coordination among different internal sections. Thus, even if the radiologists of the two organizations gather together to try to select common countermeasures, the process does not run smoothly. This process may take a lot of time and involve considerable readjustment works. Even though they use the same technologies and accompanying technological countermeasures, the best way to establish security management differs greatly depending upon each organization.

The approach that we tried in this experiment facilitates construction of the appropriate system of administration that matched the individual organization, and that can set common rules.

In addition, for the wider development of rules and manuals, the individual organization can develop these without the know-how and experience of the rule for manual making by taking the rules and manuals of another organization into account. This approach also makes it possible to develop rules and manuals that reflected the circumstances of each organization. For instance, in this experiment, the number of discussions that we needed to hold with the KCMC was less than half the number required with the YCUH. It may be said that our method was effective even if we take into consideration that the organizational size of the KCMC is smaller than that of the YCUH. It is thought that this approach reduces the workload because we were able to use the rules and manuals that we developed for the YCUH as reference materials in developing these items for the KCMC. If we continually apply this method to many different organizations, we may be able to establish a universal set of fundamental rules that may help other organizations reduce their workloads.

4.2 The Problems That Became Clear through the Experiment

Adjustment Load for Each Organization. In generally, many medical institutions already have comprehensive rules to covering personal information protection and technological security countermeasure for information and communication systems. In this case study, the YCUH already had a comprehensive set of rules and manuals covering personal data protection for both the university and the hospital. The KCMC also has rules and manuals for personal data protection for its medical center. These organizations may not have factored in the situation when connecting to outside networks or for sharing information when they developed their respective rules and manuals. Therefore, we had to review the mutual influences with these existing rules and manuals when we developed the new rules and manuals for our remote diagnostic imaging operations. This study clarified the problems encountered, the adjustment work required, and the burden concentrated on the sections concerned when we introduced a new management plan in a specific section, as in this case, on the Department of Radiology. In order to solve this problem, it might be useful to introduce a governance scheme in which the central administrative section transfers authority of restrictive rule development to each section. It is desirable to have a section governance structure in which a rule can be set when the person in charge connects to the outside organizations via a network to conduct information sharing. In this structure, the comprehensive rules function as a baseline security countermeasure and the section's original, and in most cases, the rules may have a higher level of security than the comprehensive rules. Without such a structure, the person in charge of each section must put in considerable effort to seek out the best way to adjust the rules, placing considerable burden of the person in charge. Although we might be able to set the rule to a comparatively high level for the whole medical institution that assumes outside network connection, this approach may increase the workload of all sections and this may not be productive. Thus, we recommend introducing structured information security governance.

Adjustment Load with Outside Constraints and the Connected Organizations. We also experienced difficulty to cope with outside environmental changes such as laws and regulations. Over the course of the project, we had to check compliance to several guidelines that were sometimes quite similar, but not quite same, or that overlapped. These laws and regulations have been revised and we have to monitor these changes and react in a timely manner. This is accompanied with a review and the change to rules and manuals, and we must take also the approval procedure inside the organizations and of the organization interval. When we also think about preparedness to potential lawsuits, we need to record every management decision-making processes and file all relating documents. In theory, these works possibly become a continual workload of the Radiology Department rather than on the whole hospital's administration. We must discus how to solve this problem of increased workload and economic burden for practical use. In this study, we discussed the case of two organizations connected via a network and sharing information. Thus, we could use the method to exchange a documented memorandum. However, when we think about a situation in which more and more organizations join and share information in the future, this method may turn out to be a very complicated process. This may delay the spread of remote diagnostic imaging. Thus, we need to develop another approach to help formulate a formation agreement. It may be useful to establish international standards and guidelines to solve this problem, and work on this has already started. We also think that the establishment of some supportive social institutions would be useful for promoting teleradiology, including remote diagnostic imaging by networked medical organization communities (figure 6). As we discussed before, we must secure human resources or financing to deal with increased workloads. Especially, with the first process of building the security management system and auditing systems which needs much knowledge and work. Therefore, we would like to suggest developing the social institutions for supporting mainly the creation of processes and auditing. It is important to establish whether connected organizations can perform appropriate administrative tasks for security. As the number of organizations connected increases, audit work also increases. Therefore, it would be useful if the auditors of the third party inspect the security management of the individual organizations. This approach is both effective and efficient. In addition, in the medical field, hospital usability tests are performed widely. If we place security as one element of the hospital function, giving certification and rating under this framework will also be effective [9].

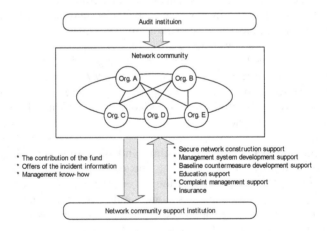

Fig. 6. Network community support institution

The network community support institution in the figure 6 is owned by the networked organizations. The institution may support a new member to develop manuals. It also can develop education tools, gather such information as legal change, standardization, and incidents from the other organization. However, these other organizations should carry out the audit.

5 Conclusion

In the medical field, a community is forming to deal with every specialized field beyond national borders. In the future, the need to share information in specialized fields is expected to increase. If we think about operations being connected in a network across borders, it is easy to assume that the issues that we discovered in our experiment will become more complicated. Especially, the differences in environmental elements, such as legal factors and healthcare policies, may influence the development of information sharing among networked medical organizations.[1]. For continual operation of information sharing, practical security management is indispensable. The implication of this study shows that the approach we tried in our project make it possible that each participating organization develops its own management system and at the same time maintains the security level for whole networked organizations. In order to promote further use of remote diagnostic imaging and other medical information sharing among medical organizations, it is useful to develop the method and social systems that can reduce the workload of medical organizations to acceptable levels and secure the security that society demands. We can expect to see further research in this field in the near future.

References

1. Hori, Y.: How to Build Common Understanding in the Implementation of Information Security Measures. Security Management 20(2), 19–27 (2006)
2. Doi, N. (eds.): Information Processing Information-technology Promotion Agency : Information Security instructional book - Guide of Information Security Practice of Organization. Jikkyo Shuppan Co., Ltd. (2008) (*translated by authors from Japanese)
3. Tanaka, M.: The significance of the Personal Information Protection Law in the Field of Japanese Medical Care. Master's Thesis of Institute of Information Security, pp.88–90/96–98 (2006)
4. Hiroshima, A.: Comments on the Personal Information Protection for Healthcare Providers. Security Management 19(2) (2006)
5. Hagihara, H., Fujimoto, M., Takeda, K., Honma, T.: Balancing of Effect and Risk of Medical Cooperation between Institutions using Information and Communication Technology. Japan Society of Security Management, 22nd National Convention Summary, 129–134 (2008)
6. Ministry of Hearth, Labor and Welfare: Guideline for Safety Management of Medical Information System, 3rd edn., pp. 12–14 (2008)
7. Ministry of Hearth, Labor and Welfare: Guideline for Appropriate Use of Personal Information in Medical and Care Institutions (2006)
8. City of Yokohama, Code of Personal Information Protection of the City of Yokohama (2008-11-28), http://www.city.yokohama.jp/me/shimin/joho/kokai/jorei/ko1.html
9. Hagihara, H., Aida, N., Sugimoto, E., Kawazoe, T., Matsuyama, K.: Establishment of Medical Cooperation System using Mutual Browsing Function of PACS. In: The 28th Joint Conference on Medical Informatics, p. 178 (2008)

---

[1] The difference of the doctor license is a big issue. However, we have excluded it from our argument in this paper.

A Secure Framework and Related Protocols for Ubiquitous Access to Electronic Health Records Using Java SIM Cards

Reza Hassanzadeh, Tony Sahama, and Colin Fidge

Faculty of Science and Technology
Queensland University of Technology
Brisbane, Australia
r.hassanzadeh@isi.qut.edu.au,
{t.sahama,c.fidge}@qut.edu.au

Abstract. Ubiquitous access to patient medical records is an important aspect of caring for patient safety. Unavailability of sufficient medical information at the patient point-of-care could possibly lead to a fatality. In this paper we propose employing emergent technologies such as *Java SIM Cards* (JSC), *Smart Phones* (SP), *Next Generation Networks* (NGN), *Near Field Communications* (NFC), *Public Key Infrastructure* (PKI), and *Biometric Identification* to develop a secure framework and related protocols for ubiquitous access to *Electronic Health Records* (EHRs). A partial EHR contained within a JSC can be used at the patient point-of-care in order to help quick diagnosis of a patient's problems. The full EHR can be accessed from an Electronic Healthcare Records Centre (EHRC).

Keywords: Electronic Healthcare Record, Java SIM Card , Next Generation Network, Smart Phone, Near Field communication, Biometric Identification, Public Key Infrastructure.

1 Introduction

Ubiquitous access to a patient's medical records is an important aspect of caring for patient safety. Unavailability of sufficient medical information at the patient point-of-care could possibly lead to a fatality. The U.S. Institute of Medicine (IOM) has reported that between 44,000 to 98,000 people die each year due to medical errors, such as incorrect medication dosages due to poor legibility in manual records, or delays in consolidating needed medical information to discern the proper intervention. Also the IOM reports the lack of well designed systems and procedures needed to handle the complexity of health care distribution caused 90 percent of medical errors [1]. Most of these medical errors could be avoided with access to patient's medical information at the point of care [2]. Ubiquitous access to patient's medical information is a technique which enables Healthcare systems to have access to patient's medical information wherever it is needed electronically. It has the potential to revolutionize next generation medical applications based on *Electronic Health Records* (EHRs). It could significantly improve the quality of healthcare services to increase patient safety and reduce medical errors and costs.

H. Takeda (Ed.): E-Health 2010, IFIP AICT 335, pp. 102–113, 2010.

Therefore, in this paper, we propose a secure framework and related protocols by taking advantage of new technologies such as *Java SIM Cards* (JSC), *Smart Phones* (SP), *Next Generation Networks* (NGN), *Near Field Communications* (NFC), and *Biometric Identification* for ubiquitous access to patient's medical information at the point-of-care.

The aim of our framework and related protocols is to overcome pervious work's limitations by taking advantage of SIM cards and the new technologies mentioned above. Briefly, our approach could offer the full benefits of accessing an up-to-date, precise, and comprehensive medical history of a patient, whilst its mobility will provide access to medical and patient information everywhere it is needed.

2 Related Work

Ubiquitous Access to patient information has been investigated by many researchers such as Abraham [2], Issa [3], Chenhui [4], and others. Finding an efficient solution that can be secure and implemented in existing Medicare systems is a challenging issue. Some researchers such as Bishop [5] and Chan [6] have proposed using a Medicare card, which is based on a Smart Card, as a potential solution to access patient's health records anywhere and anytime.

However, using Medicare cards as a repository of medical information at the patient point-of-care imposes some limitations on patients' emergency medical care and privacy. These include the inability to detect and inform patient's location, call and send patient information to an emergency room automatically, and computerise and secure interaction with the patient. Our approach aims to overcome these limitations by exploiting the additional capabilities of *Java SIM Card* and new communication technologies.

3 Framework Overview

Our framework is based on developing a secure conceptual structure to enable an *Authorised Person* (AP) such as a doctor to have *Ubiquitous Access* (UA) to a patient's medical record on a national scale. As shown in Fig. 1, the proposed framework relies on new technologies such as *Java SIM Cards* (JSC), *Smart Phones* (SP), *Near Field Communications* (NFC), *Next Generation Networks* (NGN), *Public Key Infrastructure* (PKI), *Secure Sockets Layer/Transport Layer Security* (SSL/TLS) and *Biometric Identification* (BI).

This framework includes six major parts: the *Patient* (P), a *Smart Phone* (SP), an *Authorised Person* (AP), an *Authorised Device* (AD), a *Trusted Third Party* (TTP), and an *Electronic Health Record Centre* (EHRC). The TTP and the EHRC operate at the national (N-TTP, N-EHRC) and state (S-TTP, S-EHRC) levels. The SP is utilised to computerise interaction with a patient. The AD, which is a kind of a *Smart Phone* or *Personal Computer* (PC), is used by an AP such as a doctor to communicate with the SP or TTP. The N-EHRC is a central database containing all patients' EHRs on a national scale. The N-TTP is employed to manage the whole framework's activities. The S-TTP and S-EHRC work at state levels. (For the purposes of this paper, we assume the existence of a central, national EHRC, as well as distributed state-level EHRCs; however the proposed communication framework does not rely crucially on having a centralised database. If necessary its functions can be distributed to the state level.)

Mobile phones, in general, fall into three broad categories: basic phones, multimedia phones, and *Smart Phones* [7]. A *Smart Phone* is a handheld device which has both mobile phone and PC-like abilities together. *Smart Phones* have become an emerging phenomenon for personal and business voice, data, e-mail, and Internet access, and could now form the basis of a healthcare network.

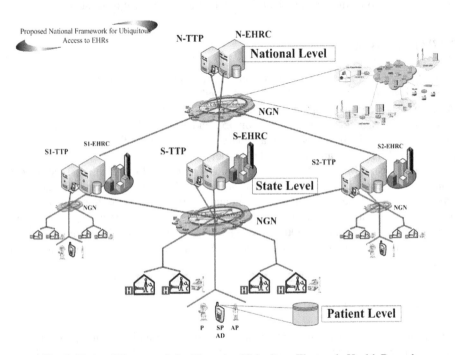

Fig. 1. National Framework for Managing Ubiquitous Electronic Health Records

The *Trusted Third Party* must be a powerful server which is able to manage very large amounts data and traffic. We assume it is facilitated with auditing, logging, authorisation, identification, and storage capabilities. Furthermore, the TTP must be connected to a database which contains all details of *Authorised Persons* and patients, including SIM IDs, devices' serial numbers, fingerprint templates, names and national IDs. Such a capability is now possible using current generation network servers from companies such as HP, IBM, or Dell.

The aforementioned characteristics of the SP, AD and TTP make them suitable for the needs of our framework. Our framework needs to provide ubiquitous access to a patient's EHR, have computerised interaction with a patient and AP, and have a central management system.

3.1 Proposed National Communication Framework

As shown in Fig. 1, our framework is divided into three levels: the national level, the state level, and the patient level. Each level has its own database which is responsible for storing patient medical records accordingly. Therefore, the framework includes three kinds of databases: a *National-Electronic Health Records Centre* (N-EHRC), *State-Electronic Health Records Centres* (S-EHRC), and patient databases (*Java SIM Cards*). Having both national and state databases is an effective strategy for achieving fault tolerance, better performance, and reliable access to large downloads of data.

The patient database stored in a JSC is responsible for storing critical medical information such as their past medical history, blood type, allergies, and the http links (*Uniform Resource Locator*) to the original records and medical images in the central database that we called the *Electronic Health Records Centre* (EHRC).

As the patient's point-of-care location cannot be prearranged, the *Java SIM Card*, due to its intrinsic nature of mobility, can play the role of a portable data repository to help quick diagnosis of a patient's problems. The JSC can make the patient's medical records available across the country or internationally even when the network is not available.

The *National-Electronic Health Record Centre* (N-EHRC) is a central database which contains all patients' EHRs on a national scale. It is responsible for storing the medical records for all the patients in a particular country. This database must be hosted and maintained by a government authorised organisation. The location of this database depends on the network topology in a particular country. The N prefix denotes the country's abbreviation, e.g., 'AU' for Australia and 'IR' for Iran. Therefore, the central database which contains all Australian medical records is designated the AU-EHRC.

The state database or *State-Electronic Health Record Centre* (S-EHRC) is the second tier database and is responsible for storing patients' EHRs at an intrastate level. The S-EHRC stores a copy of EHRs which belong to patients who reside in a specific state (or province or other relevant division within a country). This database must be hosted and maintained by a local government authority. Again the location of this database depends on the network topology in a particular country and state. The S-EHRC and N-EHRC work together to provide fault tolerance, better performance, and reliable access to EHRs. The S prefix denotes an abbreviation for the state within a country, e.g., 'QLD' for Queensland or 'NSW' for New South Wales. Hence, the central database which contains all Queensland's patients' medical records is designated the QLD-EHRC.

As shown in Fig. 1, the framework also includes two other entities the *National Trusted Third Party* (N-TTP) and the equivalent state-based *Trusted Third Parties* (S-TTP). The N-TTP operates on a national scale and S-TTPs work on an intrastate scale. The S-TTP is in charge of managing the *Smart Phones* and *Authorised Devices* while the N-TTP is responsible for managing the S-TTPs including authorising, updating, monitoring, enabling, and disabling the S-TTPs.

In terms of management, each S-TTP is responsible for managing all duties associated with the operation, communication, and maintenance of the SP, AD and S-EHRC within the particular state. For instance, the S-TTP determines an *Access Level* (AL) for the EHRs based on three factors: the identification of an *Authorised*

Device and *Authorised Person* who wants to have access to a patient's medical information, the patient's consent, and the relevant healthcare legislation. Based on these factors the S-TTP maintains three access control lists: *Discretionary Access Control* (DAC), *Mandatory Access Control* (MAC), and *Role Based Access Control* (RBAC) [8, 9]. The MAC and DAC list are made by using the patient's consent. The RBAC list is defined by legislators. The goal is to provide doctors, hospitals, and ambulances with a reasonable level of access to a patient's medical information while still preserving patient privacy.

Moreover, interoperability between different medical information systems which cannot communicate with each other is another of the S-TTP's responsibilities. They must be able to recognise a message's context and convert heterogeneous medical information into a unified format [4]. This allows medical information to be exchanged across different healthcare systems.

Accountability is possible only when the S-TTPs are able to provide strong security mechanisms such as access control, audit trails, and authentication of the patient, *Smart Phones, Authorised Persons*, and *Authorised Devices*. For example all access to the medical records must be logged and entered in an audit trail by the S-TTPs.

3.2   Data Security in the Framework

In terms of security, this framework relies on PKI, SSL/TLS, and *Biometric Identification*. The SSL/TLS protocol is used for implementing secure sessions between a *Smart Phone*, an *Authorised Device*, and a *Trusted Third Party*. The PKI is used by the SP and AD to generate *Non-Repudiable* messages. *Biometric Identification* is employed to ensure that only *Authorised Persons* can access a patient's medical information. PKI is an IT infrastructure which includes a set of procedures, policies, software, hardware, and network services that support security mechanisms such as confidentiality, integrity, authentication, and non-repudiation [10]. PKI utilises public and private keys for encryption and decryption of sensitive information [11].

Biometrics refers to automated techniques for uniquely recognising a person based on a natural physiological or behavioural feature. Features such as the face, fingerprints, hand geometry, handwriting, iris patterns, retinal patterns, veins, and voice are measured for recognition. Biometric technologies are emerging as a foundation of extremely secure identification and personal verification solutions [12].

3.3   Wireless Communications in the Framework

In relation to IP-Wireless and contactless communication, the framework uses *Next Generation Network* and *Near Field Communication* technologies respectively. The NGN is utilised to establish *Internet Protocol* (IP) based wireless communication between the *Smart Phone* and *Trusted Third Party*, and the *Authorised Device* and TTP. The NFC is used to facilitate contactless communication between the AD and SP.

A *Next Generation Network* is an IP-based network that handles multiple types of traffic (such as voice, data, and multimedia). It is the convergence of service provider networks including the *Public Switched Telephone Network* (PSTN), the Internet, and the wireless network [13]. We contend that it is possible to access a wide range of ubiquitous e-health services through this unified network. *Java SIM Cards* are already used in the NGN for authentication, communication and security; we believe it is possible to expand those functionalities by using the JSC as a portable repository of EHR data at the patient point-of-care.

Near Field Communication is a wireless connectivity technology evolving from a combination of contactless identification and networking technologies [14]. It enables convenient short-range communication between electronic devices and smart objects. In our framework NFC plays the role of a contactless communication protocol between a *Smart Phone* and an *Authorised Device*. Through this technology patients can send their consent to the *Authorised Device* and an *Authorised Person* can see the patient's critical health information contained within a patient's device when it is needed. The communication protocols in which these devices can work together via NFC are outlined in Section 4.

3.4 Data Storage in the Framework

In terms of storing medical data our framework use two large databases at the national and state level and a portable small one which is carried by patients in their *Java SIM Cards*. This portable database is responsible for storing critical medical information.

A *Java SIM Card* is a *Subscriber Identity Module* (SIM) card for mobile networks which is made based on a *Java Card*. It is highly secure, efficient, easy to manage and provides many possibilities for supporting various applications [15], and is thus well-suited to storing healthcare records.

3.5 Proposed Local Communication Framework

As shown in Fig. 2, for the purpose of storing an individual's lifetime health information, the local framework contains two central databases called the *Australian-Electronic Health Record Centre* (AU-EHRC) and *Queensland-Electronic Health Record Centre* (QLD-EHRC) in our particular example. In addition, *Java SIM Cards* are used as a patient point-of-care medical information repository. The state level QLD-EHRC database includes only a copy of records for those patients who already live in Queensland or who temporarily visit the state. If a patient visits or moves to any state in Australia, other than his/her own state and needs medical care, the medical record is automatically fetched from the national database (AU-EHRC) and inserted into the visited state's database such as the QLD-EHRC. This strategy minimises traffic to the national AU-EHRC in a way similar to GSM mobile networks [16].

For the purpose of security, various mechanisms and protocols such as *Biometric Identification*, the *Secure Sockets Layer/Transport Layer Security* (SSL/TLS) protocol and *Public Key Infrastructure* encryption must be utilised to achieve secure access to patients' medical information. As we assume the communication between the *Smart Phone* or *Authorised Device* and S-TTP is based on a *Next Generation Network* which uses the Internet as a carrier, our framework must use PKI and SSL/TLS for the purpose of data confidentiality, integrity, authentication, and non-repudiation. These technologies enable the SP, AD, and TTP to exchange sensitive information through the unsecure public network. The patient's *Private Key* is stored in the *Java SIM Card* which has the capability of operating cryptographic algorithms, while the patient's *Public Key* is stored by the AU-TTP and QLD-TTP.

Biometric Identification such as fingerprints must be used for accurately authenticating a patient or an AP. In principle, biometrics cannot be forgotten or lost, and are difficult to duplicate or share among different users [17]. A biometrics authentication system requires the physical presence of the individual. Among several biometric technologies, fingerprints have been in use for the longest time and have more advantages than others. For instance, there are many devices such as *Smart Phones* on the market that are equipped with a fingerprint scanner. A fingerprint is captured via live scan and then its features are retrieved. The retrieved fingerprint's features are then fed into the JSC, where the fingerprint template is stored, for the matching process. If a match is made, access to the medical information will be granted.

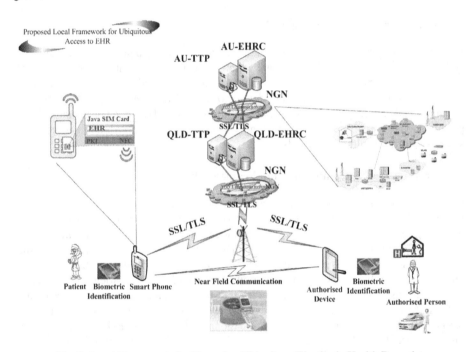

Fig. 2. Local Framework for Managing Ubiquitous Electronic Health Records

3.6   Contents of a Java SIM Card (JSC)

Fig. 3 splits the patient's *Java SIM Card* into three layers for managing ubiquitous Electronic Health Records: the application and database layer (*Applet Layer*), the *Java Card Runtime Environment* (JCRE) layer, and the *OS/Hardware* layer. While the JCRE and OS/HW layers are specific to a particular computing platform, we require an Applet Layer to address the design requirements specific to the development of *Ubiquitous Access to Electronic Health Records*.

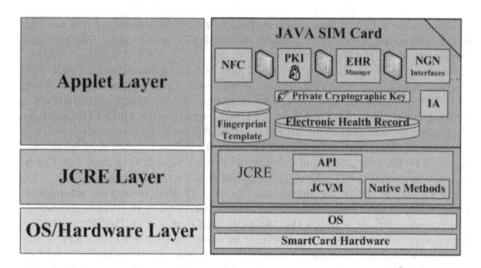

Fig. 3. Java SIM Card Architecture for Managing EHRs

The *Applet Layer* must consist of an EHR-Manager, PKI, NFC, *Identification Algorithm* (IA), NGN Interfaces and other applets as necessary. Additionally, this layer includes the *Private Cryptographic Key* and a small database which contains critical medical information such as past medical history, blood type, allergies, and the http links (Uniform Resource Locator) to original records and medical images in the central database.

The EHR-Manager interface is needed to handle communication between the state-level QLD-TTP and the *Java SIM Card* in order to update the EHRs contained within the *Java SIM Card*. After an *Authorised Person* updates a patient's EHRs within the QLD-EHRC, the QLD-TTP automatically updates the EHR within the JSC by using the *EHR-Manager* interface, *Smart Phone*, *Next Generation Network*, SSL/TLS protocol and *Over The Air* (OTA) and *SIM Tool Kit* (STK) technologies. OTA and STK technologies are widely adopted in mobile communication systems to read and write the contents of *Java SIM Cards* [18]. After a patient confirms the acknowledgement SMS message coming from the QLD-TTP, the update will be done.

The JSC must be equipped with a *Near Field Communication Application Programming Interface* (NFC API) in order to exchange information with an *Authorised Device* over about a 10 centimetre distance. The NFC enables the *Smart Phone* and *Authorised Device* to have contactless communication. By using the NFC a *Smart Phone* is able to send a patient's consent to the *Authorised Device* or the *Authorised Person* is able to see the patient's EHR within the JSC. There are many mobile phones such as the Nokia 6216 and 5800 in the market that support a SIM-based NFC interface.

The *Identification Algorithm* (IA) is needed for the challenge-response mechanism occurring between the *Smart Phone* or *Authorized Device* and the QLD-TTP. Challenge-response is important in the process of identifying a remote source as either an individual or a device. This algorithm works similarly to GSM authentication [19]. IA uses the challenge and the unique embedded information which is stored within a tamper-resistant *Java SIM Card* to generate a *Fresh ID*. The unique embedded information include the SIM ID, device serial No, scanned Fingerprint, name, and National ID.

As shown in Fig. 3, the *Java SIM Card* must also be facilitated with a *Public Key Infrastructure* API in order to implement secure sessions between the SP and AD and QLD-TTP and produce *Non-Repudiable* messages. We assume that all the *Public Keys* of the patients who reside in QLD are stored in the QLD-TTP and it is responsible for managing them. Therefore, if the AD needs to communicate with the SP, it must first connect to the QLD-TTP to get the patient's *Public Key*. Moreover, the AU-TTP must be able to put the patients' *Private Keys* on their *Java SIM Cards* remotely by using *Over The Air* (OTA) and *SIM Tool Kit* (STK) technologies.

For the sake of clarity, we suppose that when the SP needs to send any information to the AD or QLD-TTP, this information must be encrypted by the *Private Key* which is contained within the patient's JSC. An *Authorised Device* or QLD-TTP can decrypt the message received from a *Smart Phone* by using the patient's *Public Key*. If the AD needs to send any information to the SP, first it must get the patient's *Public Key* from the QLD-TTP, and then it must encrypt the information with the patient's *Public Key*. The SP can decrypt the message received from the AD or QLD-TTP by using its own *Private Key* within the JSC.

The *Java SIM Card* is a multi-application environment. Multiple applets from different vendors can coexist in a single card, and additional applets can be downloaded after card manufacture. An applet often stores highly sensitive information, such as EHRs, fingerprints, private cryptographic keys, and so on. Sharing such sensitive data among applets must be carefully limited [20]. Therefore, for further security the JSC must have a firewall between the applets in order to achieve isolation and restrict access to the data of one applet from another as shown in Fig. 3.

Furthermore, in the case of the *Java SIM Card* being lost or stolen, the JSC can protect the information within the card by requiring a fingerprint and PIN code to access the patient's medical information. Also after the QLD-TTT is aware of a card going missing, it can remotely disable the card and delete all personal information inside the card.

4   Communication Protocols

In Section 3, we introduced a framework in which an Authorised Person such as a doctor is able to have Ubiquitous Access to a patient's medical record on a national scale. We also saw what components the framework needs and how the components fit together in general terms. In this section we briefly summarised the three different protocols needed for communication between the *Smart Phone* (SP), *Authorised Device* (AD), and *Trusted Third Party* (TTP). All three protocols work on the application layer which means they are independent of the underlying protocol layers for end-to-end communication. The application layer is the 7th layer in the Open Source Interconnection (OSI) reference model [21] and is closest to the end user. The SP, AD, and TTP protocols define the processes and procedures that must be followed when these agents want to request data from, respond to and communicate with each other. The protocols are designed to cover different emergency and non emergency scenarios.

The *Smart Phone* (SP) protocol is used when a patient wants to request data from, respond to, or communicate with *Authorised Devices* (AD) or a *Trusted Third Party* (TTP). In total the SP protocol requires seven major processes and procedures: *Authenticating the Patient, Modifying an Access Control List, Viewing EHRs, Identifying the Patient, Granting Consent, Generating Non-repudiable Consent,* and *Handling an Emergency situation.* The *Authenticating the Patient* process is used by an SP to prevent an unauthorised person from using a patients' *Smart Phone* to access their medical information. The *Modifying an Access Control List* process is used to give the power to patients to decide who can access their medical record. The *Viewing EHRs* process is used to enable a patient to view his or her centralised *Electronic Health Record* via a *Smart Phone.* The *Identifying the Patient* procedure is used by the TTP to identify a patient when they want to request data from the TTP. The *Generating Non-repudiable Consent* procedure is used to make a patient accountable when he or she gives consent. The *Handling an Emergency* process is used to detect and inform a patient's location, and automatically call and send a patient's details to an Emergency Room.

The AD protocol is used when an *Authorised Person* (AP) such as a doctor wants to request data from, respond to, or communicate with patient's *Smart Phone* (SP) or a *Trusted Third Party* (TTP). In total the AD protocol requires seven major processes and procedures: *Authenticating an Authorised Person, Identifying an Authorised Person, Getting Consent, Establishing NFC Communication, Generating Referral Letter, Non-Repudiable Setup Message,* and *Verifying a Referral Letter.* The *Authenticating an Authorised Person* process is used by an AD to prevent an unauthorised person from using the AD to access the patient's medical information. The *Identifying an Authorised Person* procedure is used by a TTP to identify an AP accurately when he or she wants to have access to data from the TTP. The *Establishing NFC Communication* process is used by an AD to establish an NFC session with the SP. The *Generating Referral Letter* process is used by an AP to send a RL to a specialist. The *Non-Repudiable Setup Message* procedure is used by the AD to introduce itself to the SP. The *Verifying a Referral Letter* process is used by an AP to have access to a patient's RL from the TTP.

The *Trusted Third Party* (TTP) protocol is used when the TTP wants to request data from, respond to or communicate with the *Smart Phone* (SP) and *Authorised Device* (AD). In total the TTP protocol requires five major processes: *Establishing a SSL/TLS Session, Verifying a Setup Message, Verifying Patient Consent, Identifying the SP or AD,* and *Storing or Retrieving a Referral Letter.* All these processes are used to link the SP's and AD's processes and procedures.

While complex, all of these protocols can be implemented using existing technologies. Elsewhere we have modeled the protocols in ISO's Specification and Description Language and have simulated their behaviour in the UPPAAL model checker.

5   Conclusion

Ubiquitous access to a patient's medical records is an important aspect of caring for the patient. Using new technologies such as *Java SIM Cards* to address the challenges of ubiquitous access to EHRs is vital for current healthcare systems. While full EHRs can be accessed from an *Electronic Health Records Centre* (EHRC), partial EHRs contained within a *Java SIM Card* can be used at the patient point-of-care to help quick diagnosis of a patient's problems. By taking advantage of the *Java SIM Card* and related communication and security technologies, we proposed a secure framework and communication protocols which provide a solution for ubiquitous access to EHRs without imposing any major changes on existing infrastructure.

Acknowledgments

We wish to thank the anonymous reviewers for their helpful comments.

Reference

1. Institute-of-Medicine. To err is human: Building a safer health system 2000, http://www.nap.edu/books/0309068371/html (cited September 23, 2008)
2. Abraham, C., Watson, R.T., Boudreau, M.-C.: Ubiquitous access: on the front lines of patient care and safety. Communications of the ACM 51(6), 95–99 (2008)
3. Issa, O., Gregoire, J.C., Belala, Y., James, W.: 3G Embedded Communication System for Medical Applications. In: 2nd Annual IEEE Systems Conference (2008)
4. Chenhui, Z., Huilong, D., Xudong, L.: An Integration Approach of Healthcare Information System. In: International Conference on BioMedical Engineering and Informatics (2008)
5. Bishop, B., Maloney, D., Wilson, P., Nader, N., Sembritzki, J., Meazzini, G., Morency, D.: US cards hold medical records. Card Technology Today 12(6), 14–15 (2000)
6. Chan, A.T.S., Cao, J., Chan, H., Young, G.: A web-enabled framework for smart card applications in health services. Communications of the ACM 44(9), 76–82 (2001)
7. Chang, Y.F., Chen, C.S., Zhou, H.: Smart phone for mobile commerce. Computer Standards & Interfaces 31(4), 740–747 (2009)
8. Kim, D.-K., Mehta, P., Gokhale, P.: Describing access control models as design patterns using roles. Paper Presented at the Proceedings of the, Conference on Pattern Languages of Programs (2006) (retrieved)
9. Alhaqbani, B., Fidge, C.: Access Control Requirements for Processing Electronic Health Records. In: ter Hofstede, A.H.M., Benatallah, B., Paik, H.-Y. (eds.) BPM Workshops 2007. LNCS, vol. 4928, pp. 371–382. Springer, Heidelberg (2008)
10. Kambourakis, G., Maglogiannis, I., Rouskas, A.: PKI-based secure mobile access to electronic health services and data. Technology & Health Care 13(6), 511–526 (2005)
11. Articsoft. Introduction to Public Key Infrastructure (2009), http://www.governmentsecurity.org/forum/index.php?showtopic=1630 (cited May 10, 2009)
12. The Biometric Consortium. An Introduction to Biometric (2009), http://www.biometrics.org/html/introduction.html (cited May 10, 2009)
13. ITU-T Next Generation Network. Definition of Next Generation Network (2009), http://www.itu.int/ITU-T/studygroups/com13/ngn2004/working_definition.html (cited May 10, 2009)
14. Morak, J., Hayn, D., Kastner, P., Drobics, M., Schreier, G.: Near Field Communication Technology as the Key for Data Acquisition in Clinical Research. In: First International Workshop on Near Field Communication, NFC '09 (2009)

15. Pak, T.: JAVA SIM card (2009),
    `http://www.tele-pak.com/plastic-cards/javacards.html`
    (cited December 23, 2009)
16. Peersman, C., Cvetkovic, S., Griffiths, P., Spear, H.: The Global System for Mobile Communications Short Message Service. IEEE Personal Communications 7(3), 15–23 (2000)
17. Hu, J.: Mobile fingerprint template protection: Progress and open issues. In: 3rd IEEE Conference on Industrial Electronics and Applications, ICIEA 2008 (2008)
18. Chin, L.-P., Chen, J.-Y.: SIM card based e-cash applications in the mobile communication system using OTA and STK technology. In: 2006 IET International Conference on Wireless, Mobile and Multimedia Networks (2006)
19. Haverinen, H., Asokan, N., Maattanen, T.: Authentication and key generation for mobile IP using GSM authentication and roaming. In: IEEE International Conference on Communications, ICC 2001 (2001)
20. Chen, Z.: Technology for Smart Cards: Architecture and Programmer's Guide 2000. Pearson, London (2000)
21. ITU-T X.210, ITU-T Recommendation X.210. Open Systems Interconnection - Basic Reference Model: Conventions for the Definition of OSI Services (1993)

Capturing and Analyzing Injection Processes with Point of Act System for Improving Quality and Productivity of Health Service Administration

Atsushi Koshio[1,2] and Masanori Akiyama[1,2]

[1] Todai Policy Alternatives Research Institute, The Univerisity of Tokyo, Tokyo, Japan
[2] Sloan School of Management, Masachusettus Institute of Techonology, MA, USA
{koshio,makiyama}@pp.u-tokyo.ac.jp

Abstract. The objective of this paper is to show process data captured with barcode administration system and the results of data analyses and visualizations for improving quality of care and productivity. Hospital Information System named Point-of-Act System that was designed to capture every process of all medical acts was employed to capture data of medical processes. Data of injection process was analyzed based on operative timeliness. The result shows nursing workload didn't be allocated equally through the day and some parts of injections hadn't been administrated at the right time. Improving operative timeliness can contribute to improve quality of care and productivity. This kind of process information has a possibility to provide new research opportunity to analyze outcome with context information including process information.

Keywords: Hospital Information System, Process Management, Electrical Data Capturing, Data Analysis, Visualization.

1 Introduction

Utilizing data captured and stored by hospital information systems is quite important issue to make hospital IT systems more effective for improving health care quality and productivity. After the report of medication errors and health care quality by Institute of Medicine, these data have been regarded as significant sources for managing hospital environments [1-2]. The data can be constructed as indicators evaluating health care process and outcome. The movements such as "e-indicators" have been trying to analyze and publish these data for the purpose of health outcome management with bench marking and public disclosure [3-11]. Outcome information has a possibility to affect patient's decision and make health care system more patients centered. In addition to this outcome information, process information is also important to understand reality of health care service provision. Process indicators provide context of outcome indicators and show practices to improve quality and productivity [12-15].

Data captured through daily use of hospital information systems are containing data of medication processes. Utilizing process data for understanding daily medication process is an useful way to plan resource allocation in hospitals to

H. Takeda (Ed.): E-Health 2010, IFIP AICT 335, pp. 114–121, 2010.
© IFIP International Federation for Information Processing 2010

improve operation and management of service delivery. Process information has an ability to provide why differences of outcome are coming from. And this activities capturing process information and managing medical process also have a possibility to make health care industry more transparent and accountable through publishing the information. Transparency is one of the prioritized areas to be solved to construct better health care systems [16-18].

The objective of this paper is to show process data captured with barcode administration system and the results of analyses and visualizations for achieving the targets described above. This study will emphasize benefits of hospital information system named Point of Act System based on process management and real time data capturing and capturing every activity in the hospitals. In this study, we focus injections and utilize injection process data to analyze medical activities and visualize process in the hospital.

2 Methods

2.1 Things That Need to Be Addressed

Point of Act System (POAS) is a real time bar-code capturing health information system in International Medical Center of Japan (IMCJ) in Tokyo, Japan [19-22]. POAS has a function to prevent medical errors by certifying correctness of medical activities with capturing bar cords on patients, worker and drugs. It ensure not only the correctness of patients, drug, dose but also route and time based on real time information. At the same time, POAS captures implementation records at each process of medical activities including 6W1H information (When, Where What, Why, for what, to whom and How) of the activities. The basic requirement for successful measurement and data capturing, they must be integrated with the routine provision of care and whenever possible should be done using IS and this system satisfied this requirement [6].

There are basic characteristics of POAS captured data. The data is including every activity in the hospital that means it concludes complete data of the administration. This implies the research based on not sampling data but all data of the medications. The second characteristic is process management of administration. The first target of process management is restraining skipping processes that would sometimes be causes of medication errors. The system record the data at each point of action of processes described by figure 1 showing injection process as an example.

By capturing the data routinely at each process of activities, the data provides information on returned and wasted injections as well as normal injections without entering additional information at end points.

2.2 Data and Analysis Methods

Injection process was chose as a target of this study to analyze process data and visualize processes of medical activities. As a standard injection process physicians order for patients and pharmacists pick up and audit the order. These drugs deliver to

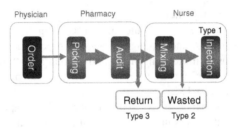

Fig. 1. Data capturing points of Injection processes

nurse stations and nurses mix and inject them to patients. 6W1H information have been captured at each point of action; Order, Picking, Audit, Mixing and Injection. In addition to these data, data on order is including "scheduled order time" that shows the scheduled time to inject to patients. These data were liked by serialized ID on each drug and order. Data from July to September 2007 that is including 306768 drugs taken in all injections during the term at every ward in IMCJ was used to analyze. The data was merged from different partial information system such as physician order entry system, pharmacy system and risk management system. Data from other term was also referred if necessary. Basic descriptive analyses and some visualization techniques are applied for analyzing injection process. Especially we described frequency of injection processes minutes by minutes to analyze business of the hospital and time differences including scheduled time and actual administration time to assess time precision of the administration processes to scheduled plan.

3   Results

Figure 2 shows the distribution of scheduled injection order time by physicians. Enormous portion of orders were scheduled on 6AM, 10AM and 6PM. Figure 3 shows actual number of activities including mixing of drugs for injections and injections of drugs by minutes. As the peak of order by physicians was 6AM, the time of peak of actual injections is around 6AM. The orders scheduled 6AM were injected

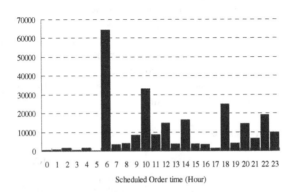

Fig. 2. Distribution of scheduled time

from around 4AM to 7AM, because the number of orders surpassed capacity of nurses at the time. Nurses adjusted to variation of number of orders by time by injecting earlier than scheduled time.

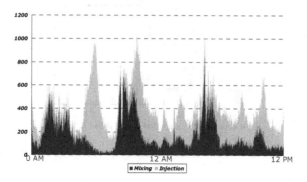

Fig. 3. Distribution of scheduled time of injections

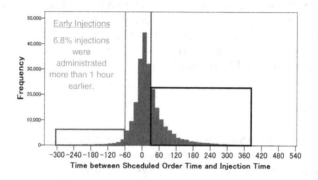

Fig. 4. Distribution of difference between scheduled time and actual time of injections

As described above, nurses adjusted to high frequency of scheduled order by injecting earlier or later. Figure 4 shows Distribution of time difference between scheduled order time and injection time. Time between scheduled order time and injection were calculated by the formula and a minute unit.

(Time between scheduled order time and injection) = (Scheduled Order Time) − (Injection Time)

Positive numbers shows early administration of injections, negative number shows lately administration of injections and 0 means right on time. It might be regarded as positive to close to 0 from the point of view of right time administration. Mean of the time is 10.63 minutes. The most frequent category is from 0 to -15 and the second most frequent category is from 15 to 0. Most of injections are around 0. 6.8 % of injections were regarded as early administration that was defined by one hour early administration[33].

Figure 5 shows time between mixing and scheduled order time. Time between mixing and scheduled order time was calculated by the formula and a minute unit.

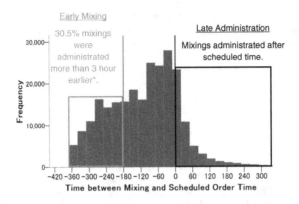

Fig. 5. Distribution of difference between drug mixings and injections

(Time between mixing and scheduled order time)= (Mixing time) – (Scheduled Order time).

For example, 180 minutes means mixing before 3 hour. Mean of the time is 108.5 minutes. The highest frequency is from 0 to 30 minutes. According the guideline for safe medication in the hospital, drug mixing shouldn't be implemented 3 hours before injection. However, 30.5 % of injections were regarded as early mixing and this information hadn't informed by the nurses.

4   Discussion

We captured data by POAS that was designed by the concept of process analysis and management. This concept provided the system a structure to capture the data. According to the survey of system use, the system covered more than 99.9% mixing drugs and injections. Process management prohibits workers from skipping each activity on the process and that contribute to ensure the correctness of medical activities through the process.

Secondly these process data suggests the importance of process indicator related to outcome indicators. Outcome data and process indicator have been used as measurement indicators of performance. The advantage of outcome indicators is that it explain the achievements of targets itself. Outcome measurement will reflect all aspect of the processes of care and not simply those that are measurable or not [24- 28]. However, as Mant said, difference in outcome might sometimes be due to case mix, how the data were collected, chance, quality of care or other factors such as nutrition, life style. Outcome indicators can be improved if efforts are made to standardize data collection and case mix adjustment systems are developed and validated [7]. Process data can be redeeming indicators to understand meanings of outcome indicators. Process data is providing context information to understand the setting for the case [29-36].

This is the example of research linking process data to some outcome indicators. In this example, we set wasted rate of drugs. If physicians change their order after

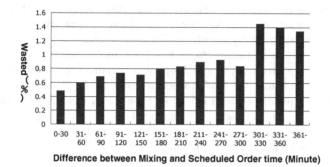

Difference between Mixing and Scheduled Order time (Minute)

Fig. 6. Time difference between drug mixings and injections and drug wasted rate

nurse's mixing drugs, these drugs must be wasted. It is of course necessary to inject right drugs based on up data decisions of physicians, but drug wasting would cause inefficacy of hospital management.

Figure 6 shows the result of analysis that beforehand mixings for laborsaving whose intervals are relatively longer have tend to be wasted by order changes. Analysis on data in unit of wards also shows wards whose intervals between mixing and injection are longer tend to waste more.

Just measuring drug wasted rate is not enough to analyze the cause of high drug wasted rate. By linking process information to outcome information and capturing process routinely, the data make us possible to investigate the reason of some outcomes.

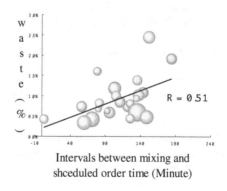

Intervals between mixing and
shceduled order time (Minute)

Fig. 7. Relationship between intervals and drug wasted rate

5   Conclusion

In this study, we show clearly that data captured by hospital information system provide us new research opportunities to improve quality of care and productivities. Many hospitals have been introducing hospital information system to improve operational efficiency. Secondly use of data captured by HIS hasn't become widely yet, though it has a possibility to improve quality and safety of care as well as productivity. The important thing to spread utilization of bust amount of data is providing evidences that secondly use of data can improve them.

Concern on performance measurement has been increasing rapidly and many organization including government and hospital associations and researches have been trying to set indictors for performance measurement [2]. As discussion of process and outcome indicators, both indicators have useful meanings for patients to chose hospitals and acquire healthcare information. This study will help to understand the benefits of process data and contribute to measure quality of care and improve hospital management on health care quality and safety.

References

1. Institute of Medicine. To error is human. National Academies Press, Washington (1999)
2. Institute of Medicine: Crossing the quality chasm: A New Health System for the 21st Century. National Academies Press, Washington (2001)
3. Fowles, J.B., Kind, E.A., Awwad, S., Weiner, J.P., Chan, K.S.: Performance Measures Using Electronic Health Records: Five Case Studies. The Commonwealth Fund (2008)
4. Baker, D., Persell, S., Thompson, J., Soman, N., Bugner, K., Liss, D., Kmetik, K.: Automated Review of Electorical Health Records to Assess Quality of Care for Outpatients with Heart Failure. Annal of Internal. Medicine (February 2007)
5. Weiner, M., Stump, T.E., Callahan, C.M., Lewis, J.N., McDonald, C.J.: Pursing integration of performance measures into electronic medical records: beta-adrenergic receptor antagonist medications. Qual. Saf. Health Care 14, 99–106 (2005)
6. Bates, D.W., Pappius, E., Kuperman, G.J., Sittig, D., Burstin, H., Fairchild, D., Brennan, T.A., Teich, J.M.: Using information systems to measure and improve quality. International Journal of Medical Informatics 53, 115–124 (1999)
7. Davies, H.T., Marshall, M.N.: Public disclosure of performance data. Lancet 353, 1639–1640 (1999)
8. Epstein, A.: Rolling down the runway: the challenges ahead for quality report cards. JAMA 279, 1691–1696 (1998)
9. Kassirer, J.P.: The use and abuse of practice profiles. N. Engl. J. Med. 330, 634–635 (1994)
10. Lansky, D.: Overview: performance measures. Comm. J. Qual. Improv. 22, 439–442 (1996)
11. Ådahl, K.: Validation of Transparency in e-Health – Turning Information Visible Through Design. In: The IRIS29 Conference (2006) (Keynote paper)
12. Nelson, R., Ball, M.J.: Consumer Informatics – Applications and Strategies in Cyber Health Care. Springer, New York (2004)
13. Rindebäck, C., Gustavsson, R.: Why Trust is Hard – Challenges in e-Mediated Services. LNCS (LNAI). Springer, Heidelberg (2005)
14. Smith, R.: Transparency: a modern essential. BMJ 328, 7448.0-f (2004)
15. Weinberg, S.L.: Transparency in Medicine: Fact, Fiction, or Mission Impossible?
16. Mant, J.: Process versus outcome indicators in the assessment of quality of health care. International Journal of Quality in Health care 13(6), 475–480 (2001)
17. Marshall, M.N., Shekelle, P.G., Leatherman, S., Brook, R.H.: The Publication of Performance Data in Health Care. Nuffield Trust, London (2000)
18. Becker, J., Kugeler, M., Rosemann, M. (eds.): Process Management: A Guide for the Design of Business Processes, 2nd edn. Springer, Berlin (2007)

19. Akiyama, M., Kondo, T.: Risk Management and Measuring Productivity with POAS - Point of Act System. Medinfo., 208–212 (2007)
20. Akiyama, M.: Migration of the Japanese Healthcare Enterprise from a Financial to Integrated Management: Strategy and Architecture. Medinfo., 715–718 (2001)
21. Akiyama, M.: Risk Management and Measuring Productivity with POAS- Point of Act System. Methods inf. Med. 46, 686–693 (2007)
22. Akiyama, M.: A Medical Information System as ERP (Enterprise Resource Planning) for the Hospital Management. Medinfo. 11, 1502 (2004)
23. Westphal, C., Blaxton, T.: The process of discovery begins by getting an overall picture of the available data Data Mining Solutions – Methods and Tools for Solving Real-World Problems. John Wiley & Sons, New York (1998)
24. Noon, C.E., Hankins, C.T.: Spatial Data Visualization in Healthcare: Supporting a Facility Location Decision via GIS-based Market Analysis. In: Proceedings of the 34th Hawaii International Conference on System Sciences (2001)
25. Ammenwerth, E., Ehlers, F., Eichstädter, R., Haux, R., Kruppa, B., Parzer, P., et al.: Analysis and modeling of the treatment process characterizing the cooperation within multiprofessional treatment teams. In: Hasman, A., Blobel, B., Dudeck, J., Engelbrecht, R., Gell, G., Prokosch, H.U. (eds.) Proceedings of the MIE 2000, pp. 57–61. IOS Press, Amsterdam (2000)
26. Fung, A., Graham, M., Weil, D., Fagotto, E.: Transparency Policies: Two Possible Futures. Taubman Center Policy Briefs (May 2007)
27. McNaughton, H., McPherson, K., Taylor, W., Weatherall, M.: FRACP. Relationship Between Process and Outcome in Stroke Care
28. Mant, J., Hicks, N.: Detecting differences in quality of care: the sensitivity of measures of process and outcome in treating acute myocardial infarction. BMJ 311, 793–796 (1995)
29. Mant, J., Hicks, N.R., Fletcher, J.: Correcting outcome data for case mix in stroke medicine: study should have had more patients or longer time scale. BMJ 313, 1006 (1996)
30. Davies, H.T., Lampel, J.: Trust in performance indicators. Qual. Health Care 7, 159–162 (1998)
31. Thomson, R., Lally, J.: Clinical indicators. Qual. Health Care 7, 122 (1998)
32. Staccini, P., Joubert, M., Quaranta, J.-F., Fieschi, D., Fieschi, M.: Modelling health care processes for eliciting user requirements: a way to link a quality paradigm and clinical information system design. International Journal of Medical Informatics 64, 129–142 (2001)
33. Sakowski, J., Leonard, T., Colburn, S., Michaelsen, B., Schiro, T., Schneider, J., Newman, J.M.: Using a Bar-Coded Medication Administration System to Prevent Medication Errors. American Journal of Health-System Pharmacy 62(24), 2619–2625 (2005)
34. Ammenwerth, E., Ehlers, F., Eichst'adter, R., Haux, R., Kruppa, B., Parzer, P., et al.: Analysis and modeling of the treatment process characterizing the cooperation within multiprofessional treatment teams. In: Hasman, A., Blobel, B., Dudeck, J., Engelbrecht, R., Gell, G., Prokosch, H.U. (eds.) Proceedings of the MIE 2000, pp. 57–61. IOS Press, Amsterdam (2000)
35. Lenz, R., Reichert, M.: IT Support for Healthcare Processes. In: van der Aalst, W.M.P., Benatallah, B., Casati, F., Curbera, F. (eds.) BPM 2005. LNCS, vol. 3649, pp. 354–363. Springer, Heidelberg (2005)
36. Plsek, P.E.: Systematic design of healthcare processes. Qual. Health Care 6, 40–48 (1997)
37. Kueng, P., Kawalek, P.: Goal-based business process models: creation and evaluation. Business Process Manage. J. 3, 17–38 (1997)
38. Dadam, P., Reichert, M.: Towards a new dimension in clinical information processing. Stud. Health Technol. Inform. 77, 295–301 (2000)

Analysis on Data Captured by the Barcode Medication Administration System with PDA for Reducing Medical Error at Point of Care in Japanese Red Cross Kochi Hospital

Masanori Akiyama[1,2], Atsushi Koshio[1,2], and Nobuyuki Kaihotsu[3]

[1] Todai Policy Alternatives Research Institute, The Univerisity of Tokyo, Tokyo, Japan
[2] Sloan School of Management, Masachusettus Institute of Techonology, MA, USA
[3] Japanese Red Cross Kochi Hospital
{makiyama,koshio}@pp.u-tokyo.ac.jp

Abstract. Our study aim to understand complete picture and issues on medical safety and investigate preventive measures for medical errors by analyzing data captured by bar code system and entered by Personal Digital Assistance. Barcode administration system named Point-of-Act-System was designed to capture every activity at the bed sides. Complete activity data including injection, treatment and other nurses' activity and warning data showing mistakes on injections were used for our analyses. We described the data and analyze statistically by accumulating data by hour to find potentially risky time and understand relationship between business and errors. The warning rate as a whole was 6.1% in average. The result showed there was a negative correlation between number of injections and injection warning rate (-0.48, $p<0.05$). Warning rate was relatively low in the hours that numbers of administrating injections are high. Bar code administration system is quite effective way not only to prevent medical error at point of care but also improve patient safety with analyses of data captured by them.

Keywords: Barcode administration system, Point-of-Act-System, Point of Care, Patient Safety, Warning data.

1 Introduction

It is widely believed that patient safety is an important issue for health care systems. Many organizations and hospitals have been trying to gather information and evidences on patient safety for the purpose to improve patient safety based on the data collected. These data is accumulated to provide information on threats for patent safety including bottle neck of administration and high risk areas. Such data are quite useful in understanding the threats and actual situations related to medication errors in hospitals. However, most of evidence is basically information on medical accidents and incidents, compiled from voluntary reports submitted by medical workers and the workers need to write reports to inform the situation to them. This information is not detailed enough to enable the discovery of underlying general principles, because

H. Takeda (Ed.): E-Health 2010, IFIP AICT 335, pp. 122–129, 2010.

accidents and errors are part of the reality in a hospital setting. A complete picture of the situations in hospitals, including details of medical accidents and incidents, is essential to identifying general causes and frequency of medical errors. However, it is extremely costly to obtain by observational research sufficient data to enable an understanding of all the activities conducted in a hospital, and furthermore, the accuracy of data collected by observation is sometimes defective.

Information technology such as electrical medical record and barcode administration system at point-of-care have the potential to provide new opportunities for us to understand the overall picture of medical activities by digital capturing data on patient care through daily medications in hospital settings. By using information systems for all patients in all wards, data captured by the systems become useful resources to understanding various phenomena in medical situations and investigating research questions. In terms of medication accidents, the point of care is potentially risky area in medical activities [1-3]. Barcode medication administration systems prevent medication errors by authenticating the "5 rights" of medication: right patient, right drug, right dose, right time, right route. Performed at the bedside, the system offers an excellent opportunity to gather data on medications. In addition to their contribution to the authentication of the 5 Rights, data captured by barcode administration systems have the potential to provide sources of research to improve patient safety in terms of actual injections and medication data.

Our study aims to use and analyze complete data on medical activities captured at the point of care by the system to understand complete picture and issues related to medical safety, and to investigate preventive measures for medication accidents. We focused on injections, which are one of the major causes of medical accidents and, investigated the relation between errors and the contexts of medication activities including how busy staffs were, and shift works.

2 Methods

2.1 Settings and Items to Be Addressed

Japanese Red Cross Kochi Hospital located on southern part of Japan has 482 registered beds and approximately 290,000 out-patients and 9,355 in-patients per year. The hospital implemented a hospital information system called "Point of Act System" or POAS, in 2004. POAS is a real time bar-code capturing health information system designed to prevent medication errors by capturing the barcodes of patients, workers and drugs, and then authenticating the 5 Rights of each medical action with real time information [4-6]. At the same time, POAS captures complete data of each medical action including 6W1H information (When, Where What, Why, for what, to whom and How) and stores the data to access in an instance. The system was designed to use data secondly for improve quality and productivity of health care. The basic requirement for successful measurement and data capturing, they must be integrated with the routine provision of care and whenever possible should be done using IS and this system satisfied this requirement The principal characteristics of data captured by this system are (1) complete data including every action in real time and accurately and (2) process management that enables POAS to ensure right process of medication and assure capturing complete data. Complete data capture through routinely use of hospital information system including 6W1H information is an innovative source to understand real situations directly without estimations and investigate solutions to prevent errors.

2.2 Data

Data captured at the sites of injection process was used for our analyses of medication administration, especially nursing care. Data on injections means both injections and IVs. 6W1H information was captured at each point of the injection process; Order to give injection, Drug picking, Drug audit, Drug mixing and Injection. Although the first objective of a bar code administration system is to ensure patient safety by verifying medication rightness including the 5 Rights of medication, another objective is to capture activities of nurses enforcing medications for patients. At the point of care or activity, nurses uses PDAs to scan the barcode of ambles or vials containing the medication to be injected or other activities including treatment, care, observation, counseling and emergency to enter information on their actions. This information is primary used for the documentation of nursing activities. However, this information can also be used not only for hospital management through understanding the workloads of nurses and the actual costs of administering medications but also for patient safety by understanding the prevailing situations when warnings are made. In addition to these data entered by nurses, we also used warning data demonstrating mistakes that can be made in scanning the barcodes on bottles of drugs. Warning data do not directly mean data on errors. However, warning data is useful sources to analyze causes of medical errors, because warned activities have potential possibility of medical errors without barcode administration system. Therefore, high warning rates in some specific times, places, situations and workers mean risky times, places, situations and workers for patient safety. Types of warning are basically wrong bottle, wrong patient and mixing error meaning incorrect mixing of drugs. All data from January 2005 to June 2008 was used for the analyses. Total numbers of activities are 14,824,046 and number of injections are 604,847. That covered almost 100 % injections and 99% of activities by nurses.

2.3 Data Analysis

We accumulated the data by each hour (24 hours) to find high risk times to understand big picture of medical activities and medical error in hospital wards. Warning rates were computed by each hour. These rates were treated as indicators to show risky times and situations.

We described these data and analyzed statistically to investigate correlations between situations and warning rates. Total number of injections per hour, total number of activities, total number of injection per PDA by hour and total number of activities per PDA by hour were used as indicators for workload at the time. Fraction of injections among total activities and fraction of treatments among total activities were used as indicators for variation of hours. We employed Pearson Correlation Analysis to investigate relationships and significant level was 5%.

3 Results

3.1 Description

Total number of activities data was 14,824,046 including 69,276 injections (0.4%), 535,571 IV starts (3.6%), 483,770 IV finishes (3.3%), 1,979,804 cares (13.3%), 10,437,250 observations (70.4%), 14,713 counseling (0.1%), 824,743 treatments (5.6%) and 478,919 emergency (3.2%). Total injections combining injections and IV drops were 604,847 and total warning on injections is 37,046 (6.1%). Figure 1 shows trend of injection warning rate at point of care. After a half year of implantation, the warning rates were relatively higher. The injection warning rate has been gradually decreasing.

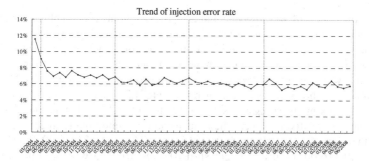

Fig. 1. Trend of Injection warning rate from March 2003 to June 2008

Figure 2 shows number of total entered data by nurse hour by hour. This data imply the workload at the time, though every activities were treated as same workload and actually the workloads are depend on the activities. Number of activities are higher on around 6AM and 10 AM.

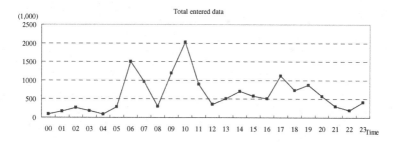

Fig. 2. Number of Total Entered Data by hour

Figure 3 shows number of running PDA by hour. In Japanese Red Cross Hospital, Patients to nurse ratio during day time twice as high as during night time. The data implys actual working people at the time.

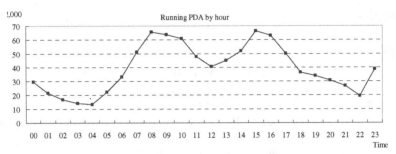

Fig. 3. Number of running PDA by hour

3.2 Data Analysis

Figure 4 shows trend of warning rate and activities by hour. Bar graph shows number of injection by hour. There was variability in number of injections by hour. There are three points that nurses administrate injections in volume. Those were 9AM, 3PM and 11PM. Two line graphs show injection warning rates and mixing warning rates by hour. Mixing warning means drugs for injection are not mixed correctly. Minimum and maximum of the injection warning rates were 4.2% and 10.5%. Minimum and maximum of mixing warning rates were 1.0% and 3.2%. This graph shows the warning rate was relatively lower when nurses administrated many injections. In this hospital, there are three working shifts for nurses. These are Day shift (8:00-16:40), Evening Shift (16:00-0:40) and Night shift (0:00-8:40). The warning rates for each shift were 5.5% (Day shift), 7.3% (Evening shift) and 6.0% (Night shift). The tendency of injection warnings and mixing warnings have somewhere same tendency. Especially during day shift, this tendency was demonstrated quite clearly.

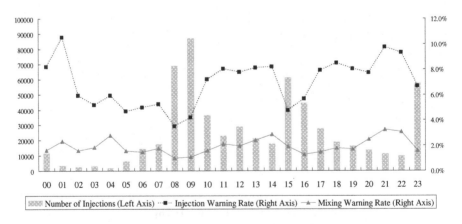

Fig. 4. Number of Injections and Warning rate by hour

According to the results of correlation analysis, there was a negative correlation between number of injections and injection warning rates. The correlation coefficients between number of injections and injection warning rates was -0.48 ($p<0.05$) and between number of injections per PDA and injection warning rates was -0.34 (p<0.05) (Figure. 5). Both results are significant and implied negative relationships between error rate and business.

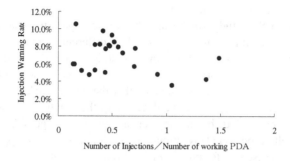

Fig. 5. Scatter plot on Number of Injections and Warning rate by hour

Variation of activities had negative effects to warning rate. Figure 6 is scatter plot to show relationship between fraction of injections among total activities and injection warning rates. We chose proportion of injections among total number of activates at the time as an indicator for variation activities. In our assumption, nurse concentrating on administering injections tend to operate more safely. This figure implies negative correlation between the two indicators. The correlation coefficient between fraction of treatments among total activities and injection warning rates was 0.35 (p<0.05). High fraction of treatment means nurses should administrate injections with other kinds of treatments for patients and discourage nurses against concentrating on injections.

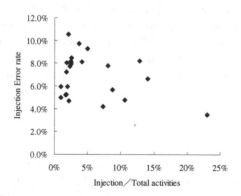

Fig. 6. Scatter plot on proportion of injections among total number of activities adn Injection error rate

4 Discussion

In the literatures on patient safety, many studies had mentioned workloads and busyness are the principal cause of medical errors [7.8]. It was acceptable for workers that rushing and fatigue would cause lack of attentions to medications. However, this study demonstrated opposite tendency of medical errors. This study implied that people would make mistakes because of not doing too many things but too many kinds of things. Literatures on human factor engineering indicated same kinds of conclusions to ensure quality of activities [9.10].

Warning rates in this study was relatively high compare to other literatures on administration errors of injections [1-3, 7, 8]. This difference came from accuracy of data and detections of mixing errors. In this study, data was collected through routinely work by hospital information system. People tend to be careful when they are observed by other. Therefore, we indicate that the data captured by PDA is more bias free data compared to conservative data. And other study also could not detect wrong bottle errors caused by mixing error, because forgetting mixing drugs sometimes difficult to be found by human eyes. Single item management of drugs with serialized ID is essential for preventing and finding mixing errors [5]. Distinction of bottles and other drugs with single item level is an only method to distinguish mixed and unmixed bottle systematically.

It is possible to accumulate the data by wards and nurses to realize risky place and working style. In this study, we tried to investigate relationship between number of injections and injection warning rate by each ward. This analysis doesn't show clear relationship between two indicators, because each ward provides health care service to different patients. When we focus on the difference of error rate by ward, we need to consider some risk adjustment method to compare fairly. This policy can be applied in comparing results among multi hospitals. Accumulating by nurses submitted new issues on privacy of workers. The system anonymized data of each nurse and their attribution, but researchers could sometimes identify nurse through patterns of work and other aspects. Researcher should be cautious to publish results.

Beside, the other issue is weighting of each activity. We treated injections and other activities as same workload activities, though actually there are quantitative and qualitative differences among activities. It is necessary to decide weighs of each activity to analyze more deeply and accurately with time study or other research methods.

5 Conclusion

This study showed general tendency of possible medical errors in practice with data captured in real time and accurately. The result suggested that high variation of activities might have negative effects for patient safety, though busyness is not one of the main causes of errors. Our study also demonstrated the effectiveness of bar code administration system. According to the result, injection warning rate was about 6% and these warning had been prevented nurses against errors and accidents with the system. In conclusion, bar code administration system is quite effective way not only to prevent medical error at point of care but also improve patient safety with analyses of data captured by them.

References

1. Keohane, C.A., Bane, A.D., Featherstone, E., Hayes, J., Woolf, S., Hurley, A., Bates, D.W., Gandhi, T.K., Poon, E.G.: Quantifying Nursing Workflow in Medication Administration. The Journal of Nursing Administration 38, 19–26 (2008)
2. Shane, R.: Current status of administration of medicines. Am. J. Health-Syst. Pharm. 65, 62–68 (2009)
3. Sakowski, J., Leonard, T., Colburn, S., Michaelsen, B., Schiro, T., Schneider, J., Newman, J.M.: Using a Bar-Coded Medication Administration System to Prevent Medication Errors. Am. J. Health-Syst. Pharm. 62, 2619–2625 (2005)
4. Akiyama, M.: Migration of Japanese Health care enterprise from a financial to integrated management: strategy and architecture. Stud. Health Technol. Inform. 10, 715–718 (2001)
5. Akiyama, M.: Risk Management and Measuring Productivity with POAS- Point of Act System. A medical information system as ERP (Enterprise Resource Planning) for Hospital Management. Methods Inf. Med. 46, 686–693 (2007)
6. Akiyama, M., Kondo, T.: Risk Management and Measuring Productivity with POAS - Point of Act System. Stud. Health Technol. Inform. 129, 208–212 (2007)
7. Fitzpatrick, J.J., Stone, P.W., Walker, P.H.: Annual Review of Nursing Research. Focus on Patient Safety 24
8. Tissot, E., Cornette, C., Demoly, P., Jaquet, M., Barale, F., Capalleier, G.: Medication errors at the administration stage in an intensive care unit. Intensive Care Med. 25, 353–359 (1999)
9. Dean, B.S., Allan, E.L., Barber, N.D., Barker, K.N.: Comparison of medication errors in an American and a British hospital. Am. J. Health Syst. Pharm. 52, 2543–2549 (1995)
10. Larrabee, S., Brown, M.: Recognizing the institutional benefits of barcode point-of-care technology. Joint Comm. J. Qual. Saf. 29, 345–353, 295–301 (2003)
11. Bates, D.W., Pappius, E., Kuperman, G.J., Sittig, D., Burstin, H., Fairchild, D., Brennan, T.A., Teich, J.M.: Using information systems to measure and improve quality. International Journal of Medical Informatics 53, 115–124 (1999)

Blended Clustering for Health Data Mining

Arshad Muhammad Mehar, Anthony Maeder, Kenan Matawie, and Athula Ginige

School of Computing & Mathematics, University of Western Sydney,
Locked Bag 1797 Penrith South DC, NSW 1797 Australia
{a.muhammad,a.maeder,k.matawie,a.ginige}@uws.edu.au

Abstract. Exploratory data analysis using data mining techniques is becoming more popular for investigating subtle relationships in health data, for which direct data collection trials would not be possible. Health data mining involving clustering for large complex data sets in such cases is often limited by insufficient key indicative variables. When a conventional clustering technique is then applied, the results may be too imprecise, or may be inappropriately clustered according to expectations. This paper suggests an approach which can offer greater range of choice for generating potential clusters of interest, from which a better outcome might in turn be obtained by aggregating the results. An example use case based on health services utilization characterization according to socio-demographic background is discussed and the blended clustering approach being taken for it is described.

Keywords: data mining, data clustering, health data, health services utilization.

1 Introduction

Exploratory data analysis using data mining techniques is becoming more popular for investigating subtle relationships in health data, for which direct data collection trials would not be possible. Some examples of such problems include data collected for operational health service purposes (such as hospital admissions, or GP consultations, over a lengthy period of time), and population health data (such as longitudinal surveys of health status, or disease management and outcomes records).

Health data mining involving clustering for large complex data sets in these cases is often limited by insufficient richness in key decision variables. For example, in seeking to establish whether there is a difference in preventative health program outcomes for patients with different dietary habits, in the absence of explicit nutritional data, typically surrogate variables such as socio-economic status or even geographical location will be used as the indicative quantities.

A major deficiency with this approach is that the surrogate variables may be poorly or unstably correlated with the health outcomes under study. Consequently when a conventional clustering method is applied, the results may be too imprecise, or may be inappropriately clustered according to reasonable expectations. In the above example, if a standard method such as k-means clustering was applied to distinguish 3 groups (of poor, intermediate and good outcomes), it is possible that each of the clusters would include data points from across the whole range of surrogate variable values.

H. Takeda (Ed.): E-Health 2010, IFIP AICT 335, pp. 130–137, 2010.

This paper suggests an approach which can offer greater range of choice for generating potential clusters of interest, from which a better data analysis outcomes might in turn be obtained by aggregating the results. By systematically applying a given clustering technique repeatedly, with different control parameters, a related succession of different clusters can be obtained, and the structure of these can be combined to yield regions in the data space for which greater strength of cluster membership may be inferred.

2 Health Services Utilization Studies for Large Data Sets

Health data research makes use of many different statistical and data mining techniques, to improve and maintain our health system and processes. As storage density increases and cost decreases exponentially, more and more transactional data is being collected in health. For example there are 5.7 million hospital admissions, over 200 million visits to doctors, and a similar number of prescribed medicines dispensed, that are captured electronically annually in Australia [1]. Analysis of this type of data offers benefits in many different areas such as health administration, adverse events, drug safety, disease diagnosis, population health and epidemiology. Often such analyses focus on well established performance indicators or quality metrics, such as length of stay or mortality. However, considerably more subtle structure is present in the data but is not easily extracted by simple clustering approaches. Some examples of attempts to find such structure in our area of interest of health services utilization characterization (specifically for hospital services) according to socio-demographic background are described below.

A study by [2] to investigate and compare hospital utilization in Victoria among Australian born and 8 different refugee source countries, showed that people born in refuge countries have lower or similar rates of hospitalization compared with Australian born. A random sample of 100,000 admissions of Australian born patients between 1998 and 2004 was compared with the total number (49,835) of admissions from non-Australian born patients from the source countries. Similar research in 1997 by [3] to determine the effect of hospital utilization between Danish born patients and non-Danish born immigrant patients showed that for certain types of cases Danish born patients consistently stay longer in hospitals than immigrants, and vice versa for other types of cases. This study included 5,310 persons discharged as inpatients, outpatients or emergency room patients who were born outside the Nordic countries, compared with a random sample of 10,000 patients born in Denmark. Another study on emergency hospital services (EHS) utilization in Spain by [4] was carried out to examine differences between immigrant and Spanish born people. This data set included patients between 15 and 64 years old for 96,916 hospital visits during the years 2004 to 2005. The results showed that people born outside Spain use EHS differently and more frequently than native born people in Spain. In Portugal an investigation of hospital utilization [5] collected data for 1,513 migrants. This work showed that age, length of stay, legal status and economic situation were interrelated in health services usage.

Narrower studies than the above have also been conducted, where specific types of disorder are of interest. An Australian study by [6] examined people with mental health problems who frequently attend the emergency department (ED) in tertiary referral metropolitan hospitals. The data was collected for 12 consecutive months between 2002 to 2003 year for 45,671 patients, from which 869 psychiatric patients and 1,076 presentations of these patients were identified. Significant differences were found for different age and diagnosis categories, for example younger people appeared more prominently in the frequent presenters group and also contained more anxiety/mood diagnosis than other groups. Another study in Spain was undertaken by [7] for 11,578 tertiary hospital admissions to psychiatric emergency services. Data collected included socio-demographic and clinical information that could be used to identify the difference between homeless and non-homeless patients and their admission patterns.

3 Data Mining Techniques for Health Data

To investigate patterns within large volumes of complex health data, some well established statistical methodologies are usually applied, based on hypothesis testing. In the past these efforts were limited primarily to epidemiological studies on clinical administrative and claims databases, due to lack of richness of other information [8]. Analogous problems to determine subtle patterns in patient cohort medical data have recently gained more attention. These problems have been addressed by applying techniques from machine learning and pattern recognition fields collectively, referred to as data mining [9].

The use of the term data mining originated from statistical computer science and is typically used in the context of large datasets [10]. It is a new generation approach to data analysis and knowledge discovery which has grown rapidly out of the need to derive useful knowledge from massive amounts of high dimensional data. Data mining is seen as exploratory rather than confirmatory in its approach [11]: a process of analyzing data from different perspectives and summarizing it into useful information (and hence also known as knowledge discovery [12]). Technically, it is the process of finding correlations or patterns among multiple data fields in large databases, using methods for searching through the data for patterns. Data mining leading to the extraction of hidden predictive information from large databases can help companies and organizations to focus on extracting important information to optimise their operations.

Data mining techniques are categorized into two different approaches: directed (or supervised) and undirected (or unsupervised). Supervised data mining is used mostly for hypothesis testing or verification, while unsupervised data mining is used mostly for new knowledge discovery [13]. Classification, estimation, and prediction are example of supervised data mining. Association rules, clustering and feature extraction are examples of unsupervised data mining. In this work we will take a simplified approach to demonstrate the principle we wish to describe, and so will concentrate on the use of clustering methods in unsupervised data mining.

Cluster analysis is the process of grouping a set of physical or abstract objects into classes according to some measure of similarity of the objects. It results in grouping of data objects that are similar to one another within the same cluster and are dissimilar to the objects in other clusters [14]. For example, in medicine, clustering of symptoms of diseases can lead to very useful taxonomies for diagnosis. In psychiatry studies to find better therapies, correct diagnosis depends on clusters of symptoms to distinguish closely related disorders such as paranoia, schizophrenia, etc. Some commonly used clustering techniques which have been applied to health data mining are discussed below.

K-means clustering is a technique that separates a given set of data into k number of clusters (represented by centroids) in such a way that objects within a cluster are closer to their centroid than to the centroids of any other clusters [15]. Given n number of objects we choose arbitrarily k initial centroids where k is the number of desired clusters specified by the user. Each point is assigned to the closest centroid and each collection of points assigned to a centroid is a cluster. For each cluster the centroid position is updated based on the points assigned to the cluster, and this assigning and updating process is repeated until convergence or termination.

Hierarchical clustering techniques produce a structure of multi-scale hierarchical clusters, from small to large [16]. Agglomerative and divisive clustering are two different types of hierarchical clustering algorithms [17]. Agglomerative hierarchical clustering is constructed in a bottom up fashion in such a way that each data point is initially assigned to its own cluster, and these initial clusters are then successively combined according to their proximity. Divisive clustering takes a top-down approach, beginning with all of the objects in the same cluster. In each successive iteration, a cluster is split up into smaller clusters, until each object is in only one cluster, or until some termination condition holds.

Density based clustering techniques discern clusters of arbitrary shape in the database using models for data density and noise [18]. This approach determines height density regions for objects in data space, separated by a region of low density. The algorithm for density based clustering defines core points, border points and noise points. It has two input parameters MinPts and Eps, where MinPts is the minimum number of data points in any cluster and Eps is the threshold or maximum radius of cluster. Any two core points which are close enough to each other are assigned to the same cluster. Similarly, any border point which is close enough to a core point is assigned to the same cluster, while any noise points are eliminated [19].

4   Blended Clustering Approach

Data clustering techniques typically used in health data mining as identified above are generally based on fixed parameter choices, as there tend to be certain intuitive expectations about the number or nature of the clusters sought. For example, the number of clusters may be predetermined, or the variables used for the clustering may be selected from the overall set of variables in a data element. The nett effect of fixed parameter choices is that clustering results are usually obtained without any indication (or consideration) of sensitivity to the range of possible parameter choices. This means that the clusters obtained may be accepted as strongly formed, whereas in fact they may be arbitrarily dependent on the parameter choices. It also provides a result which defines cluster membership (or boundaries) in absolute terms, whereas considerable variations in the strength of membership may exist for elements which are quite close in the data space, or by the distance metric. These matters are exacerbated when the data sets are highly complex with subtle interdependencies, or when they have few variables that provide strongly correlated relationships with the nature of the clusters that are sought.

Our approach to overcoming these limitations is based on multiple applications of the clustering technique, and then combining the results of these applications to gain insights on the issues above. This approach requires different aspects of variation to be addressed, and in this paper we will consider only one such aspect, viz. the construction of *different numbers of clusters*. At least adjacent consecutive numbers, or a range around a value regarded as reasonable number (i.e. at least marginally more and less than the intuitively expected number of clusters).

Formally, we may describe our approach as follows. For a given choice of k = number of clusters, a given choice of clustering technique U, and a given choice of V = set of parameters $v_1..v_n$ used to control the clustering technique, we first construct a set of clusters $C_k(U,V) = \{c_{k,i}\}$ with i=1..k. Next, we construct sets of clusters $C_{k-1}(U,V)$, and $C_{k+1}(U,V)$ using the same clustering technique. In the work reported here, we will not vary U and V so we may write these cluster sets more simply as C_{k-1}, C_k and C_{k+1}.

In general, if k is somewhat less than the overall number of items being clustered, many items will be common between pairs of clusters across these three sets. If the items in common are fairly uniformly spread across all the clusters (i.e. changing the number of clusters has the effect of slightly increasing or decreasing membership of any given cluster, implying that clusters are of comparable strength) we have what we will term a "stable" clustering. On the other hand, if we find that items in common are non-uniformly spread across a few clusters (i.e. some clusters split fairly evenly into two or more clusters while other clusters are only slightly changed, implying that some clusters are of much greater strength than others), we will term this an "unstable" clustering.

Clustering is sensitive to choice of the related number of clusters and issues such as labeling, for the given data set. Due to this sensitivity, evaluation of the optimality of clustering is a common challenge. Stability is an indication of whether the algorithm fits the data points into the clusters strongly or not. Many validation measures such as Purity, Normalized Mutual Information, Rand index and F measure etc. are applied by [20] to evaluate the stability of clusters. A theoretical analysis on evaluation and stability was carried out by [21],[22] without any application to real datasets. Another study by [23] for evaluation of stability for k-means cluster ensembles with respect to random initialization, by using pairwise and nonpairwise methods. This study used only small and artificial data sets.

We can compute stability properties for the clusterings as follows. First we compare each of the k clusters in C_k with all of the k-1 clusters in C_{k-1}, and compare each of the k clusters in C_k with all of the k+1 clusters in C_{k+1}, to assess the proportion of data elements which are in common in each case. We denote the proportion of data elements in common between a particular pair of clusters, say cluster $c_{k,i}$ from C_k and cluster $c_{k-1,j}$ from C_{k-1} by $p(c_{k,i}, c_{k-1,j})$, which can be abbreviated to $p_{k,k-1,i,j}$. The set of maximum values of $p_{k,k-1,i,j}$ for each cluster $c_{k,i}$ in C_k compared with all the clusters in C_{k-1} is denoted by $P_{k,k-1}$. Similarly, we can compute $P_{k,k+1}$. Note that in general $P_{k,k-1}$ is not equal to $P_{k-1,k}$ as they have different cardinality. If each element of $P_{k,k-1}$ is above a given threshold T (i.e. for every cluster of C_k there is at least one cluster in C_{k-1} which has >T fraction of elements in common), we denote the clusterings as T-1 stable for k; similarly we define T_{+1} stability for k. If the clusterings are both T_{-1} and T_{+1} stable as above, we call them T_1 stable for k.

T_1-stability indicates that the k-1, k or k+1 clusterings may all be considered to be valid options for interpreting the data, subject to the commonality constraint of threshold T. In this case we may wish to proceed with further analysis by tightening the value of T, or by constructing sets C_{k-2} and C_{k+2} to assess their T_2 stability. If either T_{-1} or T_{+1} stability holds but not the other, C_k must represent a point at which some degree of change or discontinuity occurs for structural properties in the data set. If neither T_{-1} nor T_{+1} stability holds, we may wish to consider whether another value for T may be more appropriate.

5 Sample Experimental Results

Consider the example of investigating different patterns of hospital service utilization for a highly heterogeneous population which has a wide mix of age, ethnicity and socio-economic status factors. In a typical hospital admissions dataset, very few variables directly indicative of these factors are available, and therefore surrogates such as country of birth or home language must be used. The occurrence and number of distinct classes for different utilization patterns is unknown a priori. The above stability analysis approach thus offers one way to evaluate plausible options for both number and membership of classes, and choices of variable values to achieve these.

To explore this approach, we constructed a sample data set of 20 elements with properties similar to population characteristics for residents of Greater Western Sydney (see Table 1). This data set contains a range of patient profiles from 4 different ethnic origins, aged from 20 to 70 years old, and with disease severities coded on a 10 point scale.

We made a single, randomly seeded application of k-means clustering, based on joint age and severity variables with k=2, 3, 4. The results of this clustering (see Table 2) were used to determine that at the level T=0.5, $C_{3,1}$ and $C_{3,3}$ are T_1-stable. By inspection, it was found that $C_{3,1}$ comprised membership of 50% from country A, while $C_{3,3}$ comprised membership of 50% from country B. This allowed us to nominate k=3 as a closer match with the data than either k=2 or k=4, and furthermore to infer that subjects of ethnic origin from countries A and B were more self-similar in the relationship between their age and disease severity characteristics, than those of countries C and D.

Table 1. Sample data set of 20 patients from 4 countries, varied by severity and age

Patient#	1	2	3	4	5	6	7	8	9	10
Country	A	A	A	A	A	B	B	B	B	B
Severity	9	5	4	9	7	5	8	4	7	8
Age	55	45	65	25	50	20	25	35	45	50

Patient#	11	12	13	14	15	16	17	18	19	20
Country	B	C	C	C	C	D	D	A	D	D
Severity	9	7	6	4	3	5	4	7	3	7
Age	55	65	55	70	25	20	60	20	65	20

Table 2. Results of k=2, 3, 4 k-means clusterings for the data of Table 1

Cluster	C2,1	C2,2	C3,1	C3,2	C3,3	C4,1	C4,2	C4,3	C4,4
Members	1	4	1	3	4	1	2	3	4
	2	8	2	12	6	5	7	8	9
	3	9	5	14	7	6	13	14	10
	5	10	9	17	8	12	17	19	11
	6	11	10	19	15	16			15
	7	15	11	20	16				18
	12	17	13		18				20
	13	18							
	14	19							
	16	20							

The above approach does not take into account some other aspects of data clustering techniques which might also affect the results, such as choice of different clustering algorithms, choice of different cluster membership (or distance) functions, choice of different control parameters to control the clustering algorithm, or choice of different subsets of variables describing items in the data set to influence the nature of the clusters. While these aspects may in principle be treated in a similar manner, they are substantially more complex in the nature of the choice, and likely to have far stronger effect than the number of clusters choice. Blending involving these aspects is intrinsically more expensive and is likely to require more careful control than the stability-based strategy described above. Consequently they have not been considered further here.

6 Conclusion

The work described here offers a first step towards what may be seen as a blended form of an "adaptive" or "learning" approach to clustering, which identifies patterns emerging from repeated application of "perturbed" configurations of the chosen data mining method based on the simplest control aspect of clustering, viz. the number of clusters. In some sense this approach is closer in philosophy to a genetic algorithm technique than a rule-based technique, as preconditions for the allowable configurations are much looser than would be determined by a hypothesis driven conception. In order to gain greater efficiency, it would be desirable to limit the range over which perturbed configurations can occur. It would also be beneficial to develop more structure in the approach to inform the choice of perturbations, and the ways of combining them to reach the improved conclusions about the data.

References

1. McAullay, D., et al.: A delivery framework for health data mining and analytics. Australian Computer Society Inc., Darlinghurst (2005)
2. Correa-Velez, I., et al.: Hospital utilisation among people born in refugee-source countries: An analysis of hospital admissions, Victoria, 1998-2004. Medical Journal of Australia 186(11), 577 (2007)

3. Krasnik, A., et al.: Effect of ethnic background on Danish hospital utilisation patterns. Social Science & Medicine 55(7), 1207–1211 (2002)
4. RuÃc, M., et al.: Emergency hospital services utilization in Lleida (Spain): A cross-sectional study of immigrant and Spanish-born populations. BMC Health Services Research 8(1), 81–90 (2008)
5. Dias, S.n.F., Severo, M., Barros, H.: Determinants of health care utilization by immigrants in Portugal. BMC Health Services Research 8, 1–8 (2008)
6. Brunero, S., et al.: Clinical characteristics of people with mental health problems who frequently attend an Australian emergency department. Australian Health Review 31, 462–470 (2007)
7. Pascual, J.C., et al.: Utilization of psychiatric emergency services by homeless persons in Spain. General Hospital Psychiatry 30(1), 14–19 (2007)
8. Prather, J., et al.: Medical data mining: knowledge discovery in a clinical data warehouse. American Medical Informatics Association (1997)
9. Harrison Jr., J.H.: Introduction to the mining of clinical data. Clinics in Laboratory Medicine 28(1), 1–7 (2008)
10. Dominique, H., et al.: A review of software packages for data mining. The American Statistician 57(4), 290 (2003)
11. Tukey, J.: Exploratory data analysis. Addison-Wesley, Reading (1977)
12. Fayyad, U.M.: Advances in knowledge discovery and data mining. AAAI Press/MIT Press (1996)
13. Berger, A.M.M.M.R., Berger, C.R.M.M.: Data Mining as a Tool for Research and Knowledge Development in Nursing. CIN: Computers, Informatics, Nursing 22(3), 123–131 (2004)
14. Han, J., Kamber, M.: Data mining: concepts and techniques. Morgan Kaufmann series in data management systems. Morgan Kaufmann, San Francisco (2006)
15. Mwasiagi, J., Wang, X., Huang, X.: The use of k-means and artificial neural network to classify cotton lint. Fibers and Polymers 10(3), 379–383 (2009)
16. Hair, J.F.: Multivariate data analysis. Prentice Hall, Upper Saddle River (1998)
17. Crowley, J., Ankerst, D.: Handbook of statistics in clinical oncology. CRC Press, Boca Raton (2006)
18. Berry, M.W., Brown, M.: Lecture notes in data mining. World Scientific, Hackensack (2006)
19. Tan, P.-N., Kumar, V., Steinbach, M.: Introduction to data mining. Pearson Addison Wesley, Boston (2005)
20. Wu, J., Xiong, H., Chen, J.: Adapting the right measures for k-means clustering. In: Proceedings of the 15th ACM SIGKDD international conference on Knowledge discovery and data mining, pp. 877–886. ACM, Paris (2009)
21. Ben-David, S., et al.: Stability of k-means clustering. In: Bshouty, N.H., Gentile, C. (eds.) COLT. LNCS (LNAI), vol. 4539, pp. 20–34. Springer, Heidelberg (2007)
22. Rakhlin, A., Caponnetto, A.: Stability of k-means clustering. Advances in Neural Information Processing Systems 19, 1121–1127 (2007)
23. Kuncheva, L.I., Vetrov, D.P.: Evaluation of Stability of k-means Cluster Ensembles with Respect to Random Initialization. IEEE Transactions on Pattern Analysis and Machine Intelligence 28(11), 1798–1808 (2006)

Flexible Genome Retrieval for Supporting In-Silico Studies of Endobacteria-AMFs

S. Montani[1], G. Leonardi[1], S. Ghignone[2], and L. Lanfranco[2]

[1] Dipartimento di Informatica, University of Piemonte Orientale, Alessandria, Italy
[2] Dipartimento di Biologia Vegetale, University of Turin, Italy

Abstract. Studying the interactions between arbuscular mycorrhizal fungi (AMFs) and their symbiotic endobacteria has potentially strong impacts on the development of new biotechnology applications. The analysis of genomic data and syntenies is a key technique for acquiring information about phylogenetic relationships and metabolic functions of such organisms.

In this paper, we describe a modular architecture meant to support in-silico genome sequence analysis, which is being developed within the project BIOBITS. In particular, we focus on a flexible genome retrieval tool, which supports optimized and customized comparative genomics searches.

1 Introduction

Arbuscular mycorrhizal fungi (AMFs) are obligate symbionts which, to complete their life cycle, must enter in association with the root of land plants. Here, they become a crucial component of soil microbial communities, and exert positive impacts on plants health and productivity: in particular, they furnish a better mineral nutrition, and act as crucial means for increasing tolerance to stress conditions [13,19].

AMFs are thus a significant resource for sustainable agriculture; in addition, they could also be exploited as a still unknown resource to promote green (agriculture) and white (industrial) biotechnologies. For instance, plants release molecules (strigolactones) which are perceived by AMFs, and cause the extensive branching essential for a successful colonization. Similar molecules have a large relevance in chemistry, since they induce seed germination from parasite plants, like Striga, which infest the two-thirds of crop lands in Africa.

AMFs are often in further symbiosys with uncultivable bacteria, living inside the AMF itself [4]. The resulting tripartite system (i.e. (i) endobacterium; (ii) AMF; (iii) plant roots) is a complex biological object, whose extensive study requires a comparative genomics approach, in order to answer fundamental questions concerning the biology, ecology and evolutionary history of the system and of its composing elements. As a matter of fact, comparative genomics represent a key instrument to discover or validate phylogenetic relationships, to give insights on genome evolution, and to infer metabolic functions of a given organism, which is particularly useful when biochemical and physiological data are not available and/or hard to obtain.

H. Takeda (Ed.): E-Health 2010, IFIP AICT 335, pp. 138–147, 2010.
© IFIP International Federation for Information Processing 2010

Studying the tripartite system has potentially strong practical impacts, given the assumption that the symbiotic consortia may lead to new metabolic pathways, and to the appearance of molecules which might be of interest for biotechnological applications.

While bacterial endosymbionts in the animal kingdom are excellent models for investigating important biological events, such as organelle evolution, genome reduction, and transfer of genetic information among host lineages [17], examples of endobacteria living in fungi are limited [12]. A key part of the study about the tripartite system mentioned above is therefore represented by the analysis of the genomic data of the endobacteria themselves. In particular, large-scale analysis and comparison of genomes belonging to phylogenetically related free-living bacteria can provide information about the events that led to genome down-sizing, and insights about the reason of the strict endosymbiotic life style of the bacteria themselves.

In this paper, we present the design of a computational environment for the genomic study of the AMF Gigaspora margarita (isolate BEG34) and of its endobacterium *Candidatus Glomeribacter gigasporarum*, which are currently used as a model system to investigate endobacteria-AMFs interactions. In particular, we are developing a modular architecture, composed by a database, in which massive genomic data are imported and stored, and of genomic comparison (synteny) and visualization tools.

To achieve such an aim we plan to exploit as much as possible the available tools built around GMOD, the Generic Model Organism Database project [18], which brought to the development of a whole, and still under expansion, collection of open source software tools for creating and managing genome-scale biological databases. In particular, we are choosing to resort to the GMOD database Chado [9], and to some freely available and freely adaptable GMOD facilities to search for syntenies like CMap, GBrowse_syn, SyBil.

However, we are extending the functionalities offered by GMOD, in order to properly meet the needs of our specific comparative genomics research. In particular, we are working at a *flexible* similar genomes retrieval tool, implementing the *retrieval* step of Case-Based Reasoning (CBR) [1], an Artificial Intelligence methodology which supports human reasoning by recalling past experiences similar to the current one. Our tool allows to search in the genomes database by expressing queries at *different levels of detail*, also in an interactive fashion. Moreover, it takes advantage of *multi-dimensional orthogonal index structures*, which make retrieval faster, allowing for early pruning and focusing.

The work, which is still in its early implementation phase, is supported by the BIOBITS project, a grant of Regione Piemonte, under the Converging Technologies Call, which involves the University of Turin, the University of Piemonte Orientale, the CNR and the companies ISAGRO Ricerca s.r.l., GEOL Sas, Etica s.r.l.

The paper is organized as follows: section 2 provides a deeper description of the biological problem under examination; section 3 sketches the general architecture we are implementing for genome analysis in the project; section 4 focuses on our flexible retrieval tool, and section 5 is devoted to conclusions.

2 Description of the Biological Domain

AMF species, belonging to the family Gigasporaceae, represent a specialized niche for rod shaped bacteria, which due to their current unculturable status have been grouped into a new taxon named *Candidatus Glomeribacter gigasporarum* [8]. The AM fungus Gigaspora margarita (isolate BEG34) and its endobacterium *Ca. Glomeribacter gigasporarum* are currently used as a model system to investigate endobacteria-AM fungi interactions. Microscopical observations have shown that the endobacteria are Gram-negative, rod-shaped, approx. 0.8-1.2 µm by 1.5-2.0 µm; they occur singly or in groups and are often inside fungal vacuoles. The analysis of the 16S ribosomal RNA sequence demonstrated that these bacteria are phylogenetically related to the beta-proteobacterial family, clustering with the Burkholderia, Pandorea and Ralstonia genera [6, 12]. Morphological and molecular studies have shown that *Ca. G. gigasporarum* is a homogeneous population, which is vertically transmitted through the fungal generations [7]. The main limitation to studying *Ca. Glomeribacter gigasporarum* is that it has not been isolated in pure culture even after testing several growth conditions [10]; therefore, this bacterium is considered an obligate endocellular component of its fungal host. A sufficient amount of endobacterial DNA was obtained from fungal spores and used to estimate a genome size of about 1.3 Mb, depending on the method used, consisting of a chromosome and a plasmid [10]. This small genome size is consistent with a strict endosymbiotic nature. Indeed small chromosomes have only been encountered in other well known obligate endocellular species [21, 4, 23, 16]. Because *Ca. G. gigasporarum* does not grow in pure culture, traditional genetic or physiological studies can not be applied. Therefore, the analysis of the genome sequence may offer a valuable tool to infer its metabolic functions; at the moment the bacterial genome is being sequenced by two complementary strategies, classical Sanger sequencing of fosmid clones combined to high-throughput pyrosequencing using the 454 platform (Roche).

3 System Architecture

In our project, genome sequence analysis is supported by a modular architecture, which permits:

(1) to store and access locally all the information regarding the organisms to be studied, and
(2) to provide algorithms and user interfaces to support the researchers' activities (e.g.: search and retrieval of genomes, comparison and alignment with a reference genome, investigation of syntenies and local storage of potential new annotations).

The system architecture has been engineered exploiting the standard modules and interfaces offered by the GMOD project [18], and completed with custom modules to provide new functionalities (see Figure 1).

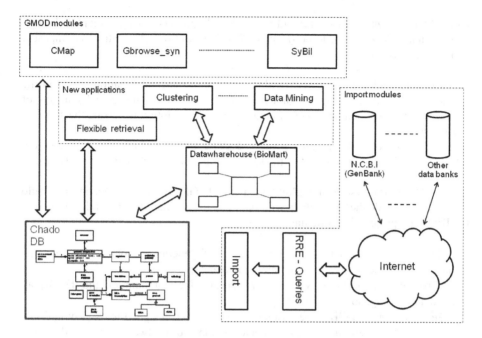

Fig. 1. The system architecture

The main module of the system contains the database which provides all the data needed to perform the in-silico activities. We adopted the Chado database schema [9], to take advantage of its completeness and of its support for controlled vocabularies and ontologies. Furthermore, Chado is the standard database for most of the GMOD modules, therefore we can reuse these modules to support the main activities of the project, and extend the system incrementally as the researchers' needs evolve. The database in this module stores and provides all the information about the organisms to be studied (i.e. bacteria), their genomes, their known annotations, their proteins and metabolic pathways, and the newly discovered annotations, which can be stored and managed locally until they are confirmed and published.

As explained, our database contains information to be used and stored locally, but we have added the possibility to populate and update the database with information retrieved from the biological databases accessible through the Internet. This feature is provided by the set of modules in the *Import modules* section (see Figure 1). The main module (*RRE - Queries*), which is built on the basis of a previously published tool [11], performs queries to different biological databases through the Internet (e.g. the GenBank [26]) and converts the results into a standard format. Afterwards, the *Import* module inserts or updates the retrieved information into the Chado database. This process can be started on-demand, or performed automatically on a regular basis, in order to maintain the local database up-to-date.

Chado also acts as the data interface for the software layers implementing the functionalities and tools used by the researchers. From the architectural point of view, we offer two types of services: the services implemented through existing modules of

GMOD (*GMOD modules* section in Figure 1), and new services implemented through new modules, developed ad-hoc (*New applications* section). The latter is composed, at the time of writing, of:

- a module called *BioMart* [25], which reorganizes the information stored in the Chado database into a data warehouse, in order to analyze the data by means of clustering and other data mining techniques (whose description is outside the scope of this paper) and
- a *flexible retrieval* module, described in section 4, which supports efficient retrieval strategies in the context of the search for genomic similarity and syntenies.

The *GMOD modules* section exploits the available GMOD modules using the Chado database to provide the researchers with the tools for comparative genomics needed in the BIOBITS project. In particular:

- CMap allows users to view comparisons of genetic and physical maps. The package also includes tools for maintaining map data;
- GBrowse is a genome viewer, and also permits the manipulation and the display of annotations on genomes;
- GBrowse_syn is a GBrowse-based synteny browser designed to display multiple genomes, with a central reference species compared to two or more additional species;
- SyBil is a system for comparative genomics visualizations.

All the tools in this system use a web-based interface to be more user-friendly and easy to use. Many GMOD modules can be reused as they are, but they can be customized to meet the researchers' recommendations before being integrated in our software architecture. Furthermore, every new module added in the *New applications* section of our architecture, or every customized module in the *GMOD modules* section, connects to the other modules of our architecture using GMOD standard interfaces. Therefore, every new or customized module can be published to the GMOD community, in order to extend and enrich this platform.

4   Flexible Retrieval of Similar Genomes

The *flexible retrieval* module we have designed in the project architecture implements the *retrieval* step of the Case-Based Reasoning (CBR) [1] cycle. CBR is a reasoning paradigm that exploits the knowledge collected on previously experienced situations, known as *cases*. The CBR cycle operates by:

(1) *retrieving* past cases that are similar to the current one and by
(2) *reusing* past successful solutions after, if necessary, properly
(3) *adapting* them; the current case can then be
(4) *retained* and put into the system knowledge base, called the *case base*.

Purely retrieval systems, leaving to the user the completion of the reasoning cycle (steps 2 to 4), are however very valuable decision support tools [24], especially when automated adaptation strategies can hardly be identified, as in biology and medicine [14]; in the project, we are following this research line.

In our module, cases are genomes as sequences of nucleotides, each one taken from a different organism, and properly aligned with the same reference organism. For each nucleotide, a percentage of similarity with the aligned nucleotide in the reference organism is also provided.

However, depending on the type of analysis which is required, a "view" of the genomes at the nucleotide level may not always be the most appropriate: sometimes, a "higher level" view, abstracting the available data at the level of genes, regions, or even complete chromosomes, would be more helpful. Our tool supports this need, by allowing the retrieval of the available cases at any level of detail, according to a taxonomy of granularities, which is depicted in figure 2.

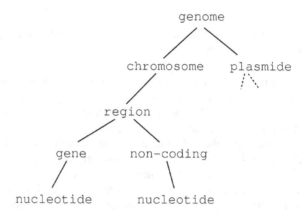

Fig. 2. A taxonomy of sequence granularities

Moreover, a sequence of consecutive granules, sharing the same *qualitative level* (e.g. low, medium, high) of similarity with respect to the reference organism, can be abstracted into a single interval, labeled with the qualitative level of similarity itself: such an abstraction process is very similar to the Temporal Abstractions (TA) methodology, described in [20,5], even if in our domain the independent variable is the granules sequence instead of time. As in TA, in fact, we move from a *point-based* to an *interval-based* representation of the data, where the input points are the granules, and the output intervals (*episodes*) aggregate adjacent points sharing a common behavior, persistent over the sequence. In particular, we rely on *state* abstractions [5], to extract episodes associated with qualitative levels of similarity with the reference organism, where the mapping between qualitative abstractions and quantitative values (percentages) of similarity can be parameterized on the basis of domain knowledge.

Space occupancy in the database can be optimized by storing the abstracted data instead of the original ones. Moreover, on abstracted data, case retrieval can benefit from the use of pattern matching techniques (see e.g. [22]).

Also in the state abstractions dimensions, we allow the user to express her queries at different levels of detail, depending on her current analysis interests, according to a state abstractions taxonomy like the one described in figure 3 - which can be properly modified depending on specific domain needs.

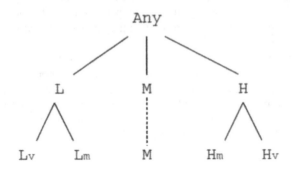

Fig. 3. An example taxonomy of state abstraction symbols; for instance, the high (H) symbol specializes into very high (Hv) and moderately high (Hm)

In synthesis, our retrieval framework allows for *multi-level abstractions*, according to two *dimensions*, namely a taxonomy of state abstraction symbols, and a variety of sequence granularities. In particular, we allow for *flexible querying*, where queries can be expressed at any level of detail in both dimensions.

Moreover, our framework takes advantage of *multi-dimensional orthogonal index structures*, which make retrieval faster, allowing for early pruning and focusing. The root node of each index structure is represented by a (string of) symbol(s), defined at the highest level in the state abstraction taxonomy (i.e. the children of *Any*, see figure 3) and in the sequence granularity taxonomy. A (possibly incomplete) index stems from each root, describing possible refinements along the symbol and/or the sequence granularity dimension. An example multi-dimensional index, rooted in the H symbol, is represented in figure 4.

Each node in each index structure is itself an index, and can be defined as a *generalized case*, in the sense that it summarizes (i.e. it indexes) a set of cases. This means that the same case is typically indexed by different nodes in one index (and in the other available indexes). This supports flexible querying, since, depending on the level at which the query is issued, according to the two taxonomies, one of the nodes can be more suited for providing a quick answer.

To answer a query, in order to enter the more proper index structure, we first progressively generalize the query itself in the state abstractions taxonomy direction, while keeping sequence granularity fixed. Then, we generalize the query in the granularity dimension as well. Following the generalization steps backwards, we can enter the index from its root, and descend along it, until we reach the node which fits the original query sequence granularity. If an orthogonal index stems from this node, we can descend along it, always following the query generalization steps backwards. We stop when we reach the same detail level in the state abstraction taxonomy as in the original query. If the query detail level is not represented in the index, because the index is not complete, we stop at the most detailed possible level. We then return all the cases indexed by the selected node.

Interactive and *progressive* query relaxation or refinement are supported as well in our framework, in a conversational fashion [2]. Query relaxation (as well as refinement) can be repeated several times, until the user is satisfied with the width of the retrieval set.

The interested reader may find additional technical details in [15]. Very encouraging experimental results have already been obtained by resorting to the same flexible retrieval framework, in the field of haemodialysis [15].

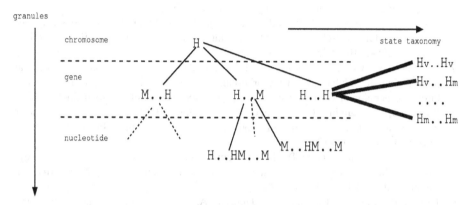

Fig. 4. An example multi-dimensional orthogonal index. Note that indexes may be incomplete with respect to the taxonomies: here, for instance, the region level is missing in the granularity dimension.

5 Conclusions

In this paper, we have described a modular architecture for supporting in-silico comparative genomics analysis, being developed within the BIOBITS project. In particular, we have focused on the main features of a genome retrieval tool, which implements the first step of the CBR cycle. Such a tool provides researchers with flexible retrieval capabilities, also in an interactive fashion. Moreover, retrieval performances are optimized by resorting to multi-dimensional orthogonal index structures, allowing for a quick query answering. In the next months, we will complete the tool implementation, and work at the collection of the first evaluation results, initializing the tool case base with a selection of genomes (in particular, from symbiotic microorganisms) available in the RefSeq NCBI database.

References

1. Aamodt, A., Plaza, E.: Case-based reasoning: foundational issues, methodological variations and systems approaches. AI Communications 7, 39–59 (1994)
2. Aha, D., Munoz-Avila, H.: Introduction: interactive case-based reasoning. Applied Intelligence 14, 78 (2001)

3. Akman, L., Rio, R.V.M., Beard, C.B., Aksoy, S.: Genome size determination and coding capacity of sodalis glossinidius, an enteric symbiont of tsetse flies, as revealed by hybridization to escherichia coli gene arrays. J. Bacteriol. 183, 4517–4525 (2001)
4. Anca, I.A., Lumini, E., Ghignone, S., Salvioli, A., Bianciotto, V., Bonfante, P.: The ftsZ gene of the endocellular bacterium 'Candidatus Glomeribacter gigasporarum' is preferentially expressed during the symbiotic phases of its host mycorrhizal fungus. Molecular plant-microbe interactions: MPMI 22(3), 302–310 (2009)
5. Bellazzi, R., Larizza, C., Riva, A.: Temporal abstractions for interpreting diabetic patients monitoring data. Intelligent Data Analysis 2, 97–122 (1998)
6. Bianciotto, V., Bandi, C., Minerdi, D., Sironi, M., Tichy, H.V.: An obligately endosymbiotic fungus itself harbors obligately intracellular bacteria. Appl. Environ. Micro biol. 62, 3005–3010 (1996)
7. Bianciotto, V., Genre, A., Jargeat, P., Lumini, E., Baecard, G., Bonfante, P.: Vertical transmission of endobacteria in the arbuscular mycorrhizal fungus gigaspora margarita through generation of vegetative spores. Appl. Environ. Microbiol. 70, 3600–3608 (2004)
8. Bianciotto, V., Lumini, E., Bonfante, P., Vandamme, P.: Candidatus glomeribacter gigasporarum, an endosymbiont of arbuscular mycorrhizal fungi. Int. J. Syst. Evol. Microbiol. 53, 121–124 (2003)
9. Mungall, C.J., Emmert, D.B.: The FlyBase Consortium. A chado case study: an ontology-based modular schema for representing genome-associated biological information. Bioinformatics 23(13), i337–i346 (2007)
10. Jargeat, P., Cosseau, C., Olah, B., Jauneau, A., Bonfante, P.: Isolation, free-living capacities, and genome structure of candidatus glomeribacter gigasporarum the endocellular bacterium of the mycorrhizal fungus gigaspora margarita. J. Bacteriol. 186, 6876–6884 (2004)
11. Lazzarato, F., Franceschinis, G., Botta, M., Cordero, F., Calogero, R.: Rre: a tool for the extraction of non-coding regions surrounding annotated genes from genomic datasets. Bioinformatics, 1 20(16), 2848–2850 (2004)
12. Lumini, E., Ghignone, S., Bianciotto, V., Bonfante, P.: Endobacteria or bacterial endosymbionts? to be or not to be. New Phytol. 170, 205–208 (2006)
13. Marx, J.: The roots of plant-microbe collaborations. Science 304, 234–236 (2004)
14. Montani, S.: Exploring new roles for case-based reasoning in heterogeneous AI systems for medical decision support. Applied Intelligence 28, 275–285 (2008)
15. Montani, S., Bottrighi, A., Leonardi, G., Portinale, L., Terenziani, P.: Multi-level abstractions and multi-dimensional retrieval of cases with time series features. In: McGinty, L., Wilson, D.C. (eds.) ICCBR 2009. LNCS, vol. 5650, pp. 225–239. Springer, Heidelberg (2009)
16. Moran, N.A., Dale, C., Dunbar, H., Smith, W.A., Ochman, H.: Intracellular symbionts of sharpshooters (insecta: Hemiptera: Cicadellinae) form a distinct clade with a small genome. Env. Microbiol. 5, 116–126 (2003)
17. Moran, N.A., McCutcheon, A.J., Nakabachi, P.: Genomics and evolution of heritable bacterial symbionts. Annu. Rev. Genet. 42, 165–190 (2008)
18. Brian Osborne and GMOD Community. GMOD (2000)
19. Parniske, M.: Arbuscular mycorrhiza: the mother of plant root endosymbioses. Nat. Rev. Microbiol. 6, 763–775 (2008)
20. Shahar, Y.: A framework for knowledge-based temporal abstractions. Artificial Intelligence 90, 79–133 (1997)

21. Shigenobu, S., Watanabe, H., Hattori, M., Sakaki, Y., Ishikawa, H.: Genome sequence of the endocellular bacterial symbiont of aphids buchnera sp aps. Nature 407, 81–86 (2000)
22. Stephen, G.A.: String searching algorithms. Lecture Notes Series in Computing, vol. 3. World Scientific, Singapore (1994)
23. Sun, L.V., Foster, J.M., Tzertzinis, G., Ono, M., Bandi, C., Slatko, B.E., ONeill, S.L.: Determination of wolbachia genome size by pulsed-field gel electrophoresis. J. Bacteriol. 183, 2219–2225 (2001)
24. Watson, I.: Applying Case-Based Reasoning: techniques for enterprise systems. Morgan Kaufmann, San Francisco (1997)
25. http://www.biomart.org/
26. http://www.ncbi.nlm.nih.gov/Genbank/

Medicare-Grid: New Trends on the Development of E-Health System Based on Grid Technology

Yeh-Ching Chung[1], Po-Chi Shih[1], Kuan-Ching Li[2], Chao-Tung Yang[3],
Ching-Hsien Hsu[4], Fang-Rong Hsu[5], Don-Lin Yang[5],
Chia-Hsien Wen[2], and Chuang-Chien Chiu[5]

[1] National Tsing Hua University
[2] Providence University
[3] Tunghai University
[4] Chung Hua University
[5] Feng Chia University
ychung@cs.nthu.edu.tw1

Abstract. The evolution of information technology over the last decade has brought opportunities to improvements in the state of art of medical services. One scenario is that a patient's digital health record can easily be shared among hospitals and medical centers via internet, enabling the examination performed in one location while clinical diagnosis be done by physicians in another. In this paper, we propose a Medicare-Grid — a novel grid-based E-health system proposed to ease the process of retrieving and exchanging personal health data among hospitals and medical centers. Grid and peer-to-peer technologies have been used to integrate computing and storage resources provided by hospitals, as also to develop an Electronic Health Record (EHR) center to store and share EHRs among these locations. We have also developed a system prototype using ultimate hardware resources and open source software systems to simulate a real scenario as described above. We demonstrate that the idea proposed in the project is feasible, possible to be implemented and applicable to real world.

Keywords: Grid, E-health, P2P, data mining, RFID, wearable measuring system.

1 Introduction

During the last century, the development of medical services has greatly improved regarding to the quality of medical treatments, results that successfully prolong human lives. One of major evolutions on software is the digitalization process of personal health record. The digitalized record, which is formally named Electronic Health Record (EHR), can thereby be shared easier among hospitals via internet. In order to make the EHR sharing mechanism feasible, major issues to be considered are twofold. The former one is how to digitalize personal health record to a standard form which must be recognizable by all hospitals, while the latter is regarding on how to share them among hospitals. For such a goal, we propose Medicare-Grid — a grid based E-health system addressing the above issues, facilitating the sharing and exchange of digitalized personal health record among hospitals.

H. Takeda (Ed.): E-Health 2010, IFIP AICT 335, pp. 148–159, 2010.
© IFIP International Federation for Information Processing 2010

As for the first issue, we adopted Taiwan electronic Medical record Template (TMT) [1], which is a standard EHR format established by Department of Health, Executive Yuan, Taiwan. Based on this format, we developed an application that translates specific EHR format used in each hospital or medical center into a standard TMT format. As part in this project, we developed an application for Taichung Veterans General Hospital, Taiwan which translated more than 500,000 EHR samples as testing data.

As for the second issue, we developed a Medicare-Grid platform to address the issue of exchanging EHRs. First, grid and peer-to-peer technologies were used to develop an Electronic Health Record (EHR) center as a decentralized database to store and share EHRs among participating hospitals and medical centers. For each site, we developed a client application that permits them to connect to the EHR center, to upload or download EHRs. Although this mechanism is actually a centralized approach, which has potential drawback on scalability and single point of failure, peer-to-peer is considered to decentralize this "single" server and makes it scalable, fault-tolerant and robust.

In addition to the data sharing mechanism mentioned, we also integrate computing resources provided by hospitals, to form a computational grid for medical related applications. We use the *de facto* standard grid middleware Globus [2] to build up a computing grid platform and implement a workflow-based resource broker to efficiently match and select available resources in reply to user's requests. Additionally, a web portal is also developed which supports users to utilize underlying grid resources with ease.

Based on our computing and data grid platform, we developed medical related applications to improve the in-hospital medical services. Applications include (1) a data warehouse for medical decision support system, (2) a RFID-based mobile monitoring system to precisely identify people or items, and (3) a wearable physiological signal measurement system that monitors the health condition of a patient.

The remainder of this paper is organized as follows. Section 2 describes similar projects with respect to domestic and international perspectives, while in Section 3 issues regarding to the development of grid platform and EHR sharing mechanism are discussed. Later, three medical related applications are presented in Section 4, and finally, conclusion remarks are presented in Section 5.

2 Related Works

As far as we know, the insights presented in this project are novel not only in Taiwan, since it is focused on the use of grid technology to enable EHR sharing among hospitals and to integrate various Medicare applications. Nevertheless, there are some medical related projects that utilize the computing grid platforms as underlying platform such as Knowledge Innovation National Grid (KING) project [3] and BioGrid related project [4].

There exists a similar project called National Grid [5], which is focused on enabling medical related documents such as EHR or X-ray image to be shared by using grid technology; currently, over one thousand hospitals have joined to this project. IBM cooperates with University of Pennsylvania to integrate computing resources provided by each hospital and form a computational grid environment, so that all participating hospitals can easily utilize remote resources and share medical data.

3   Medicare-Grid Platform

Medicare-Grid platform can be divided by three components, namely computing grid, data grid and EHR management system. Computing grid platform provide the computational cycles needed to the execution of Medicare related applications, while Data grid provides a virtual data storage system to support EHR sharing, which management system handles the EHR format translation among specialized HIS and standard TMT format and to provide user friendly web interface for users to operate the system. In subsections that follow next, we will describe detailed system design of these components.

3.1   Computing Grid

A grid platform is an aggregation of geographically distributed resources that working all together over the Internet as a vast virtual computing environment [6, 7, 8]. The main task of computing grid is resource brokering to optimize a global schedule for requested grid jobs matching and selecting suitable and available requested resources. With a resource broker, users are insulated from the grid middleware, thus avoiding communicative burdens between users and resources.

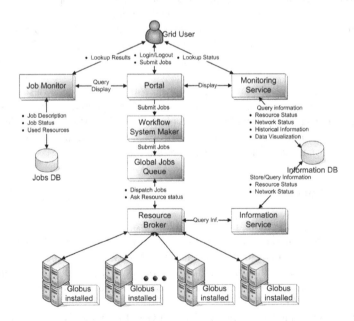

Fig. 1. The architecture of Resource Broker system and the relationships of each component

A workflow-based grid resource broker is presented whose main function is to match available resources with user requests. Also, the broker solves the job dependency problem by sorting topologically and then execution of workflows. In order to deal with communication-intensive applications, the broker considers network information statuses during matchmaking and allocates the appropriate resources, thus speeding up execution and raising throughputs. In Fig. 1, the architecture of Resource Broker system and component relationships are presented, including also functions of each component are listed in the relation link. As Grid Portals allow easy access to the system [9, 10], a schematic diagram of the complete Workflow System is shown in Fig. 2.

The achievements are described as follows. First, we construct a computational grid platform using Globus toolkit, distributed in 5 different locations (universities). Second, we have designed and implemented a resource broker which main function is to match available resources according to users' needs. Finally, we provide a uniform graphic user interface (GUI) to use Medicare-Grid platform, to achieve automatic resource discovery and efficient available resource usage. Indeed, this supports grid users to submit their jobs to the suitable grid resources without knowing in advance any information on available resources.

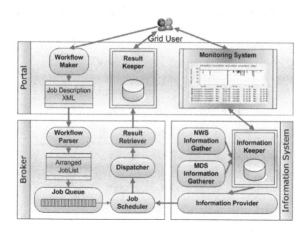

Fig. 2. A schematic diagram of the complete Workflow System

3.2 Data Grid

Data grid system is designed as distributed two-layer hierarchical peer-to-peer architecture based on the principle of locality. The bottom layer called intra-group overlay is constructed with Chord system, which the overlay clusters neighboring peers provide services within local regions; the upper layer called inter-group overlay is constructed to connect local groups together with consideration to locality. Specifically, the data grid system consists of three modules:

1. File management module: responsible for file operations, such as file insertion, file retrieve, file recovery, replicate and cache from a storage peer,

2. Intra-overlay module: to provide functions to locate peer in local group using Chord architecture,
3. Inter-overlay module: to provide API for communication need among groups.

A novel file replication mechanism is proposed, different from existing replication mechanisms such as PAST [11], OceanStore [12], and Freenet [13] that rely on global information of system. We made use of levels to control the degree of replication in our system. Peers that originally hold a file is skipped by replication level will hold a simple indicator to the peer which really holds such file.

In order to evaluate performance of the proposed system and its potential, we have implemented and deployed such proposal on Taiwan Unigrid [14] to perform large scale experiments. These experiments have been executed on the storage system located in 9 geographically distributed sites with total of 42 servers, as shown in Fig. 3(a). During the experimentation process, we selected top 10 download files from SourceForge.net as the source of testing data, and three different group bound network bandwidth {1000kbps, 100kbps, 10kbps} to cluster storage nodes.

Fig. 3(b), 3(c) and 3(d) show that we have successfully cluster some closer located peers under specific group bound. In the experiment, we noticed that the average measured bandwidth time between the newly coming peer and the measured target is less than 10 ms, and the average locate operation is less than one second.

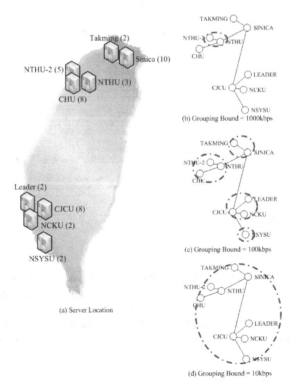

Fig. 3. (a) Server location in Taiwan Unigrid testbed, (b), (c) and (d) Server group result with different group bound 1000, 100, 10kbps

3.3 EHR Management System

EHR management system is the core service in this paper, addressing the issues of sharing standardized EHR among each participating hospital, and they are threefold. The former one is how to standardize EHR, followed by how to share them, and the latter is regarded to the user interface. For the first issue, we adopted TMT, which is a standard EHR format established by Department of Health, Executive Yuan, Taiwan, and developed a translation application to translate the specific EHR format used in each hospital into standard TMT format. Since the HIS (Hospital Information System) used in each hospital is developed by difference software company, each of them have a specific format and database schema. To make standard TMT format practicable, it requires understanding both TMT and specific hospital format in order to develop translation application for that hospital. Throughout the development of this paper, we focused our attention to the development on the transformation application between TMT and the format used in Taichung Veterans General Hospital, organization which made available more than 500,000 EHR sampling data, and translated with success to standard TMT format and stored next on data grid.

As for the second issue, we exploit the data grid as the fundamental EHR storage space to store and share EHR among hospitals, as illustrated in Fig. 4 the proposed EHR sharing mechanism. The text in black color represents the HIS used in each hospital. Physicians in each hospital make use a desktop computer to read and record patient's health record in the local database. The text in red color is the server and application developed in this paper to facilitate EHR sharing. The EHR Center is constructed using data grid as described in subsection 3.2. A client application is then implemented with the functionality of search, upload, and download data from EHR Center. In order to connect hospital with data grid, the TMT Translator is responsible for the translation of specific EHR format to stand TMT format.

A case study is used to demonstrate the entire sharing operation. For instance, a patient X has appointment with a doctor in hospital A, his/her health record is then stored in local HIS database according to operation procedure of hospital A. Patient X's EHR is then translated to TMT format (by TMT Translator) and uploaded to EHR Center (by P2P Storage Client). As patient X register in another hospital for a diagnosing session, say hospital C, the EHR of X will be downloaded partial or entirely (depending on the purpose of the appointment patient X has in this medical center) from EHR center and translated to the format used in hospital C. This mechanism enables the inspection done by one hospital to be diagnosed by doctor served in another hospital.

Advantages of this sharing mechanism are twofold. First, it is easy to deploy in hospital. Only two applications (TMT Translator and P2P Storage Client) are required to install in each hospital. P2P Storage Client is a universal application that is developed only once. Although each hospital must develop and own a personalized version of TMT Translator, this application may have been developed or under development since Taiwan government is promoting the TMT as standard and requests that all hospitals to follow this standardization process. Second, this sharing mechanism will not interfere with the procedure of taking medical treatment. All EHR translation and exchange are performed in background and on-demand. Moreover, physicians do not needed to learn how to obtain EHR from other hospitals; instead, in their perspective, all the patient's health records can just be read from its own hospital.

As listed in early this subsection, we address the third issue by developing a web portal interface, in order to demonstrate our prototype. This web-based portal integrates all enabled functions provided by computing grid, data grid, and EHR sharing mechanism and able to connect between hospital and Medicare-Grid platform to exchange the EHR data, as shown in Fig. 5.

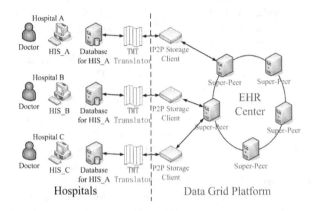

Fig. 4. The EHR sharing mechanism

Fig. 5. The web portal interface with enabled functions of Medicare-Grid platform

4   Medicare Applications

In this section, we present medical related applications developed in this project, that include (1) a data warehouse for medical decision support system, (2) a RFID based mobile monitoring system to precisely identify people or items, and (3) a wearable physiological signal measurement system that periodically monitor the health condition of patients. In subsections that follow next, we describe details on the design of these applications.

4.1 Medical Decision Support System

With the rapid growth on the amount of medical data, to find useful information among such a large dataset in an efficient way is desired. The medical decision support system, which is used to help physicians or medical professionals to make better decisions for treatment, is built based on data mining techniques. In this system, we focused on the cardiovascular disease (CVD) and made use of patients' EHR data as the source data. To build an EHR medical decision support system, we collected patients' EHRs on the data grid system and then stored them in a data warehouse, in which data mining techniques are utilized to analyze the EHR information.

There are a number of previous works on mining medical data, such as mining approaches to analyze medical database to find useful patterns, and mining personal health information and providing the results as references for doctors [15]. Data warehousing has been extensively investigated, including data preprocess and data warehouse maintenance over changing information sources [16]. On the technology of data mining, it consists of many approaches such as association rule [17] which discovers hidden and interesting rules in database, clustering which divides a data set into several groups by their characteristics, and decision tree which is used to predict the class of the new input data.

Based on related works, we considered these approaches and then developed a medical decision support system, to analyze the EHR data warehouse and provide useful results. Results obtained relate to the data we collected from some specific hospitals, since they represent the analysis of the heart disease EHR in a particular population, where the results must be confirmed by medicine experts or physicians.

Additionally, we establish a genetic database of cardiovascular diseases. In this system, we integrate 34 cardiovascular diseases and its related gene expression data, SNP, protein-protein interaction, alternative splicing and protein-protein interaction (PPI) information into a web-based interface. Through the analysis of this data model, we obtain significant result of rules for future research and tracking.

The source of cardiovascular disease related gene data is from NCBI OMIM database [18]. OMIM disease data is collected first, and then the text-mining technique is used to generate a dataset of cardiovascular disease. Next, analysis on this dataset is performed to obtain a list of cardiovascular diseases and their related genes. Lastly, we parse these annotations and store them in a database, and then filter out those incorrect results from the dataset, as in Table 1.

We use the list of cardiovascular disease related genes to search the STRING database [19], and get the PPI network graph. Due to the cardiovascular disease is multi-complex disease, these graphs can help to understand the interactions involved in these related genes. The source of alternative splicing data is AVATAR [20], which is a value-added alternative splicing database. Alternative splicing is an important event of gene transcript, and it causes the polymorphism of the gene expression. We link this database and obtain the alternative splicing result of these cardiovascular disease related genes to help us observe the form of the specific gene. The source of SNP data is HAPMAP [21], which provides plentiful SNP information, like the Linkage Disequilibrium (LD) Maps, tagSNPs and the race classification data. We performed analysis on these data and reserved the SNP data that show a high LD value that is related to the cardiovascular disease gene. These SNP data can help us research the relation of a specific SNP in a specific race between the cardiovascular diseases, and these data can also help us design the microarray experiment.

By now, the prototype system has 34 cardiovascular diseases and their genetic data. Each disease has alternative splicing form graph, protein-protein interaction graph and related gene list, and haplotype data. In addition, the number of all CVD related genes is 480 and the number of CVD related tag SNPs is 79621.

Table 1. The list of cardiovascular diseases we provided and their number of related genes

Disease Name	Gene Number
Aortic aneurysm	48
Arrhythmogenic right ventricular cardiomyopathy	22
Arterial thromboembolic disease	13
Ascending aortic disease	28
Atherosclerotic vascular disease	48
Brugada syndrome	6
Cardiac amyloidosis	9
Cardiomyopathy familial restrictive	26
Carney complex	21
Carnitine palmitoyltransferase II deficiency, late-onset form	2
Cerebral amyloid angiopathy	26
Congenital sick sinus syndrome	6
Coronary disease	212
Digeorge syndrome	79
Dilated cardiomyopathy	122
Familial hypercholesterolemia	76
Familial hypertrophic cardiomyopathy	78
Infantile dilated cardiomyopathy	18
Insulin resistance-related hypertension	21
Jervell and Lange-Nielsen syndrome	3
Myocardial infarction	146
Naxos disease	4
Orthostatic hypotension	31
Polymorphic ventricular tachycardia	21
Venous thrombosis	40
Ventricular tachycardia	46
Watson syndrome	156
Williams syndrome	514

4.2 Mobile Intelligence System

The *Mobile Intelligence System* (*MIS*) establishes an active RFID environment comprising various components and approaches for context acquisition of individuals, environment's variables and their associated values. In *MIS*, RFID-based localization, tracking and monitoring techniques were developed for enhancing context acquisition in medical-care environments. Among these functions, localization is the most important component in *MIS* and serves as the key technology for developing mobile intelligence services. The localization system termed as *Real-Time Location System* (*RTLS*), employs active RFID technologies and has three major components as shown in Fig. 6. The monitoring and tracking system can reflect the position of individuals that with active RFID Tag through web interface. In addition, for some areas that are dangerous or private, they can be marked as off limits from the system or restrict the time-duration for stay. For example, 30 minutes is set for a bathroom to avoid accident such as tumble of elder people who is not able to move or unconscious. Once an abnormal event occurred, such as illegal entrance to a limited area or over stay-duration in a specific zone, an alarm can be dispatched and email or short message is sent to the system administrator.

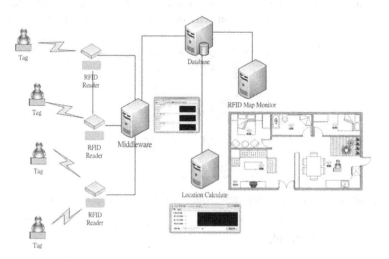

Fig. 6. The Real-Time Location System (RTLS) architecture

4.3 E-Texcare Health Care System

A number of research topics listed next have been investigated to achieve the e-Texcare health care system requirements for good functionality, portability, comfortable, endurance, and ease of use. The system configuration established and developed is listed as follow:

1. Wearable research (design, fabricate and integrate)
   - Physiological measurement
   - Electronic circuits
2. Physiological measurement research
   - Microprocessor, and micro sensor circuits for physiological measurement
   - Signal processing
3. Mobile and wireless communication research
   - RF and wireless communications
   - Information transmission and reception

A wearable and portable health care system is available for measurements on humans, as shown in Fig. 7. The wearable platform contains sensors that acquire and process vital signals such as ECG, body temperature, etc. Measured bio-signal data are transmitted via Bluetooth technology to the "Mobile Medical Information Processing Module", like PDA or Notebook, for further processing and analysis. All physiological measurement results can be sent to "Remote Mobile Medical Information Processing Module", which are e-health PC workstations in the health care centers through GSM or internet/wireless networks when connection is possible.

The e-Texcare system contains electrocardiogram (ECG/EKG), heart rate (HR), respiration rate, body temperature, and falling detection unit. Therefore, functions as the lethal arrhythmias monitoring, continuous examination of cardiovascular and cardiopulmonary functions, respiration activities, and falling detection are achieved.

Fig. 7. A prototype of e-Texcare® wearable multi-functional physiological measurement system

5   Conclusion Remarks

In this paper, we integrate grid and peer-to-peer technologies to build up a high-performance computing and storage environment as underlying backbone and proposed an EHR sharing mechanism based on this backbone to form a Medicare-Grid platform. As prototype, we closely collaborated with Taichung Veterans General Hospital, Taiwan who kindly provides us EHR sampling data for experiment purposes. These sampling data are then translated to standard TMT format and stored on Medicare-Grid platform.

In this platform, we have developed three Medicare applications: Medical Decision Support system, which provides analysis of cardiovascular diseases and its genetic data. Each disease has the alternative splicing form graph, protein-protein interaction graph and related gene list and haplotype data; RFID-based localization, tracking and monitoring techniques were developed for enhancing context acquisition in medical-care environments, and finally, the development of e-Texcare health care system and a wearable multi-functional physiological measurement system, to demonstrate that the lethal arrhythmias monitoring, continuous examination of cardiovascular and cardiopulmonary functions, respiration activities, and falling detection are achievable.

Acknowledgment. This paper is based upon work supported by National Science Council (NSC), Taiwan, under grants no. NSC97-3114-E-007-001- and NSC98-2218-E-007-005-.

References

1. Taiwan electronic Medical record Template (TMT),
   http://emr.doh.gov.tw/old/index.html
2. Foster, I., Kesselman, C.: Globus: A Metacomputing Infrastructure Toolkit. J. Supercomput. Appl. 11(2), 115–128 (1997)
3. Knowledge Innovation National Grid (KING) Project,
   http://www.nchc.org.tw/tw/about/publication/king.php
4. National Bioinformatics Applied Grid,
   http://biogrid.genomics.org.cn/index.jsp
5. NationalGrid, http://www.nationalgrid.com/corporate
6. Czajkowski, K., Fitzgerald, S., Foster, I., Kesselman, C.: Grid Information Services for Distributed Resource Sharing. In: 10th IEEE International Symposium on High Performance Distributed Computing, pp. 181–184. IEEE Press, New York (2001)
7. Foster, I., Kesselman, C.: The Grid: Blueprint for a New Computing Infrastructure. Morgan Kaufmann, San Francisco (1999)
8. Foster, I.: The Grid: A New Infrastructure for 21st Century Science. Physics Today 55(2), 42–47 (2002)
9. Yang, C.T., Lai, K.C., Shih, P.C.: Design and implementation of a workflow-based resource broker with information system on computational grid. J. Supercomput. 1–34 (2009)
10. Yang, C.T., Shih, P.C., Lin, C.F., Chen, S.Y.: A resource broker with an efficient network information model on grid environments. J. Supercomput. 40(3), 76–109 (2007)
11. Druschel, P., Rowstron, A.: PAST: A large-scale, persistent peer-to-peer storage utility. In: HotOS VIII, Germany (2001)
12. Kubiatowicz, J., Bindel, D., Chen, Y., Czerwinski, S., Eaton, P., Geels, D., Gummadi, R., Rhea, S., Weatherspoon, H., Weimer, W., Wells, C., Zhao, A.B.: OceanStore: An Architecture for Global-Scale Persistent Storage. In: 9th International Conference on Architectural Support for Programming Languages and Operating Systems (2000)
13. Clarke, I., Sandberg, O., Wiley, B., Hong, T.W.: Freenet: A Distributed Anonymous Information Storage and Retrieval System. In: Proceedings of the ICSI Workshop on Design Issues in Anonymity and Unobservability, USA (2000)
14. Taiwan Unigrid, http://www.unigrid.org.tw
15. Lloyd-Williams, M.: Case Studies in the Data Mining Approach to Health Information Analysis. In: IEE Colloquium on Knowledge Discovery and Data Mining, vol. 1, pp. 1–4 (1998)
16. Rundensteiner, E.A., Koeller, A., Zhang, X.: Maintaining Data Warehouses over Changing Information Sources. Communications of the ACM 43(6) (2000)
17. Dai, P.T., Chu, J.L., Lin, S.J., Chang, H.B., Yang, D.L.: Construction and Analysis of a Data Warehouse System for Customer Relationship Management. In: Proceedings of EC 2003, Taiwan (2003)
18. Online Mendelian Inheritance in Man, OMIM. McKusick-Nathans Institute of Genetic Medicine, Johns Hopkins University and National Center for Biotechnology Information, National Library of Medicine, http://www.ncbi.nlm.nih.gov/omim/
19. Mering, C., Jensen, L.J., Kuhn, M., Chaffron, S., Doerks, T., Krüger, B., Snel, B., Bork, P.: STRING 7 – recent developments in the integration and prediction of protein interactions. Nucleic Acids Res. 35, 358–362 (2007)
20. Chang, H.C., Yu, P.S., Huang, T.W., Hsu, F.R., Lin, Y.L.: The Application of Alternative Splicing Graphs in Quantitative Analysis of Alternative Splicing Form from EST Database. J. Comput. Appl. Technol. 22(1), 14–22 (2005)
21. The International HapMap Consortium. The International HapMap Project. Nature 426, 789–796 (2003)

A "Ubiquitous Environment" through Wireless Voice/Data Communication and a Fully Computerized Hospital Information System in a University Hospital

Eisuke Hanada[1], Shusaku Tsumoto[1], and Shotai Kobayashi[2]

[1] Division of Medical Informatics
[2] Exective Director, Shimane University Hospital,
Enya-cho. 89-1, 693-8501 Izumo, Japan
{e-hanada,tsumoto,skdr3nai}@med.shimane-u.ac.jp

Abstract. Fully computerized hospital information systems (HIS) are spreading in Japanese hospitals. Most HIS consist of server computers, terminals, a database, and a LAN. The introduction of HIS has enabled quick communication between doctors and staff and the immediate dissemination of patient information. Installation of a wireless data communication system compatible with a HIS has been reported to improve efficiency. However, also necessary is a voice communication system that can transmit instructions quickly in emergencies, such as a sudden change in the health status of an inpatient. In the Japanese medical community, "An environment in which access and the sharing of information are possible anywhere and at all times" is called a "ubiquitous environment." In order to attain such an environment, a telecom infrastructure with a mobile communications network is very important to voice and data communication. Here, we show the "ubiquitous environment" realized in Shimane University Hospital and how it has improved efficiency.

Keywords: Ubiquitous Environment, Electronic Hospital Information System, Wireless LAN, Mobile Voice Communication, Labor efficiency.

1 Introduction

Because most Japanese doctors do not employ secretaries, they have traditionally transmitted patient information and instructions for patient care in handwriting on paper. This is also true for the nursing staff. Computers have been widely installed in Japanese hospitals over the past 30 years. The original purpose was to calculate costs and to bill the patients. In recent years, with improvements in the performance of computers and databases and rapidly increasing data transfer rates for local area networks, LAN, the installation of Hospital Information Systems (HIS) has spread quickly in Japanese hospitals. Currently, the main purposes of HIS installation are to store and transmit information related to prescriptions, examinations, and the medical instructions of doctors. However, because there are no standards for HIS in Japan, each system is built around the functions needed by the hospital into which it is installed. However, because of the expense of the hardware, it has not been possible

H. Takeda (Ed.): E-Health 2010, IFIP AICT 335, pp. 160–168, 2010.

to install a sufficient number of terminals. With the evolution of HIS, it has become indispensable to place one or more terminals in outpatient consultation rooms. Few hospitals can afford terminals at each sickbed in their wards, so terminals are generally placed only at the staff stations.

The introduction of computers, databases, and LANs not only enables the rapid transfer of instructions by a doctor, but also enables the immediate sharing of patient records. However, to prepare for emergencies, such as sudden changes in the condition of an inpatient, adding a voice communication system to the data communication system is also necessary.

In the medical community in Japan, "An environment in which access and the sharing of information are possible anywhere and at all times" is called a "ubiquitous environment." In order to attain such an environment, a telecom infrastructure with a mobile communications network is very important to voice and data communication. Here, we introduce the "ubiquitous environment" currently in place in a university hospital and discuss its success in improving labor efficiency.

2   The Computerized Hospital Information System

Shimane University Hospital (hereafter, SUH) is an advanced hospital with 616 sickbeds and about 350 doctors. It has 11 general wards, a psychiatric ward, an ICU, and an NICU. Each general ward has on average about 50 sickbeds.

At SUH, many functions have been added since the HIS was introduced about 20 years ago. As a result, electronic storage of patient and nursing records (September, 2006) and the full digitalization of radiological data (April, 2008) have been realized. Also, online input and transmission of medical information, such as diagnosis, has been done since November 2006.

For about twenty years many hospitals have had electronic systems for recording prescriptions and medical examinations. However, in many hospitals patient treatment records and instructions for patient care given by doctors to the nursing staff are not yet computerized. This is also true of many functions unique to the nursing staff. Few hospitals have computerized systems to deal with the records of the co-medical staff, for example, consultations concerning medication by pharmacists or nutritional guidance by dietitians. In SUH, all aspects of the hospital have been incorporated into our HIS. SUH has an advanced system that has created a "ubiquitous environment".

In the HIS of SUH, users are categorized by their job description and affiliation and are allowed access only to that information judged necessary. Permission for access to data is classified as follows: reference only or permission to create or rewrite. For data protection, all of the server hardware, storage systems, and the networks between servers are backed up by duplicate systems. A monitoring system for the operation of the server, etc. is also in place.

Users can refer to any information within their authority using a common application to enter their ID and password at any terminal. Thus, all the staff members at SUH can work in a paperless environment, except for documents on which signatures are required. Only a few hospitals in Japan have attained an electronic environment on this scale.

In addition to the systems described above, in 2003 SUH started a patient information sharing system by linking our system to other hospitals and clinics (an inter-regional collaboration system, ICS). In Japan, a hospital in charge of a patient's treatment charges according a scale set by the Ministry of Health that is based on the requirements for treatment and the severity of a disease. Doctors often move their patients to other hospitals when specialized treatment is necessary, then again take charge of their care when they improve specialized treatment is no longer necessary. In such cases, the doctor refers the patient and writes a letter of introduction, which includes a summary of his treatment. In the ICS, all pre-registered doctors are given and ID and password, which allows them access to the system, allowing them to conveniently submit the introduction letters by computer. The ICS server is one of a number of servers in our HIS. By inserting a firewall system between the ICS server and other servers, direct access is denied to other, unauthorized areas of the HIS from outside SUH.

The functions included in the hospital information system of SUH are shown in Fig. 1.

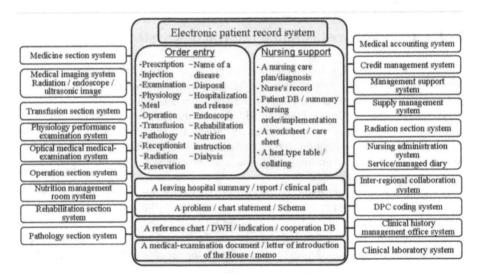

Fig. 1. Functions of the HIS at SUH (presented by Toshiba Sumiden Medical Information Systems Corp., Japan)

The HIS of SUH currently consists of about 45 servers and over 800 terminals that are connected using wired/wireless LAN.

3   Data Sharing Using Wireless LAN

The hospital building of SUH has six floors. Each floor is 110 m long, east to west, with a staff station in the center (see Fig. 2). The nursing staff on each floor is divided into two groups, one for the east and one for the west wing. In the daytime, eight to ten nurses are assigned to each nurse unit, with about three nurses working at night.

Wireless LAN (IEEE802.11a) was installed in all wards except for the ICU and NICU in October of 2003. At the time the wireless LAN was installed, 72 computers (hereafter, WLAN terminal) were connected to the HIS, as shown in Fig. 3. This number was determined based on the number of nurses working at that time. The present number of WLAN terminals is 110 at 13 access points (AP) on each floor, as shown in Fig. 2. The wireless LAN of SUH is exclusively for staff use. The system, which includes MAC Address filtering of AP, is secure and there have been no problems such as unauthorized use. The frequency of the electromagnetic signals specified by the IEEE802.11a standards is in the 5.2 GHz band, and the maximum output power is about 150 mW. The results of our irradiation experiments with 5.2 GHz electromagnetic waves on medical devices confirmed that this frequency has no influence on medical devices, if the access point and wireless network card in the PC are as approved by Japanese law [1].

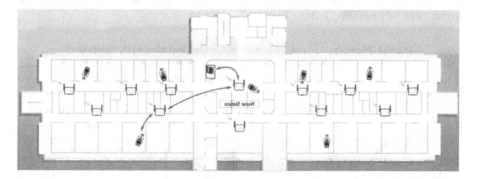

Fig. 2. Location of the SUH wireless LAN AP's on one floor (One AP, not shown, is in the "patient counseling room")

Fig. 3. A wireless LAN terminal at SUH (circle, wireless LAN card; arrow, a vibration-absorbing mat)

4   Labor Efficiency Improvement by Mobile Voice Communication

At SUH, Personal Handy-phone System handsets (PHS, WILLCOM inc.) have been distributed to almost all doctors since November of 2004, which has enabled quick voice transfer of information and medical instructions. Other designated staff members have access to these phones, as do the safety management nurse and the facility maintenance staff. Currently, approximately 450 handsets are in use. Because the output power of the electric signals emitted by PHS handsets is weak, 80 mW maximum, there is almost no influence on medical devices [2]. These PHS handsets can accept calls from any number, but are pre-set so that only three numbers can be dialed. The usage fee is the equivalent of 7 to 8 US dollars monthly per handset.

In addition, one or two PHS handsets for which the monthly charge is fixed can be assigned as needed to the pharmacy and each ward. Quick, charge-free communication with doctors can be attained using these handsets. For example, a pharmacist can confirm a prescription quickly. Also, the nurse can receive a doctor's assistance at times of sudden changes in the condition of a patient. The use of these handsets has reduced the time wasted by physically looking for a doctor, which has greatly contributed to the improvement of labor efficiency. This was confirmed in a study of the number telephone calls: The number was greatly reduced by the introduction of PHS (See Table 1 [3]).

Table 1. Number of phone calls received before and after PHS installation

a) Number of calls by place of origin and the reduction rate (Weekdays 8:30 ~ 5:00)

Origin of call	Pharmacy	Clinical lab.	Hosp. Affairs Section	Others
Before introduction	118	92	111	982
After introduction	23	66	38	412
Number Reduced	95	26	73	560
Reduction rate (%)	**80.5**	28.3	**65.8**	57.0

b) The total number of calls over five weekdays

Section	Calls before introduction	Calls after introduction
Wards	1216	588
Visitor sections	458	356
Other sections	116	212
Total	1790	1126

In addition, SUH has permitted cellular phone use under certain conditions in some areas of the hospital since January of 2004 [1]. Permission for cellular-phone use is a difficult problem for hospitals [4]. In order to insure cellular phone safely, it is necessary for measures to be taken against the following problems; electromagnetic interference (EMI) with medical devices, noise by the speaker or ring tone, improper personal information disclosure using the camera/movie recording function, and lack of concentration on work while talking over the telephone. The output power of signals emitted from Japanese cellular phone handsets is currently 250 mW or less. Thus, for the convenience of the patients, the conditional use of cellular phones in hospitals can be safely permitted.

5 Discussion

Mobile Communication System

As shown above, SUH can be considered a pioneering hospital with a "ubiquitous environment". Our follow-up data for the introduction of the electronic data retrieval and storage system and the wireless LAN to the HIS show them to have been successful in allowing us to implement our "ubiquitous environment" and that it has been safe and efficient. The nurses who work in our wards are the main users of the WLAN terminals. An important factor in our success was that we have carefully considered the merits and limits of the various systems to be used and took precautions to insure the safe and efficient usage of our wireless LAN before installing the systems.

The number of AP installed for the wireless LAN in SUH now thirteen for each floor, the minimum necessary number. Some nurses have reported that the range of the signals is not satisfactory in some sickrooms. The range of an electromagnetic wave has been shown to be influenced by the materials used in the construction of walls and doors [5]. Unfortunately, adding to the number of AP's would increase the need for equipment maintenance and require remodeling expenses due to an increased need for wiring, so we must maintain the current level. Although some simulations of electromagnetic wave range have been done [6-8], the huge computational complexity needed to perform this type of simulation in an actual hospital setting has resulted in only simple simulations having been done.

Computerization of Medical Information

Medical records have long been handwritten in Japan, and doctors often include drawings in their records. When computerized medical records are proposed, there is often opposition by these doctors. At SUH, this opposition was reduced by the introduction of a system that can scan drawings and by the executive director who exercised strong leadership.

The Ministry of Health, Labour and Welfare (MHLW) of Japan requires hospitals that computerize medical records to adopt the following conditions to insure information security.

- Confidentiality : limitation of the right to access
- Integrity   : verification and backup of data, system duplication, etc.
- Availability   : certainty of access by approved users

The HIS of SUH fulfills these conditions.

Many Japanese hospitals are introducing "critical path" (CP)" systems to standardize patient care. A CP is drawn up each disease and every surgical procedure. The CP describes the patient care that will be given during hospitalization, and in some cases, the CP is divided into timeframes. In CP, setting up a target "outcome" for every treatment and including exceptions to the treatment protocol as "variance" is recommended. CP has the benefits of promoting efficacy by eliminating unnecessary examinations and shortening the duration of hospitalization [9]. CP has been beneficial in our effort to raise medical efficiency in Japanese hospitals. From the viewpoint of the HIS manager, a CP can be considered a "packed order" that includes a wide variety of directions that can be selected from and that is used to promote standardized care. Pathological and bio-chemical tests, physiological function examinations, radiological examinations, surgeries, prescriptions, medical treatments, treatment instructions to nurses, etc. are included in each CP. Because all of the above are computerized at SUH, these standardized CP have become an integral part of the HIS. Since December 2008, SUH has been able to incorporate a unified, multidisciplinary CP that includes nursing services into our HIS. The number of CP currently registered and employed exceeds 350. The use of the CP in our HIS has reduced the time burden on our doctors and made them more efficient and effective.

Installation of the PHS and Telemedicine System

Shimane Prefecture is a rural area in western Japan. In this area, a shortage of doctors has long been a serious problem. To ameliorate this problem, doctors are dispatched from SUH to other hospitals. PHS serves as a communication medium with the doctors who work outside SUH. The number of doctors currently working at SUH is also insufficient. Therefore, communication between doctors and the co-medical staff is critical, and PHS contributes to our efficiency and patient safety.

The use of IP phones or VoIP (Voice over IP) would eliminate almost all of the cost of telephone calls, even when using public systems. Unfortunately, VoIP and IP phones are not widely used in Japan. A problem with the introduction of VoIP devices for mobile communications is that they are much more expensive than PHS and cell phone handsets. The low cost is one of the reasons SUH adopted PHS. In Japan, private corporations have no national standards or policies to guide their construction and maintenance of the regional public broadband mobile communications networks. Thus, although this service is accessible in major cities, their introduction to lightly populated areas like Shimane Prefecture has been slow, and at present no companies have plans to begin this service here in the foreseeable future. The Japanese government has a plan that proposes the use of information and communication technology (ICT) to compensate for the regional medical specialist shortage; however, because this would require a broadband communication network, it will require much time and effort to realize an environment in which this ICT strategy can be successful. Because of the above problems, SUH utilizes PHS and has introduced an online telemedicine support system [10] in which specialized medical advice is possible at a transmission speed of 1 Mbps in one direction.

6 Designs for the Future

Wireless LAN in Our New Ward Building

A new ward is under construction at SUH, with a completion date in the spring of 2011. Wireless LAN has been approved, and its specifications will meet the specifications of the current IEEE802.11n. At the time of installation, a new channel design will be used and electromagnetic shielding is being built into the ward to insure a safe electromagnetic environment.

Plans for New ICT Systems

The following new systems are also being planned: A medical device management system using wireless LAN and RF-ID tags and a nurse call system (NCS), connected to the HIS, that uses VoIP. In the medical device management system, an RF-ID tag will be attached to each medical device to prevent the loss of this expensive equipment. This system also allows us to monitor the current location of any device, to track patient information by the user of the device, and to monitor the operating condition of each device. In terms of the location of a device, high precision, such as to the nearest few centimeters, is not necessary. However, the influence of the frequency of RF-ID tags on the medical equipment with which it is to be used is important, so we are doing investigations to insure safety. Also, in large Japanese hospitals, a central office manages medical devices and distributes them to the area of the hospital they are needed. We plan to use RF-ID tags to assist in the management of this system. Because the RF-ID tag itself is expensive, their use with a bar code is also being considered. As for NCS, client/server systems with portable remote terminals are currently in use in many large Japanese hospitals. Our NCS will not only focus on voice communication as is done in the systems currently in use, but will eventually be part of our HIS that includes VoIP.

A New, Safe and Secure Server Room

The installation of a new HIS server room is also planned in order to increase security. Advanced preparation for disasters and personnel management are lacking in the HIS server rooms of many Japanese hospitals. Because Japan has many earthquakes, a quake-absorbing function is indispensable and will be built into our server room. In addition, we intend to substantially improve our firefighting equipment, take measures to protect against information leaks, and make improvements to the power supply equipment and air conditioning in the new server room Also, because of rapid changes in technology, the HIS must be upgraded and equipment replaced approximately every five years.

7 Conclusion

SUH's progressive HIS system has allowed us to realize our pioneering goal of creating a "ubiquitous environment". Our program has been so successful that the SUH staff has come to consider the use of PHS and wireless LAN with electronic medical records to be common sense. It will be important for us to continue to develop the scale of and functions included in our "ubiquitous environment".

Acknowledgement

This investigation was partially supported by the Japan Society for the Promotion of Science (No.20390151).

References

1. Hanada, E., Nakakuni, H., Kudou, T.: Safe and Efficient Use of Wireless Communication in a Large Hospital. In: Medinfo. 2007, Brisbane, p. 442 (2007)
2. Hanada, E., Antoku, Y., Tani, S., et al.: Electromagnetic interference on medical equipment by low-power mobile telecommunication system. IEEE Transactions on Electromagnetic Compatibility 42(4), 470–476 (2000)
3. Hanada, E., Fujiki, T., Nakakuni, H., Sullivan, C.V.: The effectiveness of the installation of a mobile-voice-communication system in a university hospital. Journal of Medical Systems 30(2), 101–106 (2006)
4. Derbyshire, S.W.G., Burgess, A.: Use of mobile phones in hospitals. BMJ 333, 767–768 (2006)
5. Hanada, E., Watanabe, Y., Antoku, Y., et al.: Hospital construction materials: Poor shielding capacity with respect to signals transmitted by mobile telephones. Biomedical Instrumentation & Technology 35(4), 489–496 (1998)
6. Yee, K.: Numerical Solution of Initial Boundary Value Problems Involving Maxwell's Equations in Isotropic Media. IEEE Transactions on Antenna Propagation 14(3), 302–307 (1966)
7. Ji, Z., Li, B.H., Wang, H.X., et al.: Efficient ray-tracing methods for propagation prediction for indoor wireless communications. IEEE Antennas And Propagation Magazine 43(2), 41–49 (2001)
8. Hoppe, R., Wertz, P., Landstorfer, F.M., et al.: Advanced ray-optical wave propagation modelling for urban and indoor scenarios including wideband properties. European Transactions on Telecommunications 14(1), 61–69 (2003)
9. Ramos, M.C., Ratliff, C.: The Development and Implementation of an Integrated Multidisciplinary Clinical Pathway. Journal of Wound, Ostomy & Continence Nursing 24(2), 66–71 (1997)
10. Hanada, E., Ikebuchi, K., Miyamoto, M., et al.: An Interactive Medical Support System for Rural Area in Dermatology. In: The 11th International Congress of the Iupesm, Medical Physics And Biomedical Engineering World Congress 2009, Munich, vol. 05/07, p. 1 (2009)

Towards a Diagnostic Toolbox for Medical Communication

William Billingsley[1], Cindy Gallois[1], Andrew Smith[1], Timothy Marks[1], Fernando Bernal[1], and Marcus Watson[1,2]

[1] NICTA, Level 5, Axon Building, University of Queensland,
Queensland 4072, Australia
[2] Skills Development Centre, Queensland Health, P.O. Box 470,
Herston, Queensland 4029, Australia
{William.Billingsley,Cindy.Gallois,Andrew.Smith,
Timothy.Marks,Fernando.Bernal,Marcus.Watson}@nicta.com.au

Abstract. Poor communication is a major cause of adverse patient events in hospitals. Although sophisticated simulators are in use for performing medical operations, there is comparatively little technology support being used for improving communication skills including patient history taking. Artificial Intelligence and Natural Language Processing researchers have developed sophisticated algorithms for analysing conversations. We are experimentally developing software that can visualise the combined output of these algorithms, as a diagnostic toolkit for medical communication.

Keywords: Communication, Visualisation, Patient History Taking, Natural Language Processing, Artificial Intelligence.

1 Introduction

Adverse patient events occur in between 3.7% [1] and 16.6% [2] of hospitalisations. Even the studies that have found the lower rates have concluded that a substantial amount of patient harm happens through medical management. Failures of communication have been found to be a major contributor in up to forty per cent of these events [3], and seventy per cent of those that cause serious harm [4]. One Australian study attributed communication as a major cause to approximately 14,000 preventable deaths each year [5]. If failures of communication are such a large contributor to patients being harmed or killed within the health service, then this suggests that improving medical professionals' skills and habits in communication would make a significant improvement to patient outcomes.

Technology now plays a pivotal role in diagnosing patient health issues. Particularly, visualisations of technical inspections of the body – such as ultrasound, electrocardiograms, and magnetic resonance imagery – have become a day-to-day part of diagnostic practice. We propose that technical inspections of medical communication could similarly help to diagnose and understand how it fails.

There are, of course, many different modes of communication in the health service. A failure of communication could include, for instance, that something was written

H. Takeda (Ed.): E-Health 2010, IFIP AICT 335, pp. 169–176, 2010.
© IFIP International Federation for Information Processing 2010

incorrectly on a patient chart, that a nurse was not informed of relevant information that was known to a doctor, or that a misunderstanding took place during a medical conversation. It is very unlikely that a single technology could be designed that could encompass all of these different kinds of communication and the ways they can fail. Instead, we propose starting with a kind of communication event that every patient undergoes, and that precedes every other medical interaction: patient history taking.

2 Background

Many research projects have analysed medical communication [6, 7, 8, 9]. Most studies have involved manually coding and classifying particular utterances or events in a conversation. There are a number of software tools, such as Transana[1] and Noldus's products[2], that assist observers to mark up these events manually on a transcript or video, and then analyse them, for example through connections to statistics packages. A recent meta-analysis of the analysis techniques that are commonly used [10] found that most studies, for practical reasons, focused on very short-term effects within a conversation – such as the influence of one participant's utterance on what the other participant says next. It also recommended that multiple analysis methods should be used, to better cope with the complexity of clinical communication. Besides the practical limitations of utterance coding studies, it is also clear that manual coding of a conversation is very laborious to perform.

Communications researchers are not the only academics who have an interest in analysing conversations. Within computer science, Artificial Intelligence and Natural Language Processing groups have developed a number of algorithmic techniques for analysing a conversation. For example, Leximancer [11], Latent Semantic Analysis [12], and Latent Dirichlet Analysis [13] all analyse how words co-occur within a text to discover the flow of topics. It can be difficult to prove objectively that word co-occurrence is the same thing as a topic, but comparisons against human analysis have found that the algorithms' results correlate well with human judgement [14, 15]. We are also aware of communications researchers who use these tools in their research, so the algorithmic approaches are gaining acceptance.

Applying an algorithmic analysis would make it feasible to analyse doctors' clinical conversations as part of their training or in professional development. However, we can go further. Just as Connor, et al, found in their review of manual analysis that it would be better to use multiple techniques to capture the full complexity of clinical communication, we believe the same is also true for automatic analysis. By combining different analyses, we can uncover more about the conversation. For example, colleagues of ours have developed algorithms for estimating the cognitive load of a speaker by analysing the sound of his or her speech [16]. By combining that with the text analysis, we would be able to see both what participants are saying and how much thought they are having to put into their words. Each additional algorithmic tool can add an extra dimension to the analysis.

---

[1] http://www.transana.org
[2] http://www.noldus.com

3 Concept of Operation

The analysis system we are developing has a visualisation client and a data server. Both the client and the server accept plug-ins to extend their functionality. This extensibility is necessary as it is not certain which kinds of computer analysis will prove to be informative about a medical conversation, and which will not.

The server has to make as few assumptions as possible about the data it will be handling. Different analysis components use different kinds of data. For this reason, we often depict the data repository as a bucket, as shown in Figure 1.

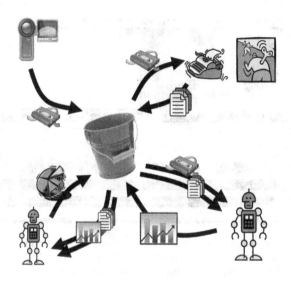

Fig. 1. The server repository acts as a generic bucket for data. When a video is uploaded, it begins to be processed through the various installed plug-ins automatically. In the figure, processing starts at the top-left and proceeds clockwise. Each plug-in takes data from the repository, passes it to an external processing component, and puts the resulting output into the repository as data that other plug-ins can then use in their processing.

When a video is uploaded into the repository, the server begins to process it automatically. At each step in the processing, a plug-in takes some form of data out of the repository, processes it, and adds a new form of data back into the repository. One of the first steps in the workflow (one of the first plug-ins invoked) is likely to be to transcribe the video. This may be a semi-automatic step, in which a speech-to-text engine produces a draft transcript, which is then edited manually using common transcription editing software. A second plug-in would take the transcript and process it through an NLP engine. A third plug-in would process the sound through a cognitive load analysis tool. Another plug-in might correlate the cognitive load data with the topic data for the video, and identify common stress patterns.

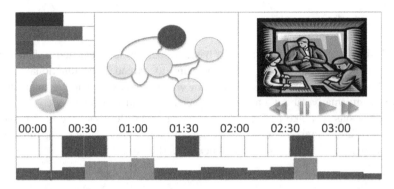

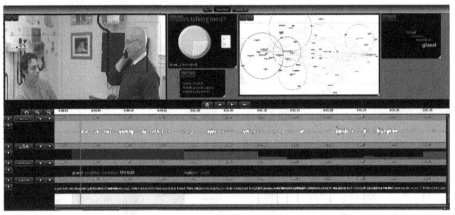

Fig. 2. Stylised and real images of the client. The client plays back visualisations of the server data alongside the video. The visualisations are linked to the video, and so can also be used to navigate the video. The client supports a plug-in architecture, both so that it can be extended for new kinds of data, and also so that different visualisations can be used for different kinds of user.

The final result of the server processing is that there is a large amount of analysis data in the repository. The data can be played back as visualisations alongside the video, as depicted in Figure 2. Just as the server supports a plug-in architecture so that we can continually extend it with new kinds of analysis, the client also supports plug-ins so we can extend it with new kinds of visualisation. The mapping of server plug-ins to client plug-ins is not one-to-one. As we describe later in the paper, the presentation of the data has to be varied for a number of different kinds of user, so we expect there to be more visualisation plug-ins than analysis plug-ins. It is also worth mentioning that advice is a kind of visualisation. By providing an appropriate plug-in, we can turn the visualisation plug-in into an explicit teaching tool.

4 Patient History Taking

One of the ways trainee doctors are taught patient history taking and communication skills is through simulated patients. An actor is trained to portray a patient scenario.

The actor is trained to portray not only the history and symptoms of the patient, but also the emotional and personality characteristics. These portrayals are often standardised ("Standardised Patients"). The trainee doctor is asked to examine this simulated patient. At some institutions, these simulated patient sessions are video recorded for later review, rather than being reviewed live. Reviewing a video session thoroughly is a time-intensive task, so there are practical limitations on how many scenarios a trainee doctor can undertake.

As the sessions are already being recorded, they make an ideal first candidate for automatic analysis. The video recording can be processed by a transcriber, sound extractor, and multiple different analysis engines. This data can then be compiled, and the video played back together with the analysis results. Because the scenarios are standardised and well-understood, they make a very good research test-bed for analysis technologies. The fact that the educators already know what is wrong with the patient and what kinds of interactions to look for means that the analysis can be pre-seeded with information. This can help to mitigate any limitations of the analysis algorithms. If the algorithmic analysis proves successful, then we can begin to apply it educationally. Because algorithmic analysis would not involve the reviewer (though it would require time from the actors and someone to correct transcription errors) it would be possible for medical students to perform additional practice sessions using the system.

There have been previous attempts at automated teaching of patient history taking. Particularly, we are aware of interactive computer simulations of patients [17, 18]. The virtual patient listens to the doctor through voice recognition or free text entry, and responds through pre-recorded video. The computer simulations are necessarily lower fidelity than using a live actor, and they are also lower fidelity in their analysis than the multi-modal detailed algorithmic analysis we have proposed. We would be interested in augmenting a computerised simulation with fine-grained AI and NLP based communication analysis, to see whether it can be effective in that situation. As the computerised patient cannot vary its intonation, body language, and emotion as effectively as the human actor, however, it is possible that doctor-computer conversations would always appear somewhat stilted.

5 More Complex Use Cases

A second scenario we are interested in investigating is the shift hand-over meeting. Shift-handover is recognised as being a critical communication system, which has informational, social, educational functions [19]. Despite the hand-over's importance, though, there are comparatively few studies into factors that make a hand-over successful or unsuccessful. Likewise, in medical practice, it is difficult to monitor how well hand-overs are being performed.

We would like to see what automated AI and NLP analysis can reveal about these meetings. By recording hand-over meetings and processing them through the analysis tools, we hope to be able to inspect them in a way that is both more detailed and more efficient than manually coding utterances.

Technically, shift hand-overs are a very much more challenging problem than simulated patient scenarios. There are many more people involved in the meeting, and the number of communication channels (the number of possible two-way conversations) grows with the square of the number of participants. Similarly, whereas the simulated patient scenarios discuss a single medical case, the shift hand-overs discuss an entire ward. Furthermore, the shift cases are not standardised, so the software would not know ahead of time what the patients' conditions and issues are. Nonetheless, it may be possible to identify common failure modes in the communication. At the very least, we hope to uncover more detail about how the meetings function.

If a hand-over meeting is transcribed and analysed by a NLP and AI components, then this also provides a way of indexing the meeting, not just against words but against topics and other measures. If other clinical conversations are also recorded and indexed, it may be possible to forensically analyze how information is conveyed from one conversation to another. For example, it might eventually be possible to follow a piece of information from one medic's interaction with a patient, through a shift hand-over, to another medic's interaction with the same patient.

6 Status and Plans

We have constructed prototype software for our diagnostic tool, which is being continuously refined. We have begun to build our first processing and visualisation plug-ins, and have established collaborations with AI and NLP teams in order to add more. There is still, however, much work to be done before we can place an educational tool in front of a doctor.

Firstly, we need to experiment with the tool. We need to process different kinds of conversation through various plug-ins, to find out what kinds of analyses combine well and add meaning – which combinations are more than the sum of their parts, and which are not. This is an experimental discovery process. Then, we need to work out ways of showing this data meaningfully to doctors. The data has been derived through complex algorithms, but must be understood by someone who has no knowledge of those algorithms, but who nonetheless works in an evidence-driven field and who will probably want to know the reasons not just the result.

The visualisations that the team needs during the discovery process might be different to those the doctors need in their professional development. So, we might find we need to develop visualisations and measures twice. The system is designed to be very adaptable, however, and can be configured differently for researchers than for doctors. We also hope to make it available to other researchers to use in their work.

Our first experiments are scheduled to take place in 2010, with the simulated patient scenarios. We also intend to apply the tool to a separate study comparing think-alouds by different practitioners. We hope that applying it in this study will help us to see how we can make the tool more useful for researchers. In 2011, we are scheduled to begin our investigations into hand-over meetings, and also hope to have developed a useful educational tool with the system.

7 Conclusion

The diagnostic toolbox we are creating is intended to be useful to both researchers and practitioners. We have a collaborative relationship with the Skills Development Centre of Queensland Health (the state hospital system), which gives us both the access to experimental subjects and scenarios that we need, and also a route to real impact if our research is successful. Our first goal is to uncover combinations of analysis that can provide meaningful insights into medical communication. Our second goal is to provide a useful educational tool that can present that meaningful analysis of communication to doctors, so they can understand more about their own communication. Through those two goals, we hope to provide a way of improving medical communication, at least in the area of patient history taking, and reduce the rates of patient harm.

Acknowledgments. The authors gratefully acknowledge their colleagues on the project: Harold Cruz and Michael Pickard. NICTA is funded by the Australian Government as represented by the Department of Broadband, Communications and the Digital Economy and the Australian Research Council through the ICT Centre of Excellence program.

References

1. Brennan, T.A., Leape, L.L., Laird, N.M., Hebert, L., Localio, A.R., Lawthers, A.G., Newhouse, J.P., Weiler, P.C., Hiatt, H.H.: Incidence of adverse events and negligence in hospitalized patients: results of the Harvard medical practice study. Quality and Safety in Health Care 13(2), 145 (2004)
2. Wilson, R., Runciman, W., Gibberd, R., Harrison, B., Newby, L., Hamilton, J.: The quality in Australian healthcare survey. The Medical Journal of Australia 163, 458–471 (1995)
3. Australian Institute of Health and Welfare. Sentinel events in Australian public hospitals 2004-05. Australian Institute of Health & Welfare (2005)
4. Leonard, M., Graham, S., Bonacum, D.: The human factor: the critical importance of effective teamwork and communication in providing safe care. Quality and Safety in Healthcare 13, i85–i90 (1995)
5. Zinn, C.: 14000 Preventable deaths in Australian hospitals. British Medical Journal 310, 14–87 (1995)
6. Roter, D., Larson, S.: The Roter interaction analysis system (RIAS): utility and flexibility for analysis of medical interactions. Patient Education and Counseling 46(4), 243–251 (2002)
7. Apker, J., Mallak, L.A., Applegate, E.B., Gibson, S.C., Ham, J.J., Johnson, N.A., Street, R.L.: Exploring emergency physician-hospitalist handoff interactions: development of the Handoff Communication Assessment. Annals of Emergency Medicine 55, 161–170 (2010)
8. Siminoff, L.A., Graham, G.C., Gordon, N.H.: Cancer communication patterns and the influence of patient characteristics: Disparities in information-giving and affective behaviors. Patient Education and Counseling 62(3), 355–360 (2006)
9. Street, R.L., Gordon, H.S.: The clinical context and patient participation in post-diagnostic consultations. Patient Education and Counseling 64(1), 217–224 (2006)
10. Connor, M., Fletcher, I., Salmon, P.: The analysis of verbal interaction sequences in dyadic clinical communication: A review of methods. Patient Education and Counseling 75(2), 169–177 (2009)
11. Smith, A.E.: Automatic extraction of semantic networks from text using Leximancer. In: HLT-NAACL 2003 Human Language Technology Conference of the North American Chapter of the Association for Computational Linguistics: Companion volume, pp. Demo23–Demo24. ACL, Edmonton (2003)

12. Deerwester, S., Dumais, S.T., Furnas, G.W., Landauer, T.K., Harshman, R.: Indexing by latent semantic analysis. Journal of the American Society for Information Science 41(6), 391–407 (1990)
13. Blei, D.M., Ng, A.Y., Jordan, M.I.: Latent Dirichlet allocation. Journal of Machine Learning Research 3, 993–1022 (1993)
14. Smith, A.E., Humphries, M.S.: Evaluation of unsupervised semantic mapping of natural language with Leximancer concept mapping. Behaviour Research Methods 38(2), 262–279 (2006)
15. Landauer, T.K., Laham, D., Rehder, B., Schreiner, M.E.: How well can passage meaning be derived without using word order? A comparison of Latent Semantic Analysis and humans. In: Proc. of the Nineteenth Annual Conference of the Cognitive Science Society, p. 412 (1997)
16. Yin, B., Chen, F.: Towards automatic cognitive load measurement from speech analysis. In: Human-Computer Interaction: HCI Intelligent Multimodal Interaction Environments, pp. 1011–1020. Springer, Berlin (2007)
17. Bergin, R.A., Fors, U.G.H.: Interactive simulated patient—an advanced tool for student-activated learning in medicine and healthcare. Computers & Education 40(4), 361–376 (2003)
18. Stevens, A.: The use of virtual patients to teach medical students history taking and communication skills. American Journal of Surgery 191(6), 806–811 (2006)
19. Kerr, M.P.: A qualitative study of shift handover practice and function from a socio-technical perspective. Journal of Advanced Nursing 37(2), 125–134 (2002)

MILXView: A Medical Imaging, Analysis and Visualization Platform

Neil Burdett, Jurgen Fripp, Pierrick Bourgeat, and Olivier Salvado

The Australian e-Health Research centre, Level 5 – UQ Health Sciences Building, Royal
Brisbane and Women's Hospital, Herston, Queensland 4029, Australia
{Neil Burdett,Jurgen Fripp,Pierrick Bourgeat,
Olivier Salvado}@csiro.au

Abstract. Medical imaging is a vital clinical and research tool that has made
significant strides in the last few decades with impressive advances in
acquisition technology. However, image analysis and interpretation is still
primarily performed manually, and is difficult to automate. In recent years,
major advances have been made that allow more automatic image analysis,
understanding, and interpretation. In this paper we introduce the 3D medical
imaging analysis and visualization platform, MILXView, and present some of
its current and potential usage for medical image analysis, understanding and
interpretation. The paper describes the design of the plugin architecture of the
software application, a general overview of the plugins and the improvements
and additions to the latest version of MILXView. As an example the cortical
thickness estimation plugin (MILXcte) is described for performing automatic
atrophy estimation of brain MRI.

Keywords: MILXView, plugins, AEHRC, ITK, VTK, WxWidgets, voxel,
image, DICOM, CTE.

1 Introduction

In this paper we introduce the MILXView 3D medical imaging analysis and
visualization platform, and its plugin architecture illustrated using Cortical Thickness
Estimate (CTE) MILXcte plugin.

Alzheimer's disease is associated with cortical atrophy, which is monitored via MR
imaging. The MILXcte plugin automates the analysis of the cortical atrophy of a brain.

The etiology of dementia is not well understood, and early diagnosis is difficult as
only subtle biological changes occur in the brain many years before cognitive
symptoms are evident. By the time a loss of cognitive function occurs and a patient is
clinically diagnosed with dementia, irreversible neuronal dysfunction has already
occurred. Obtaining early objective evidence of Alzheimer's disease (AD)
pathological lesions could allow the development and use of appropriate treatments
and care that could result in delayed onset or prevention of AD.

The aim of the Alzheimer's disease project is to develop algorithms and software to
process MRI and PET scans automatically to obtain both qualitatively and

H. Takeda (Ed.): E-Health 2010, IFIP AICT 335, pp. 177–186, 2010.

quantitatively analysis of changes in the brain for use in cross-section and longitudinal studies. Structural information from MRI is combined with functional and molecular information from PET to allow early detection of changes related to disease progression Our goal is to provide a complete assessment of individual patients and to allow the developemt of a better characterisation of Alzheimer's progression, bench-marked against healthy typical brains computed from large longitudinal study databases.

The Biomedical Imaging team at the Australian e-Health Research Centre (AEHRC) is developing a library of image processing algorithms that can be called from our core software platform: MILXView. MILXView is a 3D medical imaging analysis and visualization platform. Individual or large batch of image analysis tasks can be scheduled and run automatically from MILXView.

MILXView is designed and developed to support internal research efforts, and provide a viable and robust environment for clinical applications. It is designed to provide a familiar an intuitive user interface for radiologists and clinicians.

Both analysis and stand-alone visualization packages are usually customized solutions developed by a site to address their specific requirements. The e-Health Research Centre has a diverse set of requirements, from multimodality neuroimaging, musculoskeletal imaging, prostate radiotherapy to small animal imaging. Each of these areas requires specific requirements and analysis methods.

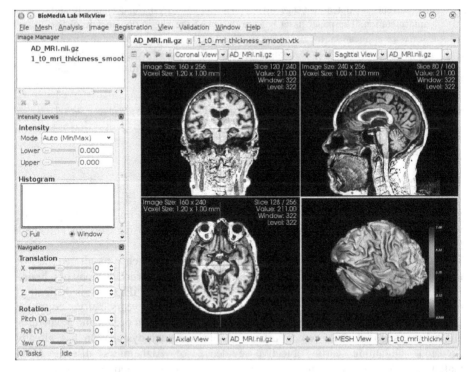

Fig. 1. Viewing an MR image in MILXView showing the orthogonal views (coronal, sagittal, axial) and 3D MESH view illustrating the grey matter cortical thickness calculated for this subject

2 MILXView Architecture

2.1 Subversion and Repository Structure

All MILXView source code and related resources are written in C++ and maintained in a subversion (SVN) repository. This is available for external access by collaborators. The source and header files are located in separate directories, so that certain areas of the code can have restrictive access. Under this scheme, collaborators can checkout include files from the MILXView repository, link against existing software libraries thus allowing to create new plugins that can be incorporated in later versions of MILXView, without distributing proprietary software source code.

Fig.2. shows part of the MILXView subversion repository structure, with a limited set of directories. All components of the MILXView application have the include and source files separated. Underneath each source and include directory, the source code (cxx) or include files (txx and h files) can be found, respectively. The core GUI directories contain the core framework that includes viewer components and basic user interface. The library directory contains the processing code and the plugins directory contains the GUI code of additional visualization tools, user interface panels and complex image analysis functions.

It is important to note that the "plugins" directory holds only the GUI code of the plugin. The "library" directory holds all the algorithmic and processing code. So CTE, for example, has its user interface implemented using the code in "cte" directory of the plugin directory, but all the processing of input files is done within the library directory, "libcte". Thus the "cte" library found in the "plugins" directory links against the "libcte" library, so that information can be passed.

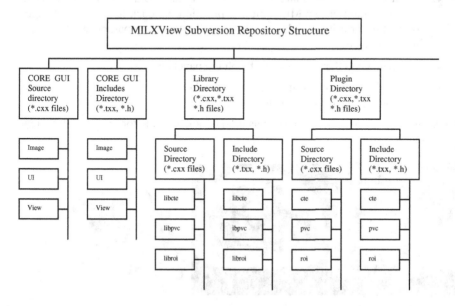

Fig. 2. Section of the MILXView repository structure

2.1 Framework

The MILXView comprises of:

- A core framework that includes viewer components and basic user interface
- A large number of plug-in components that add visualization tools, user interface panels, image analysis functions, complex image or other functionalities. (Fig 3)
- Advanced image processing, segmentation and registration pipelines i.e. co-registration (Fig 3), spatial normalization, partial volume correction, atlas creation, groupwise statistical analysis
- Cutomised plugins for particular applications and anatomical regions i.e. cortical thickness estimation, deep grey-matter segmentation, knee cartilage segmentation, lower-back muscle segmentation, prostate segmentation, breast density estimation.

The framework has been designed this way to enable multiple projects to run simultaneously, developing their own plugins, without interrupting one another. Essentially, plugins are developed as autonomous components, with their own intellectual property (IP). This allows for a large collaborative team of scientists to implement their own algorithms within the same software application, whilst still being able to manage IP. It also enables students to actively participate in the addition of new features.

New plugins GUIs are easily added to the MILXView UI. The following files are used to create a plugin;

- A plugin XML file containing the name, id and library of the plugin. The munu location on the MILXView application, its dock location (Left, right or centre), priority (its place in the menu list) and any parameters that need to be passed in.
- A plugin class that instantiates the plugin panel class.
- A plugin panel class that sets the display and position of buttons and windows using WxWidgets libraries.

Plugins are accessed via the menu options on the toolbar at the top of the MILXView application.

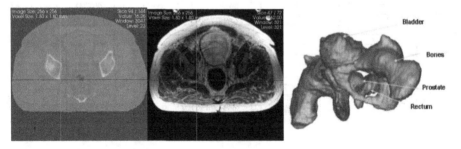

Fig. 3. Example of co-registered CT and MR image in MILXView and surface renderings of automatically obtained segmentations

2.3 Third Party Libraries

MILXView is built upon three open-source, third-party libraries:

- The Insight Segmentation and Registration Toolkit (ITK) [1] is a cross-platform system software toolkit that provides an extensive suite of tool for image analysis, performing registration and segmentation.

- The visualization Toolkit (VTK) [2] which supplies comprehensive rendering and visualization libraries.

- The MILXView GUI and plugins are built using WxWidgets cross platform library.

The above libraries were chosen as they allow MILXView to be freely distributed into the community without affecting the IP present in MILXView. They are also all cross-platform, thus allowing MILXView to be developed and distributed on Linux, Windows and Mac operating systems.

3 MILXView 3.0 Overview

MILXView 3.0 is the latest release of the MILXView platform and includes, but is not limited to, the following core features, improvements and additions:

- Support for import and export of 2D and 3D medical data in all major formats: including Analyze, DICOM, INR, MHD and Nifti.

- Fully user-customizable layout and user interface

- Improved and increased the multi-threaded architecture of the platform including preferences plug-in where the total number of threads and the maximum number of threads per task can be altered. Task manager plug-in showing the status of any running process, their queued, start and running times and their current progress.

- Standard medical imaging functions: windowing, histogram inspection, panning, slicing, zooming, and metadata inspection using a configurable multi-panel and multi-tab viewer

- 3D visualization tools: maximum intensity projection, volume and surface rendering, 3D multi-slicing screenshot, volume rendering, color map, overlay, blending, checkerboard. Loading, saving, visualization, registration and manipulation of 3D polygon meshes.

- Data manipulation in voxel or scanner space: manual rotation scaling, zooming and translation. Navigation through multiple datasets simultaneously. Manual linking and registration of two or more volumetric images.

4 A Typical Plugin - Cortical Thickness Estimate (CTE) Plugin

MILXView has forty plugins (core and others). The CTE plugin (MILXcte) is one such plugin.

Neurodegenerative diseases such as Alzheimer's are often associated with loss of gray matter in the cortex of the brain. It is therefore necessary to quantify the volume loss of the tissue and/or the cortical thickness. This can be used for one patient as a diagnostic step, or for a database of images during longitudinal studies to assess the effect of a therapy, or the progression of a disease.

Estimating the thickness of the cortex involves many image processing steps such as interpolation, filtering, registration, etc. Such a processing pipeline requires some parameters to be set and then be run on all the images (typically several hundred) present in a database. We have implemented a method to perform this computation and designed a specific plugin: MILXcte.

Clinicians are thus meant to use MILXcte, and ideally they need to select one or multiple images as inputs and run the computation as a batch processing task, which could take several hours per individual image. The results are multiple:

- New images generated after some of the processing steps, either as visual check, or because the resulting image has new information;

- Spreadsheet with numbers, in this case the thickness of the cortex for each anatomical regions of the brain;

- Custom visualization to display information hard to visually analyzed, in this case the display as a color map of the cortical thickness over the surface of the brain.

Plugins used with MILXView have a similar user interface and follow similar conventions. At the top of each plugin there are a number of tabs that hold configurable values.

Fig. 4. CTE Input (left) and template (right) Files

A clinician, in most cases, will want to add one or more images and then retrieve the result. However, scientists may want to set a variety of values. Plugins incorporated into MILXView are designed to handle both of these cases.

Generally a user will need only to add one or more image input files (see Fig. 3 below left) and then click on the "Process" button. Default values will be submitted for processing, and a short time later a result will be shown. This is the case for the MILXcte plugin. However, a scientist (or clinician) may wish to change the default values in which case they will select a tab on the plugin and change the value accordingly.

In the CTE plugin, for example, a number of selections can be altered before the CTE plugin is executed. The user can add and remove files individually using the "Add File(s)" and "Remove" buttons on the "Input Files" panel or files can be imported from a list and exported to a list, using the appropriate buttons. The same can be done for the required templates [3, 4] from the Atlas, White Matter Priors, Grey Matter Priors, Cerebrospinal Fluid (CSF) Priors, Anatomical Automatic Labelling atlas (AAL) [7] and Hippocampus mask as shown below:

The "Results" tab allows the user to specify the output directory for the CTE results, and the "Advanced" tab (shown below) allows the user to select a number of options including:

- Preprocessing
- Segmentation
- Partial Volume Estimation
- CTE Topology Correction
- Thickness Estimation
- 3D rendering

The user can view the results they are interested in using the "View" tab (shown below).

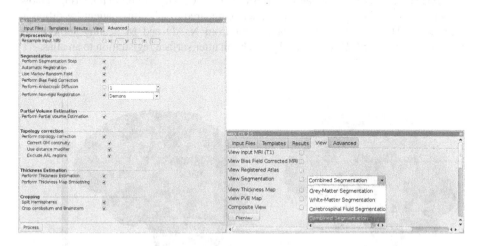

Fig. 5. Advanced (left) and View tab (right) options

As previously stated the user selects the results they want to view from the view tab and clicks on the "Display button". Sample results are shown below.

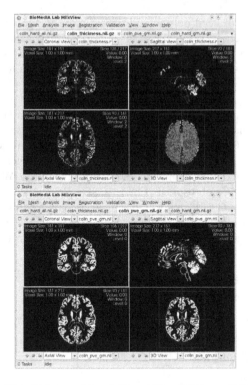

Fig. 6. View Thickness Map (left) and View PVE map [11] (right)

The CTE process also generates a mesh view (Fig. 6). The two brain renderings below show the average thickness for an AD patient compared to a healthy patient for different brain areas. They use an average atlas built from N AD and M healthy subjects by groupwise averaging CTE of each subject's brain after surface registration to an atlas.

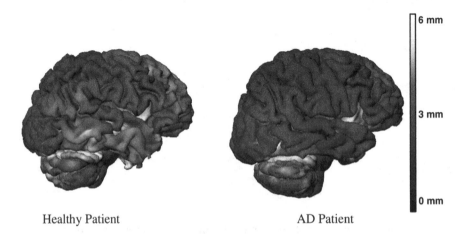

Healthy Patient   AD Patient

Fig. 7. Comparison of cortical thickness of a healthy patient and an Alzheimer's Disease patient

5 Conclusions

Our vision is to provide clinicians with a software tool easy to use and fully automatic. The physicians would read the scans from a patient, and we would compute several quantitative measurements from the images otherwise hard or impossible for a human to obtain. From our study on the Australian Imaging, Biomarker and Lifestyle cluster study (AIBL) patients we will be able to benchmark each individual patient against the typical age-matched individual and provide to physicians relevant statistics. This kind of information should be valuable not only to help in treatment planning of individual patients, but also to help design therapies and test scientific hypothesis.

Ongoing work includes increasing unit test code coverage, optimizing the code and checking for memory leaks, improving performance, validating the framework for research suitability and adding to the visualization techniques and plug-ins. Also on the road map are Microsoft Windows and Apple Macintosh versions.

References

1. Ibanez, L., Schroeder, W., Ng, L., Cates, J.: The ITK Software Guide, 2nd edn., Kitware (2007)
2. Schroeder, W., Martin, K., Lorensen, B.: The Visualization Toolkit, 4th edn., Kitware (2006)
3. Acosta, O., Bourgeat, P., Zuluaga, M.A., Fripp, J., Salvado, O.: Automated voxel-based 3D cortical thickness measurement in a combined Lagrangian-Eulerian PDE approach using partial volume maps. Medical Image Analysis (2009) doi:10.1016/j.media.2009.07.003
4. Rueda, A., Acosta, O., Bourgeat, P., Fripp, J., Dowson, N.: Partial Volume Estimation Of Brain Cortex From Mri Using Topology-Corrected Segmentation. In: 2009 IEEE International Symposium on Biomedical Imaging: From Nano to Macro, Boston, Massachusetts, USA, June, pp. 133–136 (2009)
5. Rousset, O.G., Ma, Y., Wong, D.F., Evans, A.C.: Pixel- versus region-based partial volume correction in PET. In: Carson, R., Herscovitch, P., Daube-Witherspoon, M. (eds.) Quantitative Functional Brain Imaging with Positron Emission Tomography, pp. 67–75. Academic Press, San Diego (1998)
6. Bourgeat, P., Chételat, G., Villemagne, V., Fripp, J., Raniga, P., Pike, K., Acosta, O., Szoeke, C., Ourselin, S., Ames, D., Ellis, K., Martins, R., Masters, C., Rowe, C., Salvado, O., The AIBL Research Group: AB burden in the temporal neocortex is related to hippocampal atrophy in elderly subjects without dementia. Neurology 74(2), 121–127 (2010)
7. Acosta, O., Bourgeat, P., Zuluaga, M.A., Fripp, J., Salvado, O., Ourselin, S.: Automated voxel-based 3D cortical thickness measurement in a combined Lagrangian-Eulerian PDE approach using partial volume maps. Medical Image Analysis 13(5), 730–743 (2009)
8. Raniga, P., Bourgeat, P., Fripp, J., Acosta, O., Villemagne, V., Rowe, C., Masters, C., Jones, G., O'Keefe, G., Salvado, O., Ourselin, S.: Automated ^{11}C-PiB Standardized Uptake Value Ratio. Academic Radiology 15(11), 1376–1389 (2008)
9. Fripp, J., Bourgeat, P., Acosta, O., Raniga, P., Modat, M., Pike, K.E., Jones, G., O'Keefe, G., Masters, C.L., Ames, D., Ellis, K.A., Maruff, P., Currie, J., Villemagne, V.L., Rowe, C.C., Salvado, O., Ourselin, S.: Appearance Modeling of 11C PiB PET images: Characterizing amyloid deposition in Alzheimer's disease, mild cognitive impairment and healthy aging. NeuroImage 43(3), 430–439 (2008) Note: CD-ROM paper number 234 TH-PM

10. Diep, T.-M., Bourgeat, P., Ourselin, S.: Efficient Use of Cerebral Cortical Thickness to Correct Brain MR Segmentation. In: IEEE International Symposium on Biomedical Imaging: From Nano to Macro, Washington DC, USA, April 2007, pp. 592–595. IEEE, Los Alamitos (2007)
11. Zuluaga, M., Acosta, O., Bourgeat, P., Salvado, O., Hernandez, M., Ourselin, S.: Cortical Thickness Measurement from Magnetic Resonance Images Using Partial Volume Estimation. In: Proceedings of SPIE: Image Processing, San Diego, USA, February 2008, vol. 6914, p. 8 (2008)

Advanced Telemedicine System Using 3G Cellular Networks and Agent Technology

Golam Sorwar[1] and Ameer Ali[2]

[1] School of Commerce and Management, Southern Cross University
NSW 2450, Australia
golam.sorwar@scu.edu.au
[2] Department of Computer Science and Engineering, East West University
Dhaka, Bangladesh
ameer7302002@yahoo.com

Abstract. The world's ageing population and prevalence of chronic diseases have lead to high demand for healthcare services. Telemedicine systems based on modern information and communication technology are expected to play a pivotal role in alleviating the pressure on health care services. Fortunately there have been a rapid advanced in technologies including wireless communication especially the third generation network (3G), Internet, software agent and health care devices in terms of mobility, speed and communication. However the current systems are limited in terms of mobility, flexibility and privacy issues. More over the existing solution does not provide any seamless integration of various healthcare providers to provide an effective and efficient team-based continuous care services for patients with chronic illness who prefer to stay in a community based setting. In this paper, we present a generic mobile health monitoring system based on 3G mobile network and software-agent which involves a set of intelligent agents. These software agents will work as human agents in collaborating among different health care professionals for offering team-based medical services. The proposed system can be implemented in a number of situations in a mobile environment.

Keywords: Telemedicine, cellular networks, multi-agent system.

1 Introduction

Telemedicine is increasingly gaining popularity due to its high potential for cost savings and increased efficiency in healthcare. Expert medical care through telemedicine can significantly improve the health care facilities at rural and remote locations. Advanced wireless and networking technologies coupled with recent advances in biotechnology, biosensors and software engineering has enabled the promising growth in telemedicine health care systems. These advances will have strong impact on some of the current health care services together with reshaping the workflow and practices in the delivery systems of these services [1], [2].

The widespread use and availability of wireless systems and the Internet brought new opportunities for public and healthcare providers to efficiently access the medical

H. Takeda (Ed.): E-Health 2010, IFIP AICT 335, pp. 187–197, 2010.
© IFIP International Federation for Information Processing 2010

services and information with enhanced technological tools. Most recent advancements in wireless communications systems, namely 3G mobile networks and WiMAX broadband access now have the potential to significantly enhance telemedicine services by creating a flexible and heterogeneous network within an end-to-end telemedicine framework. The data rates of current 3G networks are much higher than those of current 2G cellular systems. Furthermore, the fast growth of mobile systems and the extensive acceptance of cellular technology signify that 3G mobile phone services are an exciting new application domain for these services.

A number of emergency telemedicine solution, particularly remote monitoring, [3[, [4], [5], [6], [7], [8] have been proposed by adopting this emerging 3G network. Though these systems provide a promising opportunity, they are very limited in terms of the flexibility and application diversities. More importantly, they offer very limited communication facilities among a diverse group of service providers. In real world, patient management and medical decision making involves collaboration between a number of health professionals such as nurses, general practitioners, specialist consultants, paramedics, the patients and patients' career and social worker. This is particularly true for chronic diseases where the follow up takes place over a long period of time involving a number of people. Moreover, most of these systems do not have ability to process, analysis and inform patient locally; medical data was processed by data processing servers located remotely.

In order to model collaborative decision-making and to provide the opportunity for mobile device to analysis the results and make some recommendation locally, multi-agent systems provide a suitable solution. More recently, researchers have successfully attempted at developing systems in health care domains using this approach [9], [10]. However, the proposed systems are specific application oriented. For example, [9] proposes an agent-based e-health hospital information management system to improve the efficiency of the in-hospital healthcare services. Chan [10] proposes a multi-agent based e-heath monitoring framework to improve the doctor-patient interaction spanning multiple remote locations and hospitals. The main drawbacks of this system are: (1) limited video conferencing facilities, (2) not flexible to switch automatically from non-emergence to emergence situation, and (3) no involvement of other healthcare and technical services such as 24-hour emergency service, the out of hours GP services or technician for biomedical devices functional status monitoring. Integration with social services will often be necessary as a significant number of elderly people are also frail and require daily support, or suffer from dementia.

Addressing some of these issues, this paper proposes an advanced telemedicine framework based on the 3G cellular networks and the software-agent that seamlessly allows a team-based approach in information sharing and collaborating in decision making across different health care sectors, and that offers maximum continuity of care for the patient.

This paper is organized as follows: Section 2 presents possible heath care service scenarios. Section 3 gives an overview of the proposed system whereas Section 4 details the implementation model of the system. Section 5 presents a multi-agent based software model to be used in the proposed system while Section 6 concludes the paper.

2 Possible Healthcare Services

The proposed model is designed with the possible healthcare scenarios or service platforms that are presented in the subsequent sections.

2.1 General Web-Based E-Medicine and Treatment

In a web-based e-medicine and treatment service, the patient will be able to log into a website dedicated for this service and be able to access his/her health records together with previous history. In this system, three entities like patient, doctor and the pharmacist will be responsible for the success of this service platform. Their individual responsibilities and interaction with the system is stated below.

Patient: Firstly, a patient will register with this website will his/her full information and then provide the system with following information: (i) regular update of the patient condition, (ii) exercise details, (iii) update some vital parameters in regular basis that are related to patients, (iv) update of medication reactions, and (v) maintain appointment with the doctor for meeting such as video conferencing with the doctor.

Doctor: A doctor associated with a patient will do the followings: (i) regular monitoring of patient record and updates, (ii) updating the medication or treatment with change of the patient condition, and (iii) Updating the prescription for the patient.

Pharmacist: A pharmacist associated with the patient will do the followings: (i) regular monitoring of patient medication updates and (ii) post a confirmation of the availability of new medicines.

2.2 Home Monitoring

The senior citizens, who are suffering for chronic diseases, need constant assistance from the doctors and nurses. Moreover, the patients who are being discharged from the hospital early often require additional healthcare services and monitoring of their health status at home. Furthermore, current scenario of shortage of doctors for providing emergency operation to all patients, lack of hospital beds, and insufficient medical facilities in health care sector with the high expense involved in conventional hospital treatments, homecare monitoring is a promising telemedicine solution [11]. Home monitoring consists of two sub-service scenarios: a) regular monitoring and b) emergency monitoring. In regular monitoring system, the vital signs such as ECG, SPO2, and blood pressure can be monitored periodically in non-real-time (NRT) store-and-forward mode from the patient unit (home) to the central patient health record system (PHR) at the hospital while in an emergency home monitoring system, the patients at critical medical condition are treated in real-time (RT) monitoring mode i.e. the patient's vital signs are transmitted to the PHR in RT [12]. If any vital signs will be in alarming condition an alert message will be transmitted to PHR and from the PHR to the doctor unit. The doctor will contact with the nurse or the relatives of the patient with the facility of Video Conferencing, live video, and image transmission. In regular monitoring, if the patient condition becomes critical, the monitoring will be converted to emergency mode and hence does all the necessary actions according to emergency mode.

2.3 Community Care/Rural Health Centres

Patients at the community care and rural health centres do not often get necessary treatment because of the lack of professional doctors and the high care facilities. Applying telemedicine model, the community care patients can get high care medical support and professional doctor's treatment from the central/developed hospitals and specialist doctors. The services may range from regular treatment to emergency monitoring of patients in RT with the facilities like video conferencing between the doctor at central hospital and nurse/social worker attending the patient in the community care.

2.4 Pre-hospital Emergency Ambulance Service

Every year more than thousands of people die in the car accidents. Urgent initial pre-hospital treatment is crucial for the savings of severely injured people. In a study performed in UK, 91% of the people who die from cardiac arrest, do so outside the hospital due to lack of immediate treatment [13]. Pre-hospital emergency ambulance service can be seen as possible solution to these problems. In this emergency service, the ambulance should be equipped with necessary equipments for transferring patient data and video in RT mode through the 3G network from the ambulance to the doctors present in the hospital. The paramedics in the ambulance can initiate video conferencing with the doctors at hospital so that they can get best support and guidance from the specialist doctors in hospitals.

2.5 ICU Patient Care

Suddenly, a patient condition in the ICU may become worse. If the doctor is not at the treatment room in order to attend a meeting outside the hospital, in that situation the emergency ICU patient care may cause lifesaving of the patients. In emergency ICU care, the doctor can monitor the patient status from his mobile/notebook/Laptop in RT/NRT mode to give the attending nurse correct instructions for the savings of the patient.

3 Proposed System Model

This work aims at providing effective and mobile solutions to all kinds of healthcare needs, discussed in previous section, for both emergency and regular using 3G networks and Internet. Therefore, it is essential to develop an integrated, compact, reliable and easy to use telemedicine system which is able to provide all kinds healthcare supports that is needed to rural or remote patients outside the hospital ranging from simple regular health check-up to emergency care to the patients together with real time monitoring and care from distance.

This section presents a newly proposed telemedicine model based on *3G* cellular networks and agent-based technology. The block diagram of the respective frame work of the proposed model is depicted in Fig. 1. The proposed model is divided into the following units including patient unit, doctors unit, patient health record (PHR) database unit, technician unit and Social worker unit. Each of the modules is now detailed in the following section.

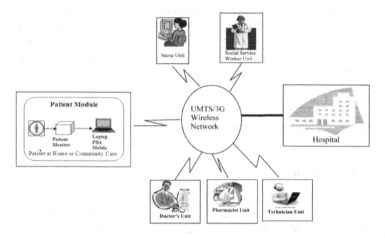

Fig. 1. Overview of the proposed System

3.1 Patient Unit

The patient unit which may be located in an ambulance, home or rural health care centres in remote areas or any other outdoor environment is implemented either on a laptop, desktop PC, mobile phone, or note book depending on the availability. Patient units which consist of vital sign monitors connected with computers/mobile phone collect and process vital medical data about patients, and transmit them through a 3G wireless link to the specialist unit which is connected to either a desktop computer within the existing hospital network or a mobile phone with 3G access capability at the physician's disposal. This enables the physicians to access the collected patient's data in a real-time mode or store-and-forward mode. After the measurement session, the acquired data can be transmitted to a database for later review and storage. For a vital signal acquisition, widely available off-the-shelf vital signal monitors will be used.

3.2 Doctors Unit

The doctors unit which may be located in a hospital, home or the outdoor environment, can be implemented like patients unit mentioned in Section 3.1 on a laptop, desk PC, mobile phone, or notebook. The specialist's or doctor's unit which is connected to either a fixed computer within an existing hospital network or a mobile phone with 3G access capability at the physician's hand receives the patient's medical data and analyses these data to provide the patients with meaningful information. As mentioned in Section 3.1, the doctors can access the collected patient's data in a RT mode or store-and-forward mode. If necessary the doctors can initiate real time video conferencing session with the patient unit or with other doctors.

3.3 Patient Health Record Database Unit

All the biological signals and patient's data are stored in the patient health record (PHR) database unit. These data are periodically sent from the patient unit to the PHR. This unit generates the alerts to the doctors for the emergency conditions either by an alert message from the patient unit or by analysing the patient data if it finds out some critical problem.

3.4 Technician Unit

The technician unit keeps track of the device error alert messages from the patient units.

3.5 Social Worker Unit

Integration with social services will often be necessary as a significant number of elderly people are also frail and require daily support, or suffer from dementia. Social Services can also be required to oversee the environmental issues and social alarms, and ideally these should be integrated with medical monitoring, as similar patient groups are involved.

3.6 Pharmacist Unit

The pharmacist unit will reside in a hospital or drug store or outdoor environment. This unit receives and monitors the medications for a patient and the outcome or results of applying the medicines. It operates through a web interface.

4 Implementation

The proposed model will provide the following RT/NRT services/operations between its various functional units as text file, image, audio, chat, whiteboard and web as shown in Fig. 2.

This system will follow a multi-collaborative design [8] and implement new RT multimedia features available for 3G wireless networks. Session Initiation Protocol (SIP) is chosen as the service control protocol along with messages defined specifically for the Internet Multimedia system (IMS) by the 3rd Generation Partnership Project (3GPP). Communication between the patient unit and one or more specialist units will take place in the form of multi-collaborative sessions through various network environments supporting various multimedia traffics. The conference model chosen is the one used in [8], [14] that consists of a central unit (CU) which is responsible for maintaining integration between different units. During the conference, each participant unit will have dialog established with the CU and the CU will ensure the media streams used in the conference are available to the appropriate users. The signals and the session management are detailed in the next section.

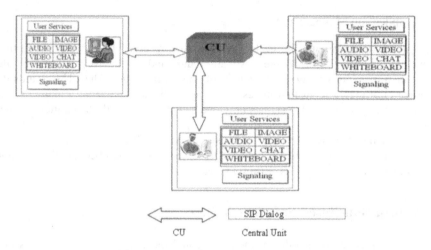

Fig. 2. Systems user services architecture

4.1 Signaling and Session Management

The SIP protocol performs signaling in the conference system by first initiating a SIP dialog with the CU. Different services are described by the use of Session Description Protocol (SDP) messages. To establish and maintain the SIP dialogs, the each unit involved in the conference is assigned a SIP user agent (UA) with a slightly modified version in CU to allow multiple dialogs concurrently.

Conference establishment, maintenance and termination are performed by the exchange of SIP messages between the conference participants. When a user enters the conference it first establishes a SIP dialog with the CU. Within the conference the different users exchange SIP messages between themselves and with the CU to vary conference characteristics and to allow for the management of the conference system. Similarly to conference joining, when a user wants to leave the conference it exchanges necessary messages with the CU for this purpose. SIP messages also carry the SDP messages which describe various medical user services. Since the CU may come to failure the users are also allowed to establish point to point sessions between them.

4.2 User Services Management

The user services in this proposed system is associated with one or more information which are going to be shared in the system. The system has services to share audio, video, still images, medical data (e.g., ECG, SPO2, blood sugar etc.), chat, electronic whiteboard and web service to access information retained in the database. There are also services for exchanging control information. Each of the medical information is associated with a user service. Each user service uses a transport according to their needs. The real-time services such as audio, video, medical data use the real-time protocol (RTP) whereas NRT services use the transmission control protocol (TCP).

4.3 Application Management

The information generated by each service is first received by the CU which then forwards this information to the destination unit and in the way defined by the application management service by means of control messages. The CU forwards the information it receives but first mixes all the audio signals and sends a unique signal to each user. In case of video signals only one signal is sent to all the entities at given moment.

The user interface will be developed using J2SE & J2ME development tools [4]. For implementation purposes, Oracle or SQL server will be used because they support data mining techniques such as clustering, decision tree [4].

5 Multi-agent Based Software Model

Providing effective and intelligent monitoring and medical care to the patients in a timely manner, and at the same time providing the doctors with decision support system which will enable them to more efficient with their tasks in the telemedicine system is of paramount importance. This will also ensure frequent patient-doctor interaction to maximize the system's utility. Towards this goal, it is necessary to develop intelligent management software for the system. A very good solution to the management software issue is the intelligent software agent [9-10], [15] which is capable of acting exactly in order to accomplish tasks with some reasoning or planning. To support telemedicine system efficiently it is necessary that the following requirements are met by the software system: (a) anticipating the information need for the users and delivering it to the user in a periodic and/or timely manner, (b) providing support for communication, coordination and cooperation among the various entities in the system such as doctors, nurses, patients and relatives, pharmacists, technicians, social service workers who are involved in the process of maintaining and delivering the health care services, (c) providing support for collaborative decision making among various entities involved in this health care system distributed information and knowledge sources, (d) relieving the people involved in the system from management of routine tasks, and (e) contributing in the automation process of the overall system [16].

The model designed especially for the 3G based telemedicine framework which depicted in Fig. 3 is based on the models in [9], [16]. This proposal aims at designing software agents (An intelligent agent is defined as one that is capable of flexible autonomous action to meet its design objectives [17]) which will work on behalf of human agents with similar characteristics. In other words, our solution delegates daily routine tasks performed by human agents to software agents. In this new approach, each actor is assigned a personalized software agent who acts as his personal human agent [9].

The software model includes an agent for each of these entities: patients, nurses, doctors (general or specialist), pharmacist and technician. These entities communicate with each other through the 3G network. Therefore, there are 7 different types of software agents in our model. They are Patient Agent (PA), Doctor Agent (DA),

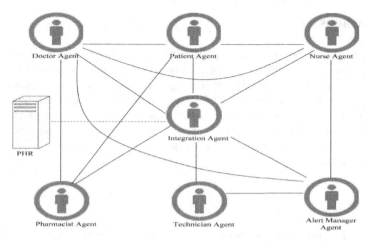

Fig. 3. Software model for advanced telemedicine framework

Nurse Agent (NA), Pharmacist Agent (PHA), Technician Agent (TA), Alert Manager Agent (AMA), and Integration Agent (IA). The PA is capable of carrying patient's data and to move the data to Patient Health Record (PHR) server where it interacts with the IA and requests IA to submit the data for the appropriate patient record. PA can also retrieve the patient's medical history records from the PHR database through the IA. PA also monitors vital signals received from the various patient side equipments and is capable of determining whether an alarm is false or real one and subsequently can forward the alert to appropriate agent (NA, DA, AMA). The IA has the ability to detect if the patient's situation is critical based on the medical data and predefined criteria, and it immediately sends an alarm to the NA which in turns notifies the nurse when the patient's medical data is abnormal. Simultaneously IA also sends the alarm notification to the AMA which keeps track of the alerts in the system. If the patient's situation becomes critical below some threshold criteria and the nurse is unable to make a decision, NA automatically forwards the alarm to the DA with a notification to the AMA. NA also provides the nurse with the summary of information of the patients associated with the nurse. The DA interacts with PA to get the required data and make decisions accordingly. DA keeps track of the patients currently under the doctor's supervision, and also provides the doctor with summary of his patients' conditions. It also keeps track of the alert messages from various PA sorts and presents them to the doctor in the order of urgency. Similarly, when the PA or DA receives device failure alert it will immediately forward the alert to the AMA and subsequently to TA where TA provides a notification to the technician. TA also keeps track of the device alerts and summarizes and presents them to the technician in some order. AMA monitors and keeps track of the alerts between different agents. The IA plays the central role and manages the total agent based architecture. It also keeps control of the PHR database. The PHA keeps tracks of the medication from the DA to PA. Whenever PA sets an alarm of medicine need to the PHA and PHA responses and then discards the alarm from its repository. Furthermore, NA, PA, DA can interact with IA and PHR at anytime with real time responses. With the agent based model presented, medical services can be provided instantly, remotely with convenience.

6 Conclusions

This paper has presented an advanced 3G network and agent-oriented approach to developing automatic architecture for a generic telemedicine system to address the ever increasing complexity in next-generation telehealth systems. The proposed system would provide flexible way of delivering care to patients than is currently available in a number of healthcare scenarios or service platforms in rural, remote and emergency settings as well as in ambulance and home care. Further works are in progress to develop a prototype and to test the system under realistic scenarios.

References

1. Kyriacou, E., Pavlopoulos, S., Berler, A., Neophytou, M., Bourka, A., Georgoulas, A., Anagnostaki, A., Karayiannis, D., Schizas, C., Pattichis, C., Andreou, A., Koutsouris, D.: Multi-purpose HealthCare Telemedicine Systems with mobile communication link support. Biomedical Engineering Online 2(7). BioMed Central Ltd. (2003)
2. Kyriacou, E., Pattichis, M.S., Pattchis, C.S., Panayides, A., Pitsillides, A.: m-Health e-Emergency Systems: Current Status and Future Directions. IEEE Antennas and Propagation Magazine 49(1), 216–231 (2007)
3. Leijdekkers, P., Gay, V.: Personal Heart Monitoring System Using Smart Phones To Detect Life Threatening Arrhythmias. In: 19th IEEE International Symposium on Computer-Based Medical Systems, Salt Lake City, Utah, pp. 157–164 (2006)
4. Sufi, F., Fang, V., Mahmoud, S.S., Cosic, I.: A Mobile Phone Based Intelligent Telemonitoring Platform. In: 3rd IEEE-EMBS International Summer School and Symposium on Medical Devices and Biosensors, Cambridge, MA, pp. 101–104 (2006)
5. Zhang, P., Kogure, Y., Matsuoka, H., Akutagawa, M., Kinouchi, Y., Zhang, Q.: A Remote Patient Monitoring System Using a Java-enabled 3G Mobile Phone. In: 29th Annual Conference of the IEEE EMBS, Lyon, pp. 3713–3716 (2007)
6. Chu, Y., Ganz, A.: A Mobile Teletrauma System Using 3G Networks. IEEE Trans. on Information Technology in Biomedicine 8(4), 456–462 (2004)
7. Kogure, Y., Matsuoka, H., Kinouchi, Y., Akutagawa, M.: The Development of a Remote Patient Monitoring System using Java-enabled Mobile Phones. In: 27th Annual Conference of IEEE Engineering in Medicine and Biology, pp. 2157–2160 (2005)
8. Navarro, E.A.V., Mas, J.R., Navajas, J.F.: Enhanced 3G-Based m-Health System. In: IEEE Eurocon 2005, pp. 1332–1335. BioMed. Central Ltd. (2005)
9. Nguyen, M.T., Fuhrer, P., Rocha, J.P.: Enhancing E-Health Information Systems with Agent Technology. Int. J. of Telemedicine and Application (2009)
10. Chan, V., Ray, P., Parameswaran, N.: Mobile e-Health monitoring: an agent-based approach. Comm. IET 2(2), 223–230 (2008)
11. Figueredo, M.V.M., Dias, J.S.: Mobile Telemedicine System for Home Care and Patient Monitoring. In: 26th Annual Conference of the IEEE EMBS, San Francisco, CA, pp. 3387–3390 (2004)
12. Istepanian, R.H., Laxminarayan, S., Pattichis, C.S.: M-Health: Emerging Mobile Health Systems. Springer, New York (2006)
13. Sandler, D.: A Call to needle times after acute myocardial infraction. BMJ (1999)

14. Rosenberg, J.: A Framework for Conferencing with the Session Initiation Protocol. Internet draft (2004)
15. Nwana, H.: Software Agents: An Overview. The Knowledge Engineering Review 11(3), 205–244 (1996)
16. Liu, P.R., Meng, M.Q.H., Tong, F.F.L., Chen, X.J., Liu, P.X.: A 3G based Network Solution to the Telehealthcare Robotic System. In: 6th World Congress on Intelligent Control and Automation, pp. 381–385. IEEE Press, Dalian (2006)
17. Chan, V.: 'Mobile health monitoring'. Thesis Presented in the University of New South Wales (2006)

User Adaptivity of Biotelemetric System for ECG Measurement and Visualization

Dalibor Janckulik, Leona Motalova, and Ondrej Krejcar

VSB Technical University of Ostrava, Center for Applied Cybernetics, Department of
Measurement and Control, Faculty of Electrical Engineering and Computer Science, 17.
Listopadu 15, 70833 Ostrava Poruba, Czech Republic
Dalibor.Janckulik@hotmail.com, Leona.Motalova@gmail.com,
Ondrej.Krejcar@remoteworld.net

Abstract. Users want a simple, intuitive and graphically attractive interface. On
the other hand, it is necessary to change dynamically the user´s experience as
they use what best viewing area of the device. The biomedical data are not all
the latest knowledge in the area. Our work focuses on exploring the possibilities
and the revelation of any deficiencies in the currently used procedures and
technologies. The main area of interest of our biotelemetric system is to provide
solution which can be used in different areas of health care and which will be
available through PDAs, web browsers or desktop clients. In paper we deals
with a problem of visualization of measured ECG signal on mobile devices in
Real Time as well as with a solution how to solve a problem of unsuccessful
data processing on desktop or server.

Keywords: Real Time, PDA, Embedded Device, Biotelemetry, ECG.

1 Introduction

The basic idea is to create a system that controls important information about the state
of a wheelchair-bound person (monitoring of ECG and pulse in early phases, then
other optional values like temperature or oxidation of blood etc.), his situation in time
and place (GPS) and an axis tilt of his body or wheelchair (2axis accelerometer).
Values are measured with the existing equipment, which communicates with the
module for processing via Bluetooth wireless communication technology. Most of the
data is processed directly in PDA or Embedded equipment to a form that is
acceptable for simple visualization. The next problem is about data processing is ECG
packets parsing which can't be processed with real-time response on PDA or
embedded device. This restriction can be solved trough the solutions proposed as
software in (Section 3) also as hardware solution in (Section 4). The sample
architecture of the developed system is sketched on (Fig. 1).

User adaptivity of the system is an important part of different platforms to work
with biomedical data. GUI should be realigned according to various parameters and
sensed perceptions so that what at first glance most of describing the situation. Our
system reacted too to stimuli from the hardware used by devices such as light sensors,

H. Takeda (Ed.): E-Health 2010, IFIP AICT 335, pp. 198–209, 2010.

accelerometers, GPS and GSM module. The main aim of the platform for patients' bio-parameters monitoring is to offer a solution providing services to help and make full health care more efficient. Physicians and other medical staff will not be forced to make difficult and manual work including unending paperwork, but they will be able to focus on the patients and their problems. All data will be accessible almost anytime anywhere through special applications designated for portable devices web browser or desktop clients and any changes will be made immediately at disposal to medical staff based on the security clearance.

For the physicians is important see the data directly and clearly on the maximum possible viewing area. This problem can be solved by dynamical programming, when we can load only important controls and functional code from database and via dynamicaly controls hiding in GUI on presentation layer. All this possibilities are described in the following sections.

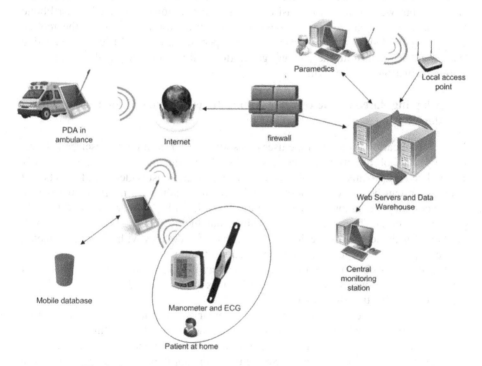

Fig. 1. Sample architecture of one option of system implementation

From the database perspective and bio-signals analyses are the data are stored and automatically analyzed by simply neuronal network.

2 The User Adaptivity of the System

The user adaptivity of the system can be divided into several areas:

- Interaction with the user is based on:
    o used equipment
    o application usage
    o used environment
- Interaction with hardware devices based on the usage of applications

2.1 Adapting Based on the Used Equipment

The application responds as the most of applications on the resolution imaging devices - displays – on the placement of elements. For client applications, where user fills in or views his personal records, the application will behave in different ways while running on personal computer or running on mobile devices such as PDAs with QVGA, VGA or WVGA resolution. For the mobile platform many controls are not available, but we also need to adjust the controls for equipment or touch SmartPhone with a keyboard. Features in one desktop application form must be in the mobile application divided into logical groups. Elderly people may have difficulties with fine resolution and small font, the younger generation will not mind that and we can put in more information into the form.

2.2 Adapting Based on the Usage of Applications in Terms of Interaction with the User

A client application for an average user is responsible for, as already described above, showing data of the user. In the case of desktop, the monitor cannot be easily manipulated and rotated as we like it. In the case of the most wide-spread tablets text information can be shown in more natural form for reading (in height of the book). On the contrary, the graph is better to be displayed in width, so that the longest record gets on the screen. The same goes for using your mobile PDA. This functionality is available for devices with accelerometer, or even for devices without accelerometer, whose display can be rotated by the user's request button.

One of the novelties is a frequently used battery indicator color change. This is for the battery of mobile devices (tablets, PDA) as well as for the battery of device designed for collecting data (ECG).

Other features are associated with the popular monitoring of heart rate during exercise. The ECG, which we get we can determine the heart rate. Blue ECG device detects a pulse back. The frequencies of training rate are obtained from the users' data and each zone is indicated by color. So the user can simply by a glance get to know in which zone his heart works.

2.3 Adaptation Based on the Environment

Here the user interface adaptation takes place according to the conditions in which it is used, at night in hospitals we do not want the monitor to light and be disruptive, but it must be legible. The solution is to switch the colors GUI so that the contrast ratio of application isn't extremely disturbed. The influence is the backlight display device that makes it possible.

2.4 Interaction with Hardware

If the user views only historical records, it does not make any sense to have the Bluetooth on; data transfer is realized using WiFi or GPRS. Compression is related, or transfer of requested data. GPRS is slow, so we transfer only data that the user actually requested, for our WiFi connection bitrates primarily confined. Shutting down the unneeded hardware is today addressed for mobile devices, where device endurance is at one of the first places.

3 Developed Software Parts of Platform

Complete proposition of solution and implementation of the patient's biotelemetry platform oriented for user adaptivity requires determination and teamwork. Every single part of the architecture has to be designed for easy application and connectivity without user extra effort, but user must be able to use given solution easily and effectively. Crucial parts of the whole architecture are network servers, database servers and client applications run-able from standard desktop operating system and client applications for Windows CE based mobile devices.

3.1 Server Part

Database background of solution is built on Microsoft SQL server. One server provides only data warehouse with stored procedures, which represent data interface for other application parts. There are stored all data of medical staff and patients. Data of patients include different records such as diagnosis, treatment progress or data which are results of measuring by small portable devices designated to home care. These data represent the greatest problem, because amount of these data rapidly increase with increasing amount of patients. Due to this fact database servers are very loaded. The stored procedures (programmed by Transact-SQL language) serve basic data parsing on weak mobile devices, which have too much problems with parsing and subsequently visualization of measured data. At this time our team is focused on implementation of analytical and reporting parts for more detailed analysis of measured/collected data. Business intelligence part of SQL server is a powerful tool which allows us to create reports faster than C# application on client side.

The only possibility of running our application on all platforms is an implementation of a view and controller layer as web application. We use two different technologies. ASP.NET is purely for web application (browser independent) and for web services. The second technology is Silverlight (only for Internet Explorer and Mozilla Firefox). Silverlight application is possible to run in Out-of-Browser mode.

In order to run a web server, an operating system supporting IIS (Internet Information Services) is needed. IIS allow to users to connect to the web server by the HTTP protocol. The web service transfers data between the server and PDA/Embedded devices. Web service also read the data, sends acknowledgments, and stores the data in the database. The service is built upon ASP.NET 2.0 technology. The SOAP protocol is used for the transport of XML data.

Methods that devices communicating with the web service can use include:

- receiving measured data,
- receiving patient data,
- deleting a patient,
- patient data sending.
- RAW data parsing
- other ...

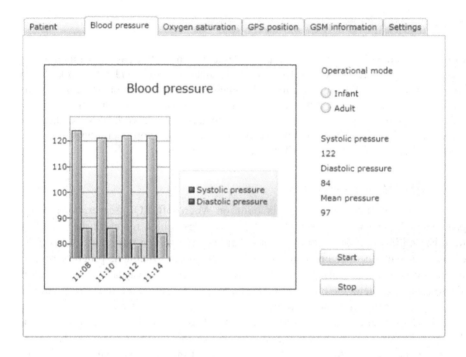

Fig. 2. Silverlight blood pressure visualization

To observe measured data effectively, visualization is needed. A type of graph as used in professional solutions is an ideal solution. To achieve this in a server application, a .NET Chart Control can be used for ASP.NET 3.5. For data analysis, neural nets are a convenient solution. However, there are problems in the automatic detection of critical states. Every person has a specific ECG pattern. The Neural net has to learn to distinguish critical states of each patient separately.

3.2 Desktop Part

The desktop client application is the main and the only part of the entire platform for patients' bio-parameters monitoring, which medical staff uses directly. It is obvious, that if Guardian should optimally replace classic paperwork, simplicity and trouble-free usage of client application are very important factors, which affect whether the doctors and medical staff accept this solution with enthusiasm and solution will be fully used or not. The options of desktop client application have to be easily upgraded. Therefore it is important to reliably design architecture which will allow that. Implementation of user functions is also important. Using the platform.NET in-build characteristics and open standards such as XML, XPath and other, is crucial. Because of that it is easy to configure or upgrade application. User interface is also easy to adjust to user request or clearance. Well designed architecture allows not only easier developing to software engineer, but brings also new and useful functions to the user. The design of appropriate architecture is crucial for the next development of implemented client application, which will be easily upgraded with new functions in the future without making any expensive and demanding changes in programmatic code.

XML represents great role in suggested solution. Options of this technology are used by dynamic assembling key components of graphic user interface, which enables its changing in dependence on roles or clearance of users. It is also used for easy application configuration.

3.3 Mobile Parts

The main part of the system is an Embedded or PDA device. The difference in applications for measurement units is the possibility to visualize the measured data in both Real-time Graph and Historical Trend Graph, which can be omitted on an embedded device. PDA is a much better choice for Personal Healthcare, where the patient is already healthy and needs to review his condition. Embedded devices can be designed for one user, with the option to use an external display used for settings or with the possibility of usage in extreme conditions.

The user adaptivity on mobile devices is control reorganization based on screen rotation provided by operating system. For automatical screen orientation change the mobile device must have accelerometer or G-sensor (HTC feature) implemented. The next step is color theme of application change. This feature is provided by measured level of actual lighting from built-in light-sensor. Devices which do not have this hardware parts can be set to defaults. Application reads default values from registry or from internal mobile database. Dynamically generated design for standard WindowsForm application is developed by dynamical programming technique, where small parts of application or controls source codes are inserted in database. When the application is running, the basic parts are loaded from database. Next choice for dynamically loaded design is XML generated design, described above in (section 3.2.).

Devices based on old PDA type (all devices developed before 2007 too) have a several limitations such as low CPU performance, low battery life or small display, which is possible to solve by embedded version of such mobile clients. We created a special windows mobile based embedded device. During the development process the several problems occurred. One of them and the most important was the need of a new operation system creation for our special architectural and device needs. We used the Microsoft PlatformBuilder for Windows CE 4.2 tools. The created operation system based on standard windows mobile has several drivers which we need to operate with communication devices and measurement devices.

At this time we use modern devices based on Windows Mobile 6 and newer. These devices have no limitations listed above; the only problem is higher price.

Measured data are stored on a SD Memory Card as a database of MS SQL Server 2008 Mobile Edition. The performance of available devices seems insufficient for sequential access parsing of incoming packets is heavily time-consuming. Pseudo paralleling is strongly required. This solution we used only in offline system implementation or when the internet connection is not available. In online (to the internet connected) system we send RAW (unparsed) data to the web service, which calls stored procedure for bitwise oriented parsing on database server. This "outsourced" data parsing is in a 12-chanel ECG measurement case faster as internal parsing, when is device unusable for overflow reason.

Table 1. BT ECG device measurement real-time packet parsing possibility

ECG device	Platform	Problem	Real Time
BT – Mobile device – Server – Visualization	.NET Framework	Memory overflow	Impossible
BT – Mobile device – Server – Visualization	C++	Memory overflow	Impossible
BT – Mobile device – Server – DB - Visualization	SQL Server procedure	-	Soft RT (2 sec deadline)
BT – MCU - Mobile device – Server - Visualization	MCU HCS08	-	Hard RT

4   Developed Hardware Parts of Platform

One of the main parts of system is a hardware background. If we want to analyze some data, we must measure and process it. This parts are realized over commercial ECG Corbelt, Blue ECG or own built ECG device for measurement and Cinterion AC75 GSM module for analysis (data parsing). GSM module is also used only in the own mobile device solution case.

4.1   ECG Device

As measurement device is possible to connect several device with Bluetooth communication possibility. In our application we use an ECG Measurement Unit (bipolar ECG Corbelt or 12 channels BlueECG) through a virtual serial port using wireless Bluetooth technology.

You can compare the increased data transfer speed in case of 12 channels ECG to 1 500 bytes per second. These data amount is very small; on the other hand the data are going as packets, so the processing is needed before the real data can be accessed. This process (called "parsing") take an unacceptable time in case of mobile device to process the data in Real Time. Same problem is growing on desktop PC, where the C# or C++ is used. In both cases the Memory Overflow is reached. The only possible way we found is in use of SQL procedure which is executed on SQL server. When the data (packets) are stored in table the procedure is call to execute and provide RAW data. In such case the data are ready to user-consumer application until 2 second deadline, so the Soft Real Time is possible to use.

The RAW data table contains full size packets received from an ECG device. Only the packets with measured data are stored to database. Those packets must contain in part of packet number bytes with a value of 0x0724.

The table with parsed data contains decimal values. Column „I" contains data from bipolar ECG; column „II" with „I" contains data from 6-channel ECG. The 12-channel ECG fills after parsing columns „I II V1 V2 V3 V4 V5 V6".

To get a real ECG data immediately after the measurement the next way can be used. We can use a special microcontroller (MCU) embedded in USB unit. This MCU unit has a full speed (12Mbit/s) USB access and BT is connected through a serial port. The MCU unit process all needed operations with parsing to provide a real ECG record to database or directly to visualizing application. In case of WPF application the Hard Real Time mode was reached.

Table 2. Stored RAW data from ECG device in database table

id	RAW data	usr_id	Stamp	parsed
5238	0xFB3708000...EAC2FDC	13	5.1.2010 12:42:33.45	1
5239	0xFB284A000...0BB7EDC	13	5.1.2010 12:42:33.45	1
5240	0xFB2A3C000...40EA4DC	13	5.1.2010 12:42:33.45	1
5241	0xFB2846000...0DBAEDC	13	5.1.2010 12:42:33.45	1
5242	0xFB2893000...0CB8EDC	13	5.1.2010 12:42:33.45	1
5243	0xFB374B000...4A92FDC	13	5.1.2010 12:42:33.45	1
5244	0xFB2B5D000...80DA2DC	13	5.1.2010 12:42:33.45	1

Table 3. Parsed RAW data stored in database table

id	I	II	V1	V2	V3	V4	V5	V6	original_id
304	9250	7934	8163	5422	5743	8924	7365	8067	10102
305	7932	7396	8534	5709	6108	6385	6313	5893	10102
306	12520	8298	7446	8462	9032	7026	6359	7204	10102
307	7552	6580	6476	7243	9834	8549	7936	6228	10103
308	8976	5783	6948	9684	5638	9336	9316	9746	10103
309	9298	6224	9682	6734	5784	6164	5652	7046	10103
310	9114	9463	7466	4624	8256	9032	8552	8592	10104
311	9773	6350	7581	8779	7365	7231	5137	7295	10104
312	8627	6278	5274	5624	8645	7405	5874	6808	10104

An example of real ECG record is shown in (Table 2) and (Table 3). In these cases, only Soft Real Time mode was reached even when a special MCU unit was used for preprocessing of data. In next subsection the use of WPF application is described as only way when the hard Real Time was reached on windows desktop PC (Windows RTX extension was used).

4.2 MCU Module and GSM Module

Other solution of parsing problem is a Java application in GSM module. The GSM module cointains own GSM communication module and processor which could be programmed by Java. The consumption of this microprocessor is acceptable, when we equals it to computing performance. Integrated processor have good computing power in bitwise operations, then the visualization application have to more time for own visualization. This is the same solution as special USB Bluetooth dongle with MCU. In other case is possible to the processed data append an informations about GPS position or data from accelerometer to visualize or send position data to user or patient keeper eg. The special USB Bluetooth dongle consists in the construction of its way "smart" bluetooth module, which, in addition to its own communication interface also included a small single-chip microcomputer (MCU) with no operating system to work according to an algorithm for parsing mentioned packages and working as a parser.

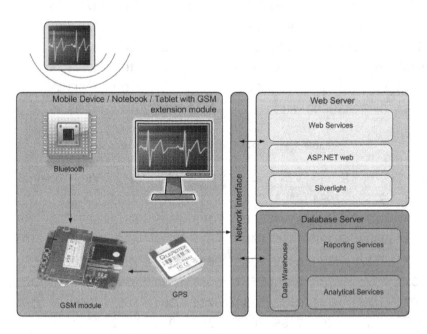

Fig. 3. Communication architecture

Program in the MCU would work with individual bytes in the packet at the lowest hardware level, which should cause that for these operations will be sufficient very simple, small and inexpensive system with negligible energy demands. Both solutions takes place reliably in real time, and the parser could be equipped with a large enough flash memory cache. This could save the processed data at a time when it is not normal Real-Time operating system was unable to read and save. This would ensure that there is, in short-term 'freeze' the system is no loss of valuable data.

5 Visualization

To make an ECG visualisation the measured data are needed at the beginning. The measurement is made on bipolar ECG corbel and 12 channels BlueECG.

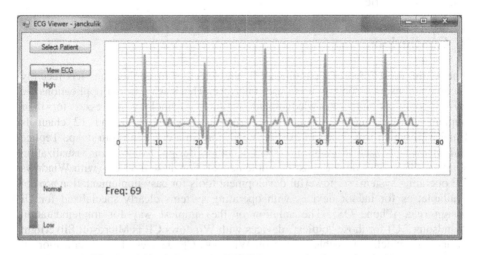

Fig. 4. UA highlighting via the ECG curve color (normal pulse)

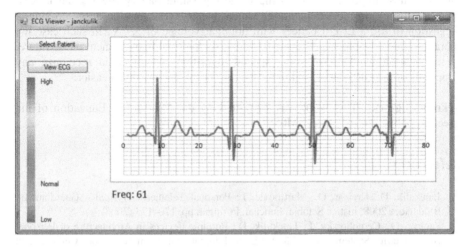

Fig. 5. UA highlighting via the ECG curve color (elevated pulse)

5.1 ECG Visualization in WPF Application

WPF (Windows Presentation Foundation) provide up to date possibilities to visualize ECG data on desktop PC. We create a WPF application to provide a full scale of graphic features to user. WPF technology runs directly on GPU possibilities (Graphic Processing Unit) which is founded on modern graphics cards. This fact is key parameter for speed of data presentation of screen. CPU has more time to compute others tasks (e.g. ECG data analyses by neural network tasks). WPF has a more design possibilities in compare to classical Windows Forms including 3D animation, pattern changes of whatever elements etc. WPF application allows viewing an ECG characteristic of measured patient in Real Time, selection of patient from database and view of historical graphs.

6 Conclusions

One of the most important parameters in the selection of applications has recently become a consumer society in the user interface. That´s why, in our applications we try to apply as much knowledge and available technology processes for their implementation. The measuring device (bipolar Corbelt ECG and 12 channels BlueECG) which was tested in extreme conditions in a cryogen room in spa Teplice nad Becvou (Czech Republic) (-136°C), other design features in visualization software on outdoor device must be implemented. For these devices, (with Windows CE operating system) so powerful development tools for easy implementation are not available; as for indoor devices with operating systems clearly specialized for UI design (e.g. iPhone OS). The solution or the simplest way for implementation "handsome" UI for those "oldiest" devices with Windows CE is Microsoft Silverlight technology which is possible startup on Windows CE devices. The visualization of the measured data was reached in case of WPF usage. On the other side, for hardware parts the most important thing is the longest possible battery life for the longest operation time for measurement. Executed battery consumption tests provide a suggestion to use a Li-Pol battery with nominal voltage of 3,7 V. In such case the operation time is going to sufficient 10 hours. As the final improvement in the future, the application would have some special algorithm, which could recognize any symptoms of the QRS curve, and make the job for the doctors much easier.

Acknowledgment. This work was supported by the Ministry of Education of the Czech Republic under Project 1M0567.

References

1. Janckulik, D., Krejcar, O., Martinovic, J.: Personal Telemetric System – Guardian. In: Biodevices 2008, Insticc Setubal, Funchal, Portugal, pp. 170–173 (2008)
2. Krejcar, O., Cernohorsky, J., Janckulik, D.: Portable devices in Architecture of Personal Biotelemetric Systems. In: 4th WSEAS International Conference on Cellular and Molecular Biology, Biophysics and Bioengineering, BIO'08, Puerto De La Cruz, Canary Islands, Spain, December 15-17, pp. 60–64 (2008)

3. Krejcar, O., Cernohorsky, J., Czekaj, P.: Secured Access to RT Database in Biotelemetric System. In: 4th WSEAS Int. Conference on Cellular and Molecular Biology, Biophysics and Bioengineering, BIO'08, Puerto De La Cruz, Canary Islands, Spain, December 15-17, pp. 70–73 (2008)
4. Krejcar, O., Cernohorsky, J., Janckulik, D.: Database Architecture for real-time accessing of Personal Biotelemetric Systems. In: 4th WSEAS Int. Conference on Cellular and Molecular Biology, Biophysics and Bioengineering, BIO'08, Puerto De La Cruz, Canary Islands, Spain, December 15-17, pp. 85–89 (2008)
5. Krejcar, O., Janckulik, D., Motalova, L., Kufel, J.: Mobile Monitoring Stations and Web Visualization of Biotelemetric System - Guardian II. In: Mehmood, R., et al. (eds.) EuropeComm 2009. LNICST, vol. 16, pp. 284–291. Springer, Heidelberg (2009)
6. Krejcar, O., Janckulik, D., Motalova, L.: Complex Biomedical System with Mobile Clients. In: Dössel, O., Schlegel, W.C. (eds.) The World Congress on Medical Physics and Biomedical Engineering, WC 2009, IFMBE Proceedings, Munich, Germany, September 07-12, vol. 25/5. Springer, Heidelberg (2009)
7. Krejcar, O., Janckulik, D., Motalova, L., Frischer, R.: Architecture of Mobile and Desktop Stations for Noninvasive Continuous Blood Pressure Measurement. In: Dössel, O., Schlegel, W.C. (eds.) The World Congress on Medical Physics and Biomedical Engineering, WC 2009, IFMBE Proceedings, Munich, Germany, September 07-12, vol. 25/5. Springer, Heidelberg (2009)
8. Penhaker, M., Cerny, M., Martinak, L., Spisak, J., Valkova, A.: HomeCare - Smart embedded biotelemetry system. In: World Congress on Medical Physics and Biomedical Engineering, Seoul, South Korea, August 27-September 01, vol. 14, PTS 1-6, pp. 711–714 (2006)
9. Brida, P., Duha, J., Krasnovsky, M.: On the accuracy of weighted proximity based localization in wireless sensor networks. In: IFIP, Personal Wireless Communications, vol. 245, pp. 423–432 (2007)
10. Cerny, M., Penhaker, M.: Biotelemetry. In: 14th Nordic-Baltic Conference an Biomedical Engineering and Medical Physics, IFMBE Proceedings, Riga, Latvia, June 16-20, vol. 20, pp. 405–408 (2008)

Help Me to Understand Your World: A Reflection on the Potential Impact of E-Health Systems on the Prognosis for Asperger Syndrome

Rudi G. Harmse and Dalenca Pottas

Faculty of Engineering, the Built Environment and Information Technology,
P.O. Box 77000, Nelson Mandela Metropolitan University, PORT ELIZABETH, 6031,
South Africa
{Rudi,Dalenca}@nmmu.ac.za

Abstract. Consumer focused e-Health systems will provide a broader spectrum of health consumers with timely, cost-effective and relevant services that will ultimately lead to a greater quality of life. This is the promise (or hope) that is increasingly being heard from health informatics researchers and practitioners. This paper looks at the characteristics of a particular minority group, namely high-functioning adults with Asperger Syndrome. It considers opportunities and risks associated with the worldwide web that has been identified in the literature and relates its implications for this community. Finally the paper concludes with some reflections on the questions that need to be answered.

Keywords: Autism Spectrum Disorder, Asperger Syndrome, e-Therapy, e-Health.

1 Introduction

There has been significant development in the understanding of the concept "Autism" over the last 3 decades. This has led to the diagnostic concept being broadened and the realization that previous prognosis expectations need to be re-examined [1].

The various diagnostic concepts are now commonly collectively referred to as Autism Spectrum Disorders (ASD) and reflects the consensus that Autistic Disorder and related disorders should be thought of as a spectrum. Individuals diagnosed with an ASD all demonstrate the same core deficits but the symptoms may manifest in diverse ways. With, for example, the intellectual function ranging from severe mental retardation to IQs in the superior range on conventional IQ tests.

While the increased awareness of ASD has led to a greater availability of support services there are still many reasons to believe that the amount of available support is inadequate and that the capacity of the traditional health care systems is insufficient. Especially in the case of higher functioning individuals they may not receive the benefit of services which could have a substantial impact on their quality of life. This is particularly evident when the situation of those who managed to avoid detection before adulthood is considered as even less services are available later in life.

H. Takeda (Ed.): E-Health 2010, IFIP AICT 335, pp. 210–221, 2010.

E-Health systems utilize information and communication technologies together with e-commerce and e-business principles to change the way health care is delivered [2]. Consumer focused e-health systems aim to empower users to take greater responsibility for their own health and wellbeing through providing relevant and cost-effective services at the point of need. In order to do this it is necessary to understand the needs of the consumers, especially when the relevant consumer population is defined by cognitive processes that differ from the norm.

This paper provides a brief outline of Asperger Syndrome (AS) followed by a consideration of the value of interventions in the life of individuals with AS. The advantages and disadvantages that web based systems have, as identified by Tantam [3], are then related to the particular AS characteristics in order to illustrate ways in which individuals with AS may benefit from these technologies, as well as how the characteristics may either mitigate threats or provide additional challenges.

2   Autism Spectrum Disorder and Asperger Syndrome

Asperger syndrome (AS) is one of 3 diagnostic categories identified in what is commonly called the Autism Spectrum Disorders (ASD). This is also sometimes referred to as the Autistic Spectrum Disorders. At one stage autism was considered a rare disorder with a prevalence of about 0.04% with 70-80% of these having significant learning disability but more recently the prevalence of the extended spectrum of autistic disorder places the figure at 0.6% with 70-90% having normal learning ability [4].

The common characteristic that links all the ASD diagnoses is the widely recognized triad of impairments in the areas of communication, social skills and behavioral flexibility. Currently the diagnosis of AS requires that speaking is not delayed and occurs at the normal age and that the level of IQ is not below normal levels.

Cashin and Barker [5] has recently suggested that, while useful for diagnosis, the triad of impairments focused on behavior is less useful for therapy. They proposed a switch to a cognitive triad of impairments that is constant and not changing at various times as is the case with the behavioral triad which is the manifestation of these underlying cognitive impairments. In this view the actual triad is seen to be visual processing, impairments in abstraction and an impaired theory of mind. If this or a similar common cognitive model could be identified and verified it would be useful for modeling and tracking progress through the life of an individual with AS using an e-health system.

Impaired theory of mind has been referred to as Mindblindness. This theory of Mindblindness can effectively explain the social and communication difficulties faced but it cannot explain non-social features, does not account for the emotional response difficulties and is also not specific to ASD as other clinical conditions also show forms of mindblindness [6].

Baron-Cohen [6] explores the educational implications of extending the theory of Mindblindness to be able to explain the non-social areas of strength present in autism and AS. This was done by adding a second factor (systemizing) and by broadening the theory of mind to include emotional response to the feelings of another (affective empathy) [6]. Systemizing refers to the tendency and ability to analyze or construct systems. There are many kinds of systems including mechanical, abstract, natural and even social systems that can be analyzed and understood by noting any regularities and underlying rules. There is evidence for intact and even unusually strong systemizing in AS for example in above the norm performance in a physics test [6].

Under this empathizing-systemizing (E-S) theory both the social-communication deficits as well as the areas of strength can be explained. The deficits are explained in terms of delays in the development of empathy and the strengths in terms of superior skill in systemizing [6]. One of the implications highlighted by Baron-Cohen [6] is that the functioning in the weak area of empathizing can be strengthened by framing learning in terms that allows its uptake by the systemizing strength in a similar way as one might teach a foreign language.

Individuals with AS generally have less severe autistic behavior, higher IQs and better language skills than individuals with Autism Disorder. They also show a desire to interact with others but lack the skills to do so successfully. These combined with the fact that AS is more often only diagnosed later in life creates a different set of opportunities and difficulties for potential intervention. In adults the difficulties are often subtle and are especially present in communication, social relationships and interests [4].

2.1 Diagnosing the Core Syndrome of AS

The ICD-10 definition of AS includes exclusion criteria, examples of stereotyped and abnormal behavior and descriptions of abnormalities in reciprocal social interaction.

With the definition of AS including an IQ in the normal or superior range together with better verbal skills a more positive prognosis could be expected. This has been confirmed by studies that found that early communication skills and intellectual level are the most significant predictors of outcomes in adults with ASD [7; 8]. The recognition of the much larger group of people with AS who have social functioning at a level sufficient to have avoided being previously diagnosed has also increased understanding of what can be achieved [9].

A difficulty in practice is that the core syndrome will manifest differently in different individuals as well as over time in the same individual [9; 10]. While present throughout life, the non-verbal difficulties become progressively harder to determine with age as the individual develops various coping strategies that disguise the difficulties.

Another difficulty is that there are psychological disorders which may be confused with AS or conversely AS could be confused for another psychological disorder [9] which could result in inappropriate treatment.

2.2 Emotional Consequences of AS and Psychological Disorders

The prevalence of anxiety and depression is high in people with AS. A complicating factor is that many people with AS attend mainstream schools where their special educational needs may not be recognized.

A common response to distress is the development of an anxiety disorder but this is difficult to diagnose as the main presentation of this may be as an apparent increase of the severity of the core AS characteristics. This may lead to an increase in rituals or an agitated state with increased bewilderment [9].

Extended periods of anxiety can lead to depression and increased levels of substance abuse. Depression can also lead to an increase in self-neglect and social withdrawal. The role of emotional factors on the prognosis should not be underestimated and should be a particular focus of assistance [9].

3 Interventions

Early detection and the provision of specific education has improved prognosis [10]. In addition, the understanding of the role that emotional and personal factors play in prognosis means that focused interventions aimed at these difficulties can lead to substantial improvements in the apparent level of disability in AS.

3.1 Quality of Life

The term "Quality of life" refers to a set of factors that together express personal well-being. There are eight quality of life domains recognized (emotional wellbeing, interpersonal relationships, material wellbeing, personal development, physical wellbeing, self-determination, social inclusion and rights).

Renty and Roeyers [11] found a relationship between the perceived quality of life of persons with ASD and the support, both perceived informal as well as received formal and informal, that they experience. They found that the various support characteristics had a greater determining factor on quality of life than the disability characteristics themselves. Interestingly their analysis did not show a strong relation with the level of received support (either formal or informal) but that a correlation was found with *perceived* informal support as well as a negative correlation with *unmet* formal support needs.

This would indicate that both the perceptions and specific needs of the individual should be addressed in any interventions to improve quality of life. In the case of unmet support needs the following were found to be most correlated: accommodation, daytime activities, ASD-specific information, and interpersonal relationships [11]. Of these it will be seen in section 4 that web-based technologies provide particular opportunities for the last two.

3.2 Value of Interventions

When there is clearly a disorder present that is susceptible to medication this could be used, but it has been shown that individuals with AS may be particularly susceptible to the side-effects of medication. They should therefore be started at lower dosage and any increases should be in smaller increments than would normally be used [9].

With the significance of met and unmet formal support needs there should be a particular focus on identifying and meeting these needs. With the findings that targeted formal support is of much more value this would appear to be an area where investments in this regard can be leveraged by ensuring it is targeted and specific. It is clear that what is required is a person-centered methodology that provides individuals with the means to strengthen their social support network as well as support that is completely tailored to their needs. Could web-based e-health provide such an environment? What other opportunities and threats does the e-health approach bring with it?

4   Opportunities and Threats

Tantam [3] explores a number of opportunities and threats posed by the worldwide web for psychotherapy in an e-health approach under the categories:

- Information
- Interactivity
- Openness
- Disembodied presence

These categories will be used here to frame the discussion. Of these categories, the first two are related to the important support needs that are strongly correlated with quality of life mentioned in section 3.1. That is the ASD-specific information and the interpersonal relationships that are related to the Information and Interactivity categories respectively. The other two categories have not yet emerged as having such a direct bearing on AS prognosis but they were considered for completeness and it will be seen that they have some implications as well.

4.1   Information

A particular advantage of the new technologies is the availability of information in its various forms. There are many sources of information available, but with this availability comes the problem of information overload. The quality of information is also of some concern with the dangers of misinformation and disinformation being ever present [3].

Through the simple expedience of a search on the Internet using for example a search engine such as Google a person with AS can gain access to a diverse collection of information but what is the value of this information? With a number of different competing theories as well as unproven treatment methods there is potential for confusion, outdated or even biased information.

If, as occurs frequently, the individual with AS makes learning about their condition a particular interest then their capacity for intense focus and persistence on their special interest becomes an asset in dealing with the amount of information available. It has also been found that for individuals with AS reading is a much more effective method of understanding than listening [4].

Individuals with AS do, however, seem to have some problems with executive control functions which make it harder for them to structure their information search and focusing on the most relevant materials. Many individuals compensate for these weaknesses by imposing strict structure on their lives and planning in detail.

There is also the concern that these individuals' trusting nature and tendency to literal interpretation may make them susceptible to misinformation or lead to misunderstanding some of the material.

Given the importance of the availability of ASD-specific information any e-health solution targeting this community will need to provide this information with the necessary quality control. Specific attention would need to be paid to ensuring that the material is clear, appropriately structured and not misleading to members of the AS community.

4.2 Interactivity

Communication technologies have created greater opportunities for interactivity than ever before. This increased communication can assist in clarifying advice and provide a channel of feedback [3]. It could also assist the healthcare customers in formulating their problems clearly.

These technologies are useful to those with an ASD in two ways in particular.

Firstly, communication technology could provide them an alternative means to communicate. This is particularly the case with those individuals with more severe communication impairments for whom communication through email and discussion forums are their primary form of communication. It is however rare for an individual with AS to be nonverbal and this is more relevant for some Autism Disorder cases unless another condition such as severe social anxiety is also present.

Secondly, the communication technology makes it possible to bring together individuals from a much larger population. Given the relatively low incidence of ASD an individual is not likely to encounter many other individuals with similar experiences without this access to a wider population. The technology could also make contact with support services possible where it might not be locally available. The wider reach could also make it easier for such specialized support services to reach enough people to justify their existence which is an important consideration for the viability of e-health systems [2].

There is a dark side to all this interactivity. This increased interactivity could lead to unreflective responses and there is the ever present danger of breaches of confidentiality if for example emails are redistributed [3]. The problems individuals with AS have with understanding social conventions and a tendency towards excessive openness could make this even more likely.

The lack of needing to worry about nonverbal communication allows the individual with AS to focus on what needs to be said but there is the danger that indirect forms of communication could be used to such an extent that the individual withdraws from other interactions. In this way any social anxiety could be reinforced and lead to excessive withdrawal.

As mentioned earlier, individuals with AS want to socialize. This means that they are likely to make use of the opportunities to interact with peers provided by the technology. There is unfortunately the danger that they may be targeted for abuse as they may be perceived as a "soft target".

A number of websites have been created by people with particular conditions and many of these incorporate some form of discussion forum where a community forms that provides support to each other held together by their common experience. As discussed in section 3.1 the level of perceived informal support has a bearing on perceived quality of life. Some of this informal support may be obtained through online support groups.

Anecdotal evidence is mixed as to the helpfulness of this support and the general lack of systematic evidence suggests that professionals need to become more involved in the provision of information and support as well in the evaluation thereof [12].

Some examples of such online support groups for ASD include:

www.wrongplanet.net
http://www.grasp.org/
http://www.aspergersyndrome.org/

Given the demonstrated value of intervention, having an increased access to relevant services is likely to be an advantage. There is however currently still the questions surrounding the quality of e-services with the susceptibility to medicine side effects in the AS population being of concern as well as some inconsistency in diagnosis. This is a factor that is not only relevant for systems specially designed for AS but is particularly of concern in more general e-health systems where a misdiagnosis of for example Schizophrenia could lead to the prescription of medication which will result in a poor prognosis for the individual with AS.

The potential for gaining access to specialists needs to be balanced with the practical problems and limitations. On the one hand the fact that so much of psychological intervention is based on communication makes it suitable with a virtual environment – certainly much more so than medical interventions requiring a physical presence. On the other hand the interaction is not as easily reduced to simple data items as would be the case in remote monitoring of simpler physical ailments such as blood sugar levels in patients with diabetes. The therapist-client relationship could also arguably be more dependent on the establishment of a trust relationship for success which may be more difficult to establish in the disembodied environment.

4.3 Openness

Very little information on the Internet can be restricted to only professionals [3]. This openness allows health consumers to view much of the same information as professionals, interpret this information themselves and even participate in professional disagreements [3].

Given the still volatile nature of our understanding of AS and the amount of ongoing research there is the danger that consumers might be exposed to findings and conclusions that may in fact be premature. The many different views and academic debates may also lead to confusion among consumers.

Individuals with AS may be prone to developing their own theories based on this information due to their extreme tendency to systemizing. Obviously this poses a danger, but at the same time if those individuals with high cognitive abilities could apply their abilities in conjunction with experts within the field it could lead to furthering our understanding of the condition.

4.4 Disembodied Presence

The risks so far mentioned are not unique to the Internet and have been present in various degrees in other media. A particular aspect where the digital media does pose a new challenge is in the aspect of disembodied presence [3].

The issue here is the unprecedented degree of anonymity and the ease of deception of even such fundamental characteristics as gender and age [3].

There is also a lack of presence that being with a person normally entails. Even when there is no verbal communication there is still the constant stream of non-verbal communication [3]. It may be possible to create a sense of presence through a computer conversation, but once again the reality that all is not what it seems due to the possibility of virtual identities is present.

Given the fact that one of the defining characteristics of ASD is a reduction in awareness of non-verbal communication it might be expected that those with ASD would be less affected by this aspect of disembodiment in the same way that a blind person is unaffected by a darkened room while it has a major impact on sighted individuals. There is still the reality that all is not as it seems with virtual identities and as individuals with ASD are seen as socially naive they may well become the targets of purposeful deception.

Tantam [3] explores the concept of embodiment further and also considers the effect that the absence of a physical awareness of the presence has on the conduct of individuals online. While a computer with a camera can have a field of vision, there is no actual gaze that could generate a sense of shame. This can be an advantage in situations such as computerized tests or to allow individuals unable to bear public scrutiny to interact but can also lead to behavior that would normally be inhibited due to the moderating effect of shame [3].

Interestingly some of the socially problematic behaviours of individuals with ASD may stem from a reduced awareness of others. It is possible that such individuals may therefore also be expected to experience less of a difference in this regard. At the same time there is the risk that an excessive amount of time spent in virtual communication could further reduce opportunities for the individual to develop an increased awareness of the presence of others and to modulate behavior appropriately.

There can also be a degree of dissociation with the Internet serving as an alternative world [3]. Given the high incidence of anxiety and depression in individuals with AS, there is always the danger that such individuals may withdraw into the virtual world. They could then use it as a method to avoid facing the difficulties of real world interactions. If this avoidance gives them access to more interaction it is a positive aspect but a reduction of real world interaction should be guarded against.

5 Summary and Discussion

Table 1 provides a summary of the information presented in this paper with the AS characteristics that have relevance for the opportunities and threats discussed. In this table those characteristics that could be considered as positive in the particular context is indicated with a + while those that provide a particular challenge to an individual with AS is indicated with a -.

As can be seen in the table AS provides a number of problems in all these areas but also present a number of particular advantages for each of the categories considered. It would therefore seem reasonable to conclude that there is reason to believe that it

Table 1. Summary of opportunity and threats related to relevant AS characteristics

Category	Opportunity	Threat	AS characteristics
Information	Availability	Information overload	+Intense focus
			+Persistence
			-Executive control issues
			-Relevance of focus
		Mis-/Disinformation	-Literal interpretation
			-Trusting
Interactivity	Clarifying advice	Unreflective responses Confidentiality breach	-Social conventions -Excessive openness
	Alternative communication	Withdrawal	+Relative verbal strength -Social anxiety
	Links with peers	Abuse	-Prone to victimization +Desire to socialize
	Access to services	Variable quality	-Inconsistency in diagnosis -Susceptible to side-effects +Value of intervention
Openness	Availability Participation	Premature information	-Develop own theories +Systemizing ability
Disembodied presence	Anonymity	Withdrawal Deception	+Nonverbal deficits -Behaviour reinforcement -Socially naïve

would be fruitful to utilize these technologies for this population but that the solutions need to be tailored to their particular difficulties to mitigate for the particular weaknesses. There are a number of ways where these technologies are already being utilized. One that has led to an increase in the number of people who realize they may have AS is online testing.

Using the Internet for testing has become very popular as it is easy to do with the current technology and has been shown to give results that are similar to those administered by a human [13]. The capabilities of computers to conduct analysis of complex tests that would be time consuming by hand as well as the ease with which tests can be converted for Internet use means that tests that are selected, administered and rated by users have become widely available. This proliferation of self-administered tests has to be balanced with questions of validity. Just because a clinical test has been converted to an Internet form does not mean that its results have the same validity. The validity of a self-administered test has to be tested, even if it is based on a test that has proven validity when conducted by another person the self-administered nature could result in effectively being a different test.

Tantam [13] believes that the main advantage of computer-based testing is the fact that these tests can be adaptive and therefore able to ask only the most discriminating questions to achieve a specific level of accuracy with only the necessary questions being asked. The efficiency of testing means that repeat testing can be used to track progress. It would be important to ensure that the tests maintain their validity and reliability after extended use and that they do not simply measure improved skill at taking the test.

An interesting finding is that, when the content could be considered shameful, computer-based tests are answered more honestly than human administered tests. So, at least in some instances, these tests could have even more validity than human administered tests.

There is the risk that individuals might take online tests without a sufficient understanding of their significance or shortcomings. A common type of message seen on online AS forums is: "I took testXYZ online and got a score of X. What now? What does that mean?" Easily available screening tests may lead to individuals seeking appropriate help which they might not have realized they need otherwise. An individual with an undiagnosed ASD might be functioning sufficiently to have escaped diagnoses and may never have been formally tested. Yet they have experienced difficulties throughout their lives and been aware of being "different". In many cases an online test provides the first step towards an improved understanding of their own mental functioning and allows them to come in contact with others that think similarly and ultimately lead to a better quality of life.

The benefit for people who would not otherwise have become aware of the origin of their problems should be balanced with the risks that people might inappropriately self-diagnose on the basis of online screening tests without understanding the limitations and purpose of the tests.

Another area where it might be possible to expand the support available is if certain services could be automated. There are some areas of psychotherapy that utilize well tried procedures which, at least to some extent, could be implemented in algorithms that a computer could follow. Tantam [13] refers to a few studies that concluded that computer based treatment could be a viable option for psychotherapy aimed at the reduction of distress.

Given the high level of incidence of anxiety and the importance of emotional and personal factors for the prognosis of individuals with AS (as discussed in section 3), it is clear that if effective computerized systems were available to assist with this, it would be of help for this community. The difference in cognitive functioning of AS individuals would need to be considered and the validity and effectiveness of these techniques for AS individuals cannot be assumed.

An area for computer therapy that has seen increasing use is the use of immersive virtual environments for various uses [13]. Some relevant uses reported include the fear and avoidance of public speaking as well as autism [13]. Besides the suitability of virtual environments for exposure therapy it has also been used for training such as for social skills training for people with AS.

6 Reflections

The use of web based e-health systems hold considerable promise but the particular characteristics of the AS community raises the possibility that response to these technologies may not follow a pattern exactly like those of the general population. It is therefore necessary to conduct further research to determine in what ways these differences impact on the way services are delivered.

A number of questions still need to be answered or require more definitive answers:

- Given the prevalence of conditions such as anxiety and depression, does the effectiveness of treatments for these differ for this population?
- Which aspects of support can be automated and safely provided? What is the long term effect of such support?
- Given the prevalence of usage of Internet based testing by consumers and the value of early detection and educational support, how can e-health systems support this process while minimizing misuse?
- Given the mixed experiences with peer support, what factors influence its success?
- How can professional and peer support more closely integrate to leverage the advantage of peer support while mitigating for its risk factors?
- To what extent does a sufficient level of trust develop in the therapist-client relationship in an e-health solution? Does the AS characteristics make this more or less likely to occur?
- The understanding of AS is continually evolving and studies of long-term prognosis is by its nature based on treatments conducted in the past. How can e-health systems assist in assessing the effectiveness of newer treatments?
- How can e-health systems utilize the systemizing strengths to assist the consumers to overcome their tendency for trusting inappropriately and being too open with self-disclosure?

7 Conclusion

This paper considered the characteristics of a particular group of potential health consumers, namely those with Asperger Syndrome (AS). It was concluded that a person-centered methodology that provides individuals with the means to strengthen their social support network and received support that is completely tailored to their needs is desired. The question was then asked: Could e-health provide such an environment?

The particular characteristics of individuals with AS were then considered in terms of the opportunities and threats that can be identified in the categories: Information, Interactivity, Openness and Disembodied presence.

This led to the conclusion that there are potential benefits and that some types of systems have already been implemented but it was also seen that this population brings a number of special considerations that need to be given attention. It cannot be assumed that their response to these systems will be the same as the general population and that the effectiveness of approaches should be verified for this population. This includes ensuring that systems aimed at the general population which include individuals with AS but are not specifically focused on their particular needs at least "above all - do no harm".

References

1. Marriage, S., Wolverton, A., Marriage, K.: Autism Spectrum Disorder Grown Up: A Chart Review of Adult Functioning. J. Can. Acad. Child Adolsc. Psychiatry 18(4), 322–328 (2009)
2. Tan, J.: E-Health Care Information Systems: An Introduction for Students and Professionals. Jossey-Bass, San Francisco (2005)
3. Tantam, D.: Opportunities and Risks in e-Therapy. Advances in Psychiatric treatment 12, 368–374 (2006)
4. Berney, T.: Asperger Syndrome from Childhood into Adulthood. Advances in Psychiatric treatment 10, 341–351 (2004)
5. Cashin, A., Barker, P.: The Triad of Impairment in Autism Revisited. Journal of Child and Adolescent Psychiatric Nursing 22(4), 189–193 (2009)
6. Baron-Cohen, S.: The Empathising-Systemising Theory of Autism: Implications for Education. Tizard Learning Disability Review 14(2), 4–13 (2009)
7. Howlin, P.: Outcome in Adult Life for more Able Individuals with Autism or Asperger Syndrome. Autism 4, 63–83 (2000) doi:10.1177/1362361300004001005
8. Howlin, P., Goode, S., Hutton, J., Rutter, M.: Adult Outcome for Children with Autism. J. Child Psychol. Psychiatry 45(2), 212–229 (2004)
9. Tantam, D.: Psychological Disorder in Adolescents and Adults with Asperger Syndrome. Autism 4, 47–62 (2000) doi:10.1177/1362361300004001004
10. Attwood, T.: The Complete Guide to Asperger's Syndrome (Softcover first edition). Jessica Kingsley Publishers, London (2008)
11. Renty, J.O., Roeyers, H.: Quality of Life in High-functioning Adults with Autism Spectrum Disorder: The Predictive Value of Disability and Support Characteristics. Autism 10, 511–524 (2006) doi:10.1177/1362361306066604
12. Tantam, D.: The Machine as Intermediary: Personal Communication via a Machine. Advances in Psychiatric treatment 12, 427–431 (2006)
13. Tantam, D.: The Machine as Psychotherapist: Impersonal Communication with a Machine. Advances in Psychiatric treatment 12, 416–426 (2006)

How the Usability of a Pen-Tablet System Varies with Response Time Retardation

Kei Teramoto, Shigeki Kuwata, and Hiroshi Kondoh

Division of Medical Informatics, Tottori University Hospital
36-1 Nishi-cho, Yonago, Tottori, 683-8504, Japan
{kei,shig,kondoh}@med.tottori-u.ac.jp

Abstract. To realize cloud computing (CC), virtualization technology has been accepted as an infrastructure of Electronic Patient Records (EPR). However, it has not been sufficiently done so far to evaluate the usability of Pen-Tablet Systems (PTS) as an input device of EPR with CC environments. From our preliminary studies, we confirmed that response time retardation, which virtualization technology inherently bears, would be an influencing factor for the usability. In this study we conducted usability questionnaires for subjects who were requested to use a drawing application that produced the pseudo retardation in order to measure an allowable range on the retardation for implementing PTS on EPR with CC environments. Usability of the PTS would drastically drop with increasing values of the scattering of delays exceeding 35 milliseconds. As a result, this study would provide useful measures for implementing PTS with CC technology.

Keywords: Cloud Computing, Pen-Tablet System, Usability.

1 Introduction

Thin-client computing, well known as cloud computing (CC) or Server-Based computing, for hospital information system has been widely accepted, because the technology is able to decrease the cost of ownership and enhance a security level [1]. However, it has not been sufficiently done so far to evaluate the usability of Pen-Tablet Systems (PTS) as an input device of Electronic Patient Records (EPR) with CC environments. This is a comparative study on the usability of a standalone PC and a thin-client as a terminal with CC technology when users utilize PTS with EPR. Response time retardation, often occurring in CC environments, was evaluated in terms of the degrees of its impact on the usability by an experiment using an application to produce the controlled pseudo retardation (delay) of response time.

2 Method

From the preliminary studies, we confirmed that the response time retardation varied with virtualization software for implementing EPR on CC environments [2]. In the current experiment, five subjects with the age ranging from 28 to 40 having over 10

H. Takeda (Ed.): E-Health 2010, IFIP AICT 335, pp. 222–223, 2010.

years of PC experience were requested to write signatures using PTS with a drawing application, subsequently to answer three-grade questionnaires on the usability (5: equal to standalone PC, 3: inferior but usable and 1: not usable). The drawing application controlled an average of the delays increased from 0 to 120 milliseconds (msec) with the interval of 20 msec, as well as a standard deviation of the delays increased from 28 to 80 with the interval of approximately 3 msec.

3 Results and Conclusion

As a result, we found that the scattering, as a standard deviation of the delays, would impact on use of PTS much more than the delay length, as an average of the delays. Since the result was also supported by our preliminary studies [3], it is reasonable to suppose that the scattering can be a useful indicator for using PTS on CC environment.

In terms of the relationship between the scattering of the delays and the usability evaluated by subjects, the best usability was obtained for subjects under the condition of the delay length within 100 msec and the scattering within 35 msec: the subjects marked approximately over 4 points on the usability questionnaires. When the scattering lay between 36 and 40 msec, the best usability was also found only with a very limited range of the delay length less than within 20 msec. When the scattering exceeded 40 msec, the results of evaluation showed the inferior usability even if PTS had no delays.

As conclusion, it would be desirable that values of the scattering range within 35 msec for using PTS with CC technology. Otherwise the usability would drastically drop with increasing values of the scattering, even if the values increased by only a few milliseconds.

Although this study would provide useful measures for implementing PTS, its applicability to hospital settings still remains limited: the number of subjects and the types of applications for virtualization were not sufficient in this study. Those limitations should be reexamined in further studies.

References

1. Kuwata, S., Teramoto, K., Yasushi, M., Kushniruk, A., Borycki, E., Kondo, H.: Effective Solutions in Introducing Server-Based Computing into Hospital Information System. Stud. Health Technol. Inform. 143, 435–440 (2009)
2. Teramoto, K., Kuwata, S., Kushniruk, A., Borycki, E., Kondo, H.: Issues on evaluating the usability of a pen-tablet system using server-based computing. Stud. Health Technol. Inform. 150, 415 (2009)
3. Teramoto, K., Kuwata, S., Kondoh, H.: Evaluation of the Usability of a Pen Tablet System Using Server-Based Computing: Evaluation of the Usability of a Pen Tablet System Using Server-Based Computing. In: Asia Pacific Association for Medical Informatics 2009, Lighthouse, Japan, vol. 27, pp. 182–186 (2009)

Stress Testing of Web Services Interface

Leona Motalova, Dalibor Janckulik, and Ondrej Krejcar

VSB Technical University of Ostrava, Center for Applied Cybernetics, Department of
measurement and control, Faculty of Electrical Engineering and Computer Science, 17.
Listopadu 15, 70833 Ostrava Poruba, Czech Republic
{leona.motalova,dalibor.janckulik,ondrej.krejcar}@vsb.cz

Abstract. The aim of this paper is a stress testing of the developed UAS for
home care agencies. The developed testing application is possible to use on any
others UAS with web service interface. The whole system, including
applications developed for the stress testing is based on Microsoft technology
.NET. By the help of our test application, the hardware solution for the server
was selected on the base of selected home care agency needs.

Keywords: Stress testing; Response Time; Mobile Device; SQL Server.

1 Introduction and Test Results Evaluation

The area of stress testing shows the tested system behavioral in case the data are
accessed by several users simultaneously. For the testing of affection on the length of
the time response by the number of the simultaneous accesses to the database, the
application was developed in C# language in the development environment of
Microsoft Visual Studio 2008. The developed application simulates simultaneous
access of any number of users, on the methods implemented by the Web service and
measure the response time of the web service for the requirement depended on the
number of users who approach to service at the moment. The application measures
and creates: (1) The duration of one call of the given method, (2) The duration of the
call of the method to the specified number of simultaneous user access, (3) The
overall response time Web service by a given number of users including travel time
requirement for Web services, (4) Build the required collection of data from the
database, (5) The way of this collection back from Web service to the application, (6)
The duration of the complete fulfillment of the requirement from the start button is
pressed to the end of the test.

Each type of tests are made in five iterations, all the values are then processed into
arranged tables. For tests in which users are gradually generation, from these values
are then calculated "MODUS", "MEDIAN" values and "arithmetic mean". Since it
was measured only 5 iterations, not always experienced the same measurements
values, therefore some items of calculated values contains value # N/A. Our
measurements are not on the accuracy and repeatability values critical and diversity of
individual measurements by a few milliseconds is not essential for us, it is only
informative measurements, detecting how long time the server needs to respond to the
request, which is also influenced by the current server utilization.

H. Takeda (Ed.): E-Health 2010, IFIP AICT 335, pp. 224–225, 2010.
© IFIP International Federation for Information Processing 2010

Application allows measurement of response time of SQL Server to query based on the number of simultaneous access to data. The application was created within the development environment Microsoft Visual Studio 2008 and the database accessed by Web services. The application allows you to measure the response time of database server, but also the time it takes delivery of the request to the server, packaging data collection and their subsequent transfer to the user. Period of the data processing in the developed application isn't at the time of the response included. The application also provides the user directing itself a Web service, which has delayed for the execution of user request a major impact. This delay includes the connection to database and subsequent compilation of web services. Data obtained by measurements are presented in a column chart and tables are summarized in text fields. The results indicate that the length of the response increases proportionally with increasing number of users and even the large number of 1000 users of the database should handle the problem of demand, which for the purposes of the agency over-sufficient. The response times but has a great influence machine on which the database server is stored. Test results shows that when using a desktop PC with a memory of only 512MB and tact 850MHz processor, amount of response for the 1000 user responses to long-7s, which is contrary to the requirement of the Agency, which called for the maximum response in 5 seconds. It is to be reckoned with the fact that the response will grow with increasing the number of records in the database.

2   Conclusion

Application has been tested by several stress tests for different numbers of simultaneous accessing users. The number of users has been gradually increased by the entered step or was generated randomness in the specified range. In the case the same number of users are accessing server, the time needed to process the query is almost unchanged. In this case the differences caused by network latency or the need to process the first request with higher priority results in the millisecond.

For smaller agencies is not a problem to use the processing requirements through Web services. For larger agencies, however, processing of large amounts of data for simultaneous access to a large number of employees could take excessive time, therefore it is preferable to use the handle requests directly to the database.

Acknowledgement. This work was supported by the Ministry of Education of the Czech Republic (1M0567) and Grant Agency of Czech Republic (GA 102/08/1429).

References

1. Krejcar, O.: PDPT Framework - Building Information System with Wireless Connected Mobile Devices. In: ICINCO 2006, 3rd International Conference on Informatics in Control, Automation and Robotics, Setubal, Portugal, August 01-05, pp. 162–167 (2006)
2. Janckulik, D., Krejcar, O., Martinovic, J.: Personal Telemetric System – Guardian. In: Biodevices 2008, Insticc Setubal, Funchal, Portugal, pp. 170–173 (2008)

Learning from Pathology Databases to Improve the Laboratory Diagnosis of Infectious Diseases

Alice Richardson[1], Fariba Shadabi[1], and Brett A. Lidbury[2]

[1] Faculty of Information Sciences and Engineering
University of Canberra, ACT 2601, Australia
[2] Centre for Biomedical and Forensic Research, Faculty of Applied Science
University of Canberra, ACT 2601, Australia

Abstract. This paper investigates the effect of data pre-processing and the use of ensemble on the accuracy of decision trees. The methodology is illustrated using a previously unanalysed data set from ACT Pathology (Canberra, Australia) relating to Hepatitis B and Hepatitis C patients.

Keywords: Decision Tree, Ensemble Classifier, Data Transformation, Hepatitis.

1 Introduction

In this paper we describe our empirical study of constructing a decision tree ensemble using different data pre-processing techniques on multi-variable pathology laboratory data for the enhanced laboratory diagnosis of infectious diseases (for this study, hepatitis B and hepatitis C viruses). We specifically use a data set of 18625 deidentified records from 1997 – 2007 made available to us by ACT Pathology. Seventeen explanatory variables and two response variables were provided.

2 Methodology and Experimental Results

In this study we employed S-PLUS decision trees and carried out a four-factor experiment to study the effect of virus, outcome, method and preprocessing on the overall accuracy rate. There are two viruses (Hepatitis B (HBV) and Hepatitis C (HepC)) and two outcomes (positive or negative). There are three methods (basic multiple, majority multiple and clear negative).

The basic multiple method consists of a standard decision tree with 2/3 of the data for training and 1/3 for testing. The 2/3 of negative outcomes are split into 72 sets, each the same size as the 2/3 of positive cases. Accuracy rate is calculated for each tree separately.

The majority multiple method uses 36 subsets for training where each subset had 282 negative outcomes and 141 positive outcomes for HBV. Furthermore, we computed the accuracy rate for each tree (using the same test dataset) based on majority voting from all trees.

H. Takeda (Ed.): E-Health 2010, IFIP AICT 335, pp. 226–227, 2010.

The clear negative method involves selecting the cases which are "certainly negative", this gave us total of 154 cases. We then combined this with 1/3 of the positive cases to construct the training set. The remaining data are used for testing.

Finally, there are four ways of preprocessing: none, scaling, logging and scale-logging. Scaling sets the range of each explanatory variable to a common range of 0 – 100. Logging uses the natural logarithm transformation. Scale-logging uses a common range of 0 – 100 then takes the natural logarithm. Note also that assignment of positive and negative to data occurs before scaling.

The analysis of variance shows that accuracy rate depends on outcome (F = 32.279, df = 1 and 23, p = .000). Positive cases have a higher accuracy rate on average than negative. There are also a significant interaction between method and outcome (F = 50.640, df = 2 and 23, p = .000). Majority multiple does better on average at predicting negatives, whereas the other two methods do better on average at predicting positives. The other significant interaction is between virus and outcome (F = 32.120, df = 1 and 23, p = .000). For HepC positive leads to higher accuracy rates on average, the reverse is true for HBV.

3 Discussion and Conclusion

Immunoassay techniques are routinely used in pathology departments to detect antibodies to disease-causing microbes, indicating previous exposure to, or infection by, the specific pathogen. This study examined the immunoassay marker HBSA to detect previous hepatitis B virus (HBV) infection/exposure, and the general HepC antigen to detect hepatitis C virus (HCV) infection.

The best approach for negative HBSA and HepC data accuracy was the "basic single" method due to the size of the dataset.

For smaller datasets, as found for both HBSA and HepC positive cohorts, other methods were required to achieve high predictive accuracy based on associated pathology data (described in Table1). Furthermore, the "clear negative" method, which used other pathology data (i.e. ALT liver enzyme) to give the most certain true negative cohort, was very effective. For this method, patient data with HBSA $\leq$ 0.01 and ALT $\leq$ 55 U/L were considered to be "clear negative" for HBV. We also considered patient data with HepC <= 0.03 as "clear negative" for HCV.

Acknowledgements

The authors wish to thank Mr Gus Koerbin, Principal Scientist, ACT Pathology, and his staff, for their support of and interest in this study. The authors also thank "Medical Advances Without Animals (MAWA)" for funding this project.

System Design for Automated Time Study of Nursing

Shohei Nakamura, Ichiroh Kanaya, Yuko Ohno, and Kazuo Kawasaki

Osaka Universiy
2-1 Yamadaoka Suita, Osaka, Japan

Abstract. There has been a shortfall in the number of nurses, so it is required to optimize the nursing service. Then, the authors proposed a new system design for automated time study of nursing to investigate nursing service easily. The system combines images from video monitoring and information from ambient sensing, and it analyzes them after combining. Besides the authors conducted video monitoring with ambient sensing in a hospital and analyzed images from the video monitoring. The authors indicated the effectiveness and potential of the system.

Keywords: Time study, Nursing, Video monitoring, Image analysis, Ambient sensing.

1 Introduction

Recently, there has been a shortfall in the number of nurses in Japan. Thus, in order to treat patients adequately with limited human resources, optimizing nursing service is required in medical site. To optimize nursing service, at first, to figure out precisely the present situation of nurses is needed; this must be based on a quantitative and detailed analysis.

Time study is just a method to record the content of work in detail and to provide data for analysis of the current circumstances. On a traditional time study, one observer always follows one subject on her or his job and documents it in detail. Normally the observed object of time study is a team of about 10 ~ 20 nurses, so at least 20 members are required for conducting time study, considering backup members. Therefore, this method needs large amount of well-trained human resources and burdens nurses both physically and mentally because of following them constantly. For these reasons, the new method of time study which clear these problems is strongly demanded. In this research, the authors proposed new method of time study and examined it in clinical practice.

2 Method

The new method of time study is required to get enough information for analysis with minimal equipments after solving the traditional method's problems. The information needed in time study is 5W information (What, When, Where, Who, Whom) about nurses' job. In this research, the authors proposed the system for time study that using

H. Takeda (Ed.): E-Health 2010, IFIP AICT 335, pp. 228–229, 2010.

Video monitoring, Ambient sensing and Image analysis organically. Video monitoring is to record nursing service by some cameras located adequate place. It can get 5W information at the same time but it has some restrictions about installation location, angle of view or background. To complement it, the authors use small sensors or devices. Ambient sensing is one method to support video monitoring and to get information that can't be got from only video monitoring by setting up them on desks, walls or nurses. After taking these data, they are integrated, processed and analyzed in computer. This system mainly uses differential analysis, because the moving object can be extracted easily. It can accomplish the automated time study with solving the traditional time study's problem if all attempts success.

3 Results and Discussion

For demonstrating the efficiency of this system, Video monitoring and Ambient sensing was conducted at Saito Yukokai hospital. The purpose of this time study was to investigate the work of managing the narcotic drug and anti cancer drug, because these works that should be controlled strictly were one reason to tie up the nurses. Therefore, the author set eight video cameras centering around the coffer of the drugs at the nurse station with careful attention to installation place not to burden nurses. Besides, the night nurse in this nurse station used a red LED device and a welsupport. In this research, LED device was used as an optical marker for picking out the object nurse from background in differential analysis. The spec of the red LED was that the luminance was 3000mcd, the angle of light direction was 120deg and covered by tracing paper to diffuse its light. Welsupport is high functional pedometer on shelves by NIPRO. It can measure movement of nurse, so it was used for measuring movement performed outside angle of view and total amount of nurse's movement.

Below figure shows the representative development of differential analysis. This difference images were calculated with 1 / 29.27 second-differential images. It could extract a body movement of nurse clearly. Moreover, it could extract specifically a light of LED device. A red strap in image before process was changed color into green in image after process, but the color of red LED was not changed. From results of graph of welsupport, its data roughly synchronized with actual movement of nurse, but it could use only for assistant information.

Fig. 1. Images before and after in differential analysis

The Impact of Electronic Medical Records on the Work Process of Outpatient Care: Extracting Use-Cases of Paper-Based Medical Records Using a Time Process Study

Sachiko Shimizu[1], Yuko Ohno[1], Hiroko Noda[1], Shohei Nakamura[2], Ichiro Kanaya[2], Kenji Yamada[1], Atsue Ishii[1], Satoko Kasahara[3], Katsumi Hirakawa[4], Rie Nakagawa[5], and Yasushi Matsumura[5]

[1] School of Medicine, Osaka University, 1-7Yamadaoka, Suita, Osaka, Japan
[2] School of Engeneering, Osaka University, 2-1Yamadaoka, Suita, Osaka, Japan
[3] School of Medicine, Kochi University, Kohasu Oko, Nankoku, Kochi, Japan
[4] School of Human Nursing, University of Shiga Prefecture, 2500Yasaka, Shiga , Japan
[5] Osaka University Hospital, 2-15Yamadaoka, Suita, Osaka, Japan
{shimizu,ohno,h.noda,atsue}@sahs.med.osaka-u.ac.jp,
{nakamura,kanaya}@design.frc.eng.osaka-u.ac.jp,
dr.kenji.yamada@gmail.com, s-kasahara@kochi-u.ac.jp,
khirakawa@nurse.usp.ac.jp,
{rnakagawa,matumura}@hp-info.med.osaka-u.ac.jp

Abstract. The goal of this study is to measure the impact of electronic medical records on both time efficiency and the work process with regard to outpatient care. In this study, we focus on examining the pre-assessment ahead of the introduction of the electronic medical records procedure applying new methodology, time process study. We extracted 12 use-cases and 82 actions in relation to paper based medical records at an outpatient department at a university hospital using time process study. The results suggest that, for nurses, indirect management of patients accounted for a higher proportion of the use-cases than was the case for direct care.

Keywords: business intelligence, electronic health records, work process, time efficiency, time process study.

1 Introduction

Electronic Medical Records system (EMRs) are intended to improve the efficiency and effectiveness of care through providing assistance to the workload of medical staff. Previous researches in relation to the impact of EMRs have concentrated on assessing the improvement of time efficiency occurring between pre- and post-introduction of EMRs. The crucial question arises as to the ways in which clinical work activities might be subject to change following the introduction of EMRs, and whether the corresponding changes to work activities will affect clinical efficiency.

H. Takeda (Ed.): E-Health 2010, IFIP AICT 335, pp. 230–231, 2010.

The goal of this study is to measure the impact of EMRs on both time efficiency and the work process with regard to outpatient care, with the focus being on examining the pre-assessment ahead of the introduction of the EMRs procedure applying time process study method. The study was undertaken at the outpatient department of Osaka University Hospital, a tertiary care facility located in Osaka, Japan.

2 Time Process Study

The Time Process Study (TPS) provided a new method for collecting data as well as for analyzing and visualizing work activity that compensates for the weaknesses of more conventional methodologies. TPS works by utilizing a unified modelling language (UML) to identify and visualize how a business procedure functions.

We suggested extending TPS in the same way as was proposed by Shiki et al. Thus, we first defined the use-case properties in order to identify the characteristics of the outpatient service in relation to paper based medical records (pMRs). In this regard, it is essential both to clarify the process and define the service properties in order that service quality might benefit in terms of improvement.

3 Results and Discussion

In this study we extracted 12 use-cases and 82 actions in relation to pMRs at an outpatient department at a university hospital using TPS. The results suggest that, for nurses, indirect management of patients accounted for a higher proportion of the use-cases than was the case for direct care. Although some of the tasks a nurse is concerned with may be similar to that of a medical clerk, nursing involves a further role providing direct patient care.

Generally, nursing consists of two roles, namely, a provider of direct patient care and a manager of the care environment. While direct care is an important component of nursing, indirect assistance with regard to care and the medical environment is crucial to the success of any intervention which also applies to all health care providers. Conversely, previous research has shown that the demands related to documentation can have a negative impact on job satisfaction. Our results showed paramedics in outpatient department provide their service to internal customer primary. According to these findings, indirect care seems to place a higher burden on the nurse than was previously thought.

This study also suggests that the items 'Searching pMRs' and 'Delivering pMRs' involve a great many actions due to the complexity of carrying out these tasks. These tasks have possibilities to involve many 'decisions'. Thus, paramedics may often be required to make informed guesses using incomplete information regarding patients due to the fact that many links occur in the process of associating with other sections of the hospital. Moreover, the tasks 'Searching pMRs' and 'Delivering pMRs' can crop up abruptly and thus lead to a disruption of more immediate task demands.

TPS was allowed to discuss about amount of work process and task properties. Future research is required to examine the validity of the TPS and describe activity diagrams of outpatient services, and further research is needed to examine the impact of EMR on time efficiency and work activities.

The Working Process and Time Efficiency of Patient Transportation in Cardiovascular Hospital Using Time Process Modeling

Hiroko Ojima[1], Yuko Ohno[1], Sachiko Shimizu[1], Shintaroh Oi[1], Yasuko Inoue[1], Atsue Ishii[1], Satoko Kasahara[2], Katsumi Hirakawa[3], Shohei Nakamura[4], Ichiro Kanaya[4], Kazuo Kawasaki[4], Atsuko Tanaka[5], Fujie Motosugi[5], and Chizuru Okada[5]

[1] School of Medicine, Osaka University, Yamadaoka1-7, Suita, Osaka, 5650871 Japan
[2] School of Medicine, Kochi University, Nankoku-shi, Kochi, 783-0043 Japan
[3] School of Human Nursing, University of Shiga Prefecture, 2500 Yasaka, Hikone, Shiga, 522-8573, Japan
[4] School of Engeneering, Osaka University, Yamadaoka2-1, Suita, 5650871 Osaka, Japan
[5] National Cardiovascular Center, 5-7-1 Fujishiro-dai, Suita, Osaka 565-8565, Japan
{h.noda,ohno,shimizu,atsue}@sahs.med.osaka-u.ac.jp,
{nakamura,kanaya}@design.frc.eng.osaka-u.ac.jp,
s-kasahara@kochi-u.ac.jp, khirakawa@nurse.usp.ac.jp,
{tanakaa,fmotosug,tokada}@hsp.ncvc.go.jp

Abstract. Patient transportation is one of the daily and frequent jobs in the hospital, however, it requires much strain and time of nurses. We carried out continuous-observation time and motion study (TMS) on the second time scale with recording by the other recorder in four wards of a cardiovascular disease hospital. Based on the recorded data, we carried out time processes modeling (TPM), that visualize the each transportation process sketchy and we could investigate the workflows of transportation as event instance.

Keywords: patient-transportation, Time Process Modeling, work process.

1 Introduction

Patient transportation is crucial issue in nursing care from the view points of both quality assurance and patient safety. In addition, the burden of the patient transportation service on nurses is both physically and mentally high and operation management is also important on the ward.

In this study, we analyze the patient transportation in the cardiovascular disease hospital to consider the process of transfer in the case of a complex situation and condition. We propose a unified modeling language (UML) based workflow modeling in order to capture the work process of the patient transportation. We describe the patient transportation prototype in the acute care hospital and propose some solutions to optimize workflow.

H. Takeda (Ed.): E-Health 2010, IFIP AICT 335, pp. 232–233, 2010.
© IFIP International Federation for Information Processing 2010

2   Materials and Methods

We conducted an observational, time and motion study in four wards. A continuous observation time study was conducted from March 9 to March 13,2009, in four different wards; 10th (department of cerebral vascular disease), 8th (department of valvular disease cardiomyopathy pulmonary hypertension), 7th western (department of cardiac dysrhythmia valvular disease cardiomiopathy) and 7th east (department of cardiac dysrhythmia valvular disease cardiac failure).

Based on time and motion studyrecords, we modeled workprocessby the time process study, expanded method for work flow and process analysis. TPM clarify the business process and analyzing the process of task, And, we apply the display technique of the UML, UML's Activity like diagram and use case like diagram help to model the detailed logic of care process.

Finally, we listed up each activity's attribute and time (named Event List). Event List is the list of work actions and is basis for structuring the business. We listed up the actors and resources for each event. And based on Time Motion Study data, we set up amount of time required.

3   Result and Conclusion

The twenty-two transportations were occurred inside the ward, and average required time is 0:05:46. Of the 22, eight diagrams have exactly the same work flow. There is no same flow diagram as Fig1. Required time for example1 is 0:02:10.

Number of diagrams modeling the outside the ward transportation are eighteen, and average required time is 0:14:40. Each diagram is different.

There are 40 events with patient transportation. There are two kinds of the actors: nurse, nurse's aid, and 5 kinds of the human resource: other nurse, contact personnel, doctor, patient, patient's family and 16 kinds of the object resource:

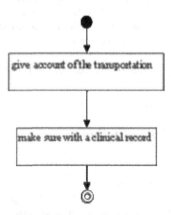

Fig. 1. Example (inside the ward)

telephone, wheelchair, gurney, clinical record, identification card, electrocardiogram, drip, urine bag, personal computer, thermometer, blood pressure meter, elevator, chair, weight scale, X-ray picture and 2 kinds of the information resource: transport information, patient information.

As the result of this study, we find different process by ward. We also clarified that the work time was affected by transport type, ward characteristics and patient age.

Analysis of Human and System Factors on Errors in ICD Coding with Electronic Discharge Summary System

Hitomi Yamada[1], Shigeki Kuwata[2], Keunsik Park[1], and Kenji Ohata[1]

[1] Department of Medical Informatics, Osaka City University Hospital,
1-5-7 Asahi-machi, Abeno, Osaka, 545-8586, Japan
[2] Medical Informatics Division, Tottori University Hospital,
36-1 Nishi-cho, Yonago, Tottori, 683-8504, Japan
{hitomiyama,kspark,kohata}@med.osaka-cu.ac.jp,
shig@med.tottori-u.ac.jp

Abstract. This study aimed at clarifying the issues of the system that needs to be improved in order to raise the precision of computer-assisted ICD-10 encoding, by analyzing the inconsistency between the codes registered by physician and encoded by experts in discharge summaries of the electronic patient record system. It was found that human related factors led to the major inconsistency at the chapter level of ICD-10. Substantial commitment of coding experts was considered practically important to correct careless mistakes in physician's entry and assign accurate codes to complicated diagnoses, while relatively small improvement of the system was thought feasible as countermeasures against the inconsistency caused by system related factors.

Keywords: Coding, Electronic Patient Records, Human Errors, ICD-10, System Errors.

1 Introduction

This study aimed at clarifying the issues of the system that needs to be improved in order to raise the precision of computer-assisted ICD-10 encoding, by analyzing the difference between the codes registered by physician (system coding) and encoded by experts (expert coding) in discharge summaries of the electronic patient record system. The authors here defined the difference as an error, on the assumption that the expert coding would always appropriately reflect the diagnoses described in the summaries. The errors were then scrutinized in terms of human and system factors that would cause them.

2 Methods

Of the cases for patients who were discharged from April 1 to 15, 2009 at a university-affiliated hospital with approximately 1,000 beds in an urban district in Japan, 210 cases were selected for which the discharge summaries were registered and completed upon onset of the study. A cording expert encoded a primary diagnosis

H. Takeda (Ed.): E-Health 2010, IFIP AICT 335, pp. 234–235, 2010.
© IFIP International Federation for Information Processing 2010

using ICD-10 for each summary, followed by the comparison with computer-assisted coding by physicians. When the errors were found, the system user interfaces were in turn examined to detect the reasons why physicians wrongly encoded. Subsequently the relationship between the error factors and the degree of the error (difference) was evaluated.

The error factors were categorized into (1) human factors and (2) system factors with subcategories of 1a. mistake or infringement, 1b. lack of details and 1c. difficult tasks for human factors, and of 2a. incorrectly assigned codes, 2b. difficult search, 2c. misleading presentation and 2d. no entries for system factors. The degree of the error was classified according to the structure of ICD-10 coding that included 22 chapters (e.g., I, XV) containing subdivided blocks (e.g., A00-A09, J90-J94). In the study, inconsistency between the system coding and the expert coding at the chapter level was referred to as major inconsistency, at the block level as middle inconsistency and at more detailed level as minor inconsistency.

3 Results

The inconsistency was found in 32% of the cases. Human factors were found in 91% of major, 79% of middle and 81% of minor inconsistency. Human factors caused a large portion of the major inconsistency, specifically careless mistakes (1a. 13/29) and too intricate coding requiring experts (1c. 14/29). Ambiguous coding (1c.) tended to frequently cause the minor consistency. On the other hand, system factors were found in 22% of major, 74% of middle and 88% of minor inconsistency, causing less major inconsistency than human factors.

4 Discussion and Conclusion

Functions or measures to prevent the errors equipped with the electronic discharge summary system are highly expected. Complicated mechanisms, such as case-based reasoning, however, would be required to reduce the careless mistakes and intricate codes that tended to cause the major inconsistency. In reality, manual encoding by experts may be the easiest way to solve those issues, hopefully with a little assistance of the artificial intelligence. On the other hand, feasible countermeasures against the faults in keyword search and data presentation would be able to be prepared by relatively facile tactics, e.g., improvement of the data quality in master files in which theoretical associations between diagnoses and ICD-10 codes are incorporated.

The inconsistency between system coding and expert coding was examined to raise the precision of computer-assisted ICD-10 encoding. It was found that human related factors led to the major inconsistency at the chapter level of ICD-10. Substantial commitment of coding experts was considered practically important to correct careless mistakes in physician's entry and assign accurate codes to complicated diagnoses, while relatively small improvement of the system was thought feasible as countermeasures against the errors caused by system related factors.

Semantic Interoperability and Health Records

Hugo Peixoto, José Machado, José Neves, and António Abelha

Universidade do Minho,
Braga, Portugal
{hpeixoto,jmac,jneves,abelha}@di.uminho.pt

Abstract. Systems Interoperability and Electronic Health Records are responsible for an exponential number of visits in electronic repository, either in terms of medical professionals or related staff. This is paramount for a better and sustainable quality-of-care in clinical assistance and of great potential to medical research. Following these lines of though, we present an agency for the diffusion, integration and archiving of medical information, and show how semantic web can enforce the use of electronic documents in order to envisage free-paper hospitals.

Keywords: Semantic, Interoperability, Electronic Health Record, Information Systems, Healthcare.

1 Introduction

Healthcare is turning into a science based on information and reputation [1]. In the last decade, information systems in healthcare have gained great importance and have grown in quality and in quantity. EHR is a repository of information concerning an individual in an electronic format, stored and transmitted securely and may be accessed by multiple users [2]. The main objective is to ensure ubiquity; i.e. information is accessible at anytime and anywhere. Demands of information handling within the healthcare sector range from clinically valuable patient-specific information to a variety of aggregation levels for follow-up and statistical and/or quantifiable reporting. On the other hand, semantic interoperability between healthcare providers is a hard task [3].

Researchers in the field of Hospital Information Systems (HIS) have focused special attention to the field of quality of information. A Health Unit is computationally represented by a heterogeneous set of applications that speak different languages and are customized by different customers. So a practical and effective communication platform between information systems is paramount taking into consideration the quality of information [3,4].

The EHR semantization is one of the latest advances, in the field of internal and external interoperability. With the inclusion of the Semantic Clinical Process it will be possible to guarantee the management of large flows of information while preserving quality, improving clinical practices and guarantying access to information over the paraphernalia of existing applications in the health unity.

H. Takeda (Ed.): E-Health 2010, IFIP AICT 335, pp. 236–237, 2010.
© IFIP International Federation for Information Processing 2010

2 Implementation

In order to fulfill this goal, it was developed, at University of Minho, an Agency for the Integration, Diffusion, and Archive (AIDA) of medical information, which allows interoperability with different HIS [4], and a EHR system.

Integration of the information from the different departments and services within healthcare institutions in order to make it available for the EHR system is also an important requisite for an efficient EHR. The electronic ordering embedded in EHR can be used not only to obtain medical equipment or pharmacological prescriptions, but also for acquiring laboratory and imaging studies outside the service where it is used. Furthermore, it may enable the centralization of exam display, allowing different services to share results concerning the same patient, diminishing costs on unnecessary exams, and above all, improving the quality of service being provided.

3 Conclusions

Semantic, a key word in our work refers to a computational paradigm that allows for interoperability, enabling intelligent ubiquitous computation and communications in order to increase quality of information and decision support. Indeed, doctors gather dissimilar types of information about patients for clinical practices. Different types of tests are visited in a user-friendly, including physical exams, imaging tests (e.g. XR, CT or MRI), laboratory tests (e.g. blood, urine, fluids or tissues), or pathology and surgical reports, i.e. in Computational Science, the scientific problem must be expressed mathematically, known as the Algorithm. Using semantic web, the algorithm is translated into one or more computer programs and implemented on one or more types of hardware. In our work, the combination of software and hardware is referred to as the Computational Architecture, the AIDA agency referred to above. It is shown that user-friendlier interfaces have a high number of visits, reducing costs and increasing the quality-of-care.

References

1. Hersh, W.: Medical Informatics - Improving Health Care Through Information. In: JAMA (2002)
2. Eichelberg, M., Aden, T., Riesmeier, J., Dogac, A., Laleci, G.: A survey and Analysis of Electronic Healthcare Record Standards. ACM Computing Surveys (20), 1–47
3. Hanzlícek, P., Precková, P., Zvárová, J.: Semantic Interoperability in the Structured Electronic Health Record. In: EuroMISE
4. Machado, J., Abelha, A., Novais, P., Neves, J., Neves, J.: Quality of Service in Healthcare Units. In: ESM. Universite du Havre, Le Havre (2008)

Author Index